TORTURE IS A MORAL ISSUE

TORTURE IS A MORAL ISSUE

Christians, Jews, Muslims, and
People of Conscience Speak Out

Edited by

George Hunsinger

WILLIAM B. EERDMANS PUBLISHING COMPANY
GRAND RAPIDS, MICHIGAN / CAMBRIDGE, U.K.

© 2008 William B. Eerdmans Publishing Company

All rights reserved

Published 2008 by

Wm. B. Eerdmans Publishing Co.

2140 Oak Industrial Drive N.E., Grand Rapids, Michigan 49505 /

P.O. Box 163, Cambridge CB3 9PU U.K.

Printed in the United States of America

13 12 11 10 09 08   7 6 5 4 3 2 1

Library of Congress Cataloging-in-Publication Data

Torture is a moral issue: Christians, Jews, Muslims, and people of
    conscience speak out / edited by George Hunsinger.
        p.   cm.
    Includes bibliographical references.
    ISBN 978-0-8028-6029-3 (pbk.: alk. paper)
    1. Torture — Moral and ethical aspects.
    2. Torture — Religious aspects.   I. Hunsinger, George.

    HV8593.T6624   2008
    364.6′7 — dc22

                                        2008016716

www.eerdmans.com

In memoriam
   Robert McAfee Brown
      and
         William Sloane Coffin Jr.

Contents

Contents

Contributors

The Editor

GEORGE HUNSINGER is Hazel Thompson McCord Professor of Systematic Theology at Princeton Theological Seminary. He is an ordained minister in the Presbyterian Church (U.S.A.). In January 2006 he founded the National Religious Campaign Against Torture.

The Authors

TAHA JABIR ALALWANI is president of Cordoba University. An internationally known scholar, he also holds the Imam Al-Shafi'i Chair in Islamic Legal Theory at Cordoba's Graduate School of Islamic and Social Sciences.

WILLIAM T. CAVANAUGH is professor of theology at the University of St. Thomas. He is author of *Torture and Eucharist: Theology, Politics, and the Body of Christ* (1998).

JOHN CONROY is a reporter for the *Chicago Reader*. He is author of *Unspeakable Acts, Ordinary People: The Dynamics of Torture* (2001). His stories on the Chicago police torture scandal are archived at http://www.chicagoreader.com/policetorture.

EDWARD FELD serves as rabbi-in-residence at the Rabbinical School of the Jewish Theological Seminary and as education director of rabbis for Human Rights-North America. His forthcoming work, *The Book of Revolutions,* is a historical and philosophical presentation of biblical law.

DAVID P. GUSHEE is the distinguished university professor of Christian ethics at Mercer University. His most recent book is *The Future of Faith in American Politics: The Public Witness of the Evangelical Center* (2008).

YAHYA HENDI is Muslim Chaplain at Georgetown University. He has met with and been an adviser to Presidents Bill Clinton and George W. Bush.

SCOTT HORTON is a New York attorney specializing in international law and human rights. He teaches at Columbia Law School and has served as chair of the International Law Committee at the New York Bar Association.

JOHN HUTSON is a retired United States Navy rear admiral, attorney, and former Judge Advocate General of the Navy. He is dean of the Franklin Pierce Law Center in Concord, New Hampshire.

TONY LAGOURANIS was a U.S. Army interrogator in Iraq from January through December 2004. He is author of *Fear Up Harsh: An Army Interrogator's Dark Journey Through Iraq* (2007).

ELLEN LIPPMANN is founder and rabbi of Kolot Chayeinu/Voices of Our Lives in Brooklyn, New York. In 2006 she chaired the first North American Rabbinic Conference on Judaism and Human Rights.

MARILYN McENTYRE is an independent writer. She has been professor of English at Westmont College, the College of New Jersey, and Mills College.

INGRID MATTSON is president of the Islamic Society of North America. She is professor of Islamic studies and Christian-Muslim relations at Hartford Theological Seminary, where she serves also as director of the Islamic Chaplaincy Program.

ANN ELIZABETH MAYER is professor of legal studies in the Department of Legal Studies and Business Ethics at the Wharton School of the University of Pennsylvania. Her widely acclaimed book *Islam and Human Rights* is now in its fourth edition (2006).

RICHARD M. O'MEARA is a retired brigadier general, USAR, a judge advocate, and former infantry officer. He teaches international relations at Rutgers University, Kean University, and Monmouth University.

Contributors

DIANNA ORTIZ, OSU, is co-founder and executive director of the Torture Abolition and Survivors Support Coalition International (TASSC), an organization of torture survivors. She is author of *The Blindfold's Eyes: My Journey from Torture to Truth* (2002).

DARIUS REJALI is professor of political science at Reed College. His book *Torture and Democracy* (2007) has been acclaimed as the most comprehensive and rigorous treatment of the subject ever written.

LOUISE RICHARDSON is executive dean of the Radcliffe Institute for Advanced Study, a senior lecturer in government at Harvard University, and lecturer on law at Harvard Law School. She is author of *What Terrorists Want: Understanding the Enemy, Containing the Threat* (2006).

KENNETH ROTH is executive director of Human Rights Watch. He has written articles on a range of human rights topics for the *New York Times,* the *Washington Post,* and *Foreign Affairs,* among other publications. He is editor of *Torture: A Human Rights Perspective* (2005).

FLEMING RUTLEDGE, a nationally known preacher, was one of the first women to be ordained to the priesthood of the Episcopal Church. Her most recent book is *Not Ashamed of the Gospel: Sermons from Paul's Letter to the Romans* (2007).

MELISSA WEINTRAUB was ordained as a Conservative rabbi at the Jewish Theological Seminary. She is co-founder of Encounter Trips to Bethlehem and Hebron for future rabbis and Jewish educators. She is currently working on a book exploring Jewish religious responses to terror.

CAROL WICKERSHAM teaches sociology at Beloit College. She is coordinator of No2Torture, a Presbyterian national organization.

Introduction

George Hunsinger

I recently purchased a copy of *Life* magazine from July 17, 1970. I had begun asking myself, what did I know and when did I know it? I could remember a haunting photo essay from years ago, which turned out to be in that issue. It was an exposé of the "tiger cages" in Vietnam. I had encountered it while I was still a seminary student. Reading it would make a lasting impression on me. Looking back I can say it was the first step down a road that would eventually lead me to found the National Religious Campaign Against Torture in 2006.

In July 1970 I was already opposed to the Vietnam War for its senselessness, its brutality, and its massive aerial bombing of civilians. To that list could then be added the sorrow and the outrage that my government was apparently complicit in torture and prisoner abuse. Here is an excerpt from the article:

> Beneath the bars crouched the prisoners. More than half of them were women, one girl was only 15. The air was foul, the heat stupefying. The bars were crusted with lime, which the prisoners say guards tip down on them as punishment, burning their eyes and choking their lungs. All the prisoners were sick: with TB, open sores, eye diseases, and malnutrition. (p. 26)

U.S. congressmen had been led to the Con Son prison, where the tiger cages lay hidden, by a Vietnamese-speaking social worker named Don

Luce. Luce worked in Vietnam with International Voluntary Service and the World Council of Churches from 1958 to 1971. He would later write:

> My best friend was tortured to death in 1970. Nguyen Ngoo Phuong was a gentle person. But he hated the war and was caught by the Saigon police in one of the many anti-government demonstrations. After three days of continuous interrogation, he died. I vowed to learn more about the police who tortured him and the prison system of South Vietnam.
>
> My apartment became a hiding place for students being chased by the police. One night in July 1970 at midnight a young congressional aide knocked on my door. He wanted to meet the student leaders, he said.
>
> "They're in the tiger cages," one of the students, Cao Nguyen Loi, said. Loi then drew us maps showing how to get between the walls of Con Son prison to find the stone cages.[1]

Elsewhere Luce would comment on the Phoenix Program, in which torture, political repression, and assassination were permitted.

> Abuses of justice are not accidental but an integral part of the Phoenix Program. The widespread use of torture during interrogation can be explained by the admissibility of confession as evidence in court and by the fact that local officials are under pressure from Saigon to sentence a specific number of high level VCI officials each month.[2]

Matters like these were troubling to me. Regarding what might be done about them, however, I had not a clue.

I was aware that Luce had assigned primary responsibility for the Phoenix Program to the CIA.

> Phoenix was created, organized, and funded by the CIA. The district and provincial interrogation centers were constructed with American funds, and provided with American advisers. Quotas were set by Ameri-

---

1. Don Luce, "Vietnam's Famous Tiger Cages Revisited," *National Catholic Reporter,* September 1, 1995. See also William Blum, *The CIA: A Forgotten History* (London: Zed Books, 1986), p. 141.

2. Holmes Brown and Don Luce, *Hostages of War: Saigon's Political Prisoners* (Washington, D.C.: Indochina Mobile Education Project, 1973), p. 24.

cans. The national system of identifying suspects was devised by Americans and underwritten by the U.S. Informers are paid with U.S. funds. American tax dollars have covered the expansion of the police and paramilitary units who arrest suspects.[3]

It should be noted that the resort to torture was never official U.S. policy.[4] Nevertheless, an ominous pattern was set that would extend, over the ensuing years, well beyond the Phoenix Program itself.[5] While the CIA would not directly conduct torture sessions, its clients would be encouraged to use torture. They would be provided with names of people to be interrogated. They would be supplied with torture equipment, trained by classes in torture, and provided with torture manuals. The CIA would be present when torture took place in order to observe and evaluate the results.[6]

The subject continued to concern me. Off and on, I would read books like *Hidden Terrors* by Langguth, *Supplying Repression* by Klare, *The Political Economy of Human Rights* by Chomsky and Herman, *Prisoner without a Name, Cell without a Number* by Timmerman, and *Instruments of Statecraft* by McClintock.[7] The scene near the end of Robert Stone's 1981 novel,

3. Brown and Luce, *Hostages of War*, p. 26.

4. See Stuart Herrington, *Stalking the Vietcong: Inside Operation Phoenix* (New York: Random House/Presidio Press, 2004), p. 145; Richard A. Hunt, *Pacification: The American Struggle for Vietnam's Hearts and Minds* (Boulder: Westview Press, 1995), p. 240. On the other hand, Michael Drosnin, CIA director William Colby's Saigon legal advisor, stated: "Everybody who was there accepted torture as routine." See Drosnin, "Phoenix: The CIA's Biggest Assassination Program," *New Times*, August 22, 1975, p. 22. See also Kurt Jacobsen, "Rehabilitating Pacification: Then and Now, Iraq and Vietnam," *Soundings* 32 (2006): 28-40.

5. For the Phoenix Program itself, see Mark Moyar, *Phoenix and the Birds of Prey* (Annapolis, Md.: Naval Institute Press, 1997); Douglas Valentine, *The Phoenix Program* (New York: William Morrow, 1990); Alfred W. McCoy, *A Question of Torture: CIA Interrogation from the Cold War to the War on Terror* (New York: Metropolitan Books, 2006), pp. 64-71.

6. See Blum, *Forgotten History*, pp. 141-45, 225-30, 248-50; McCoy, *Question of Torture*, pp. 60-107; Jennifer Harbury, *Truth, Torture, and the American Way: The History and Consequences of U.S. Involvement in Torture* (Boston: Beacon Press, 2005), pp. 26-27, 112-24, 186-87; Martha K. Huggins, *Political Policing: The United States and Latin America* (Durham, N.C.: Duke University Press, 1998); Cecilia Menjívar and Néstor Rodríguez, eds., *When States Kill: Latin America, the U.S., and Technologies of Terror* (Austin: University of Texas Press, 2005), pp. 286-300, 308-9.

7. A. J. Langguth, *Hidden Terrors: The Truth About U.S. Police Operations in Latin America* (New York: Pantheon, 1979); Michael T. Klare, *Supplying Repression* (Washington, D.C.: Institute for Policy Studies, 1981); Noam Chomsky and Edward Herman, *The Political Econ-*

A Flag for Sunrise, set in Central America, in which the activist nun, Sister Justin, is tortured to death by the Guardia chief, Lt. Campos (a figure reminiscent of Roberto D'Aubuisson) would sear itself into my mind. I became active, during the 1980s, in the Central America solidarity movement, where we would hear about torture, and sometimes meet its survivors. From 1987 until 1994 I served on the board of American Christians for the Abolition of Torture. This small and rather inconsequential group was disbanded after the U.S. ratified the U.N. Convention Against Torture in 1994. All the while, of course, as a Karl Barth scholar, I was aware of his role at Barmen in 1934 and of his leadership in the German confessing church.[8]

When the Abu Ghraib photos appeared in April 2004, the Bush administration was quick to repudiate the horrific conduct that could no longer be ignored, while denying all responsibility for it. Such practices were declared to be "un-American," the work of a "few bad apples," the mischief of "*Animal House* on the night shift," and so forth. Hearing these explanations, I felt there was room for doubt.

Darius Rejali points to a certain historical precedent. Torture when practiced by democracies, he says, on the basis of several case studies, has inevitably led them to losses. After the practice of torture is exposed, the pattern leading to downfall runs like this:

> When politicians first heard of the torture, they denied it happened, minimized the violence, and called it ill treatment. When the evidence mounted, they tried a few bad apples, disparaged the prisoners, and observed that terrorists had done worse things. They claimed torture was effective and necessary, and counterchallenged that critics were aiding the enemy. Some offered apologies, but accepted no responsibility. Others preferred not to dwell on past events.[9]

---

omy of Human Rights, 2 vols. (Boston: South End Press, 1979); Jacobo Timmerman, *Prisoner without a Name, Cell without a Number* (New York: Vintage, 1988); Michael McClintock, *Instruments of Statecraft: U.S. Guerrilla Warfare, Counterinsurgency, and Counter-Terrorism, 1940-1990* (New York: Pantheon, 1992).

8. See George Hunsinger, "Barth, Barmen, and the Confessing Church Today," in *Disruptive Grace* (Grand Rapids: Eerdmans, 2000), pp. 60-88.

9. Darius Rejali, *Torture and Democracy* (Princeton: Princeton University Press, 2007), p. 536.

The torture would continue, yielding no reliable information, while the democracies remained mired in war against weaker enemies. "Soon," states Rejali, "politicians had to choose between losing their democracy and losing their war. That is how democracies lose wars."[10] It is also, we might fear, how they lose their democracies.

Just as torture is not a new American practice, so legislative attempts to ban it are also not new. As noted by Alfred McCoy, the McCain Amendment of 2005 marked the third time in thirty years that Congress had voted to prohibit torture. "Twice before, in 1975 and 1994," McCoy observed, "investigations of horrific abuse, secret prisons, and CIA complicity led to legislation."[11] Unfortunately, however, in each case, hidden loopholes were allowed.

In 1975, according to McCoy, despite the congressional cutoff of all funds to the U.S. AID's notorious Office of Public Safety, through which the CIA had been disseminating torture techniques through police-training units throughout Asia and Latin America, a loophole was nonetheless left open for the agency to continue its operations through the Army's Military Advisor Program.[12]

Then in 1994, McCoy continues, major qualifications were introduced in ratifying the U.N. Convention Against Torture that "would effectively exempt the CIA's interrogation methods from international law."[13] The exemption pertained to what McCoy calls "no-touch" torture techniques. "Although seemingly less brutal than physical methods," he explains, "no-touch torture leaves deep psychological scars on both victims and interrogators."[14] There is nothing "lite," he says, about "torture lite." Techniques favored by the CIA like sleep deprivation, hooding, long-time standing, induced hypothermia, protracted isolation, self-inflicted pain, and other systematic attacks on the senses constitute "a hammer-blow to the funda-

10. Rejali, *Torture and Democracy*, p. 536.

11. McCoy, "New Loopholes May Exist for Abuse," *San Francisco Chronicle*, January 8, 2006.

12. McCoy, *Question of Torture*, pp. 11, 73-74. Senator Alan Cranston explained that Congress banned police training in 1974, after learning that police trained and equipped by the U.S. "in Iran, Vietnam, Brazil, and other countries were involved in torture, murder, and the suppression of legitimate political activity." Statement to the United States Senate (March 5, 1992). Available online at http://www.fas.org/irp/gao/920300-train.htm.

13. McCoy, *Question of Torture*, p. 101.

14. McCoy, *Question of Torture*, p. 9.

mentals of personal identity."[15] The iconic Abu Ghraib figure, hooded and standing on a box with fake electrical wires hanging from his outstretched arms, represents, according to McCoy, "key components of the CIA's psychological paradigm," namely, sensory deprivation and self-inflicted pain.[16]

Furthermore, in the case of the McCain Amendment of 2005, loopholes were again introduced for the CIA. Through a complex series of provisions, trademark psychological techniques were effectively legalized, evidence obtained under torture was legally permitted in court for the first time in United States history, and the bedrock right of *habeas corpus* was denied to a class of detainees.[17]

Finally, it must be mentioned that what was once hidden in the shadows is now present for all to see. On March 8, 2008, legislation was vetoed by the president of the United States (the Intelligence Authorizations Act) that would have closed all loopholes for the CIA by banning techniques like waterboarding, sleep deprivation, and stress positions. Never before in American history has "cruel, inhuman and degrading treatment," as proscribed by international and domestic law, been so openly justified. As Faulkner once wrote in another connection: "The past is never dead. It's not even past."[18]

McCoy concludes:

> As a people, Americans are now faced with a choice that will influence the character of their nation and its standing in the world. They can honor their commitments . . . to ban torture unconditionally. Or they can agree . . . to make torture a permanent weapon in America's arsenal. . . . As a powerfully symbolic state practice synonymous with brutal autocrats, torture — even of the few, even of just one — raises profound moral issues about the quality of America's justice, the character of its civilization, and the legitimacy of its global leadership.[19]

The purpose of this book is not only to underscore that torture is a moral issue, beyond all partisan politics, but also to help religious commu-

---

15. McCoy, *Question of Torture*, p. 8.

16. McCoy, "Invisible in Plain Sight," *Amnesty International Magazine*, May 4, 2006. Available online at http://www.amnestyusa.org/magazine/invisible_in_plain_sight.html.

17. McCoy, *Question of Torture*, pp. 223-24.

18. Act I, scene III of "Requiem for a Nun."

19. McCoy, *Question of Torture*, p. 225.

nities mobilize against it, so that all loopholes permitting torture by any U.S. agencies, whether military or intelligence, might be eliminated.

A Survey of the Contents

This book falls into five parts. The first part consists of background material. Kenneth Roth, the distinguished human rights advocate, looks at the policies behind Abu Ghraib, the twisted logic of torture, and the possibility of a way forward (ch. 1). A survivor's account is then offered by Sr. Dianna Ortiz (ch. 2). This was the opening statement at the 2006 Princeton conference on "Theology, International Law, and Torture" at which the National Religious Campaign Against Torture was launched. The quiet dignity with which her harrowing and yet also moving story was told will never be forgotten by those who heard it. As Tony Lagouranis, a former U.S. interrogator in Iraq, makes clear (ch. 3), torture exacts a terrible toll from perpetrators as well as survivors. His vivid firsthand account illustrates the ominous reality that torture once chosen is not easily contained. Finally, military concerns about torture must not be overlooked. As Adm. John Hutson and Gen. Richard O'Meara eloquently attest (ch. 4), the conscience of many in the military opposes torture on principled as well as pragmatic grounds.

In Part Two the case against torture is made from a Christian standpoint. Marilyn McEntyre, looking back on the Princeton conference (ch. 5), contemplates the need for courage beyond numbness as a matter of moral necessity when confronted by the enormity of torture as sponsored by our own government. A discussion of the "ticking time-bomb scenario" (ch. 6), so often invoked by those who would condone torture, then follows. By a detailed application of criteria from the just-war tradition, it is shown that torture, like rape and slavery, can never under any circumstances be justified. From an evangelical perspective (ch. 7), David P. Gushee provides six reasons why torture is always wrong. Gushee gives the lie (to say the least) to those who suppose that evangelicals are all retrograde extremists. His essay is followed by a Roman Catholic account (ch. 8), in which William T. Cavanaugh brings his extensive research about the Chilean church's response to torture under the Pinochet regime, as focused on the Eucharist, to bear on recent developments closer to home. A powerful sermon by Fleming Rutledge (ch. 9) rounds this part out. It is, if I may say so, the sermon I wish I had written myself.

The third part brings Jewish voices to the fore. Melissa Weintraub shares her groundbreaking study of torture with respect to the Jewish ethical tradition (ch. 10) with passion, elegance, and depth. Her essay promises to be a benchmark for years to come. In his theological reflections on torture (ch. 11), Edward Feld indirectly reminds us, tactfully though inescapably, that the church has much to repent of in its history regarding the persecution, including torture, of Jews, for whom the Inquisition can never be forgotten, though Christians might wish to do so. His generous and gentle though tough-minded spirit is a model of responsible ethical reflection. Painful memories are also taken up in the sermon by Ellen Lippmann (ch. 12), where they are transformed into a vision of courage and hope. Part Three ends with "What We Pray For" (ch. 13), the principles of faith espoused by Rabbis for Human Rights. That there should be rabbis with this commitment in the midst of strife-torn Israel today is a sign of hope and inspiration for us all, Jews and non-Jews alike.

Part Four occupies a place of special importance in this book. It represents a limited attempt to counteract the extreme prejudice raging against Muslims in Western societies, and not least in their religious communities, today. No great religion deserves to be judged solely on the basis of its worst aspects, as if Christian and Jewish communities had nothing to be ashamed of in their pasts, or as if nonreligious persons could find nothing in themselves but virtue. The selective vision, the phantasmagoric caricatures, the thinly veiled vindictiveness, and the self-serving propaganda directed at Muslims today is something that urgently needs to be confronted by all religious communities and all people of conscience. Demonizing the other through negative stereotyping violates the divine commandment against bearing false witness, while also paving the way toward violating the commandment against murder.

The first essay in Part Four is by Ingrid Mattson, president of the Islamic Society of North America (ch. 14). In it she sets forth, from resources of her own tradition, the obligation to stop oppression, including the oppression of women. The Islamic condemnation of torture and abuse is then explained by Taha Jabir Alalwani (ch. 15). If one did not know that he is a respected Muslim scholar responding to the concerns of his coreligionists, one might almost think one were reading the words of Desmond Tutu or Abraham Heschel. Why cannot a figure like this receive the honor and recognition he deserves? The sermon by Yahya Hendi, though not so much a sermon as a religious meditation (ch. 16), appeals to non-Muslims to enter into dialogue, that they might learn to see Muslims without prejudice. In recent years more than one "Fatwah Against Religious Extremism" has been issued by the authoritative Fiqh Council of North America, whose mission is to ensure that "the dealings of North American Muslims fall within the parameters of what is permitted by the Shari'ah." Because these Fatwahs have been ignored by the broader public as if they did not exist, the most recent one is reproduced here (ch. 17). Also reproduced is the remarkable Universal Islamic Declaration of Human Rights (ch. 18). Prepared in 1981 by representatives from Egypt, Pakistan, Saudi Arabia, and other countries affiliated with the Muslim World League, it may be less than perfect from a human rights perspective at various points,[20] but its unqualified prohibition of torture (Article VII) leaves nothing to be desired relative to comparable international human rights documents.

The book concludes with Part Five, directed toward solutions. A leading expert, Ann Elizabeth Mayer, looks back on her study of Islam and human rights over a period of more than twenty-five years (ch. 19). With a keen sense of existing complexities, she nonetheless comes to the sobering conclusion that the tables may indeed have turned, so that in the future human rights may be more credibly upheld around the world by Islamic societies than by the increasingly tainted United States. The religious roots of the global human rights movement are explored, in one of their aspects, by Scott Horton (ch. 20), who shows that the eighteenth-century anti-slavery movement as led by William Wilberforce was also unequivocally anti-torture. Convinced that the resort to torture and human rights violations will only make things worse, Louise Richardson explains how to deal with terrorists in a way that can be both principled and truly effective (ch. 21). In pointing to the high importance of encouraging moderate Muslims as a bulwark against Islamic extremists, instead of alienating them with human rights violations, Richardson concurs with Mayer. Activist Carol Wickersham offers seasoned advice to the religious anti-torture movement on how to make the case today (ch. 22). The book concludes with a brief look at the actual conditions that would need to be achieved for U.S. torture to be brought to an end (ch. 23). The conditions are at once simple

---

20. See the critical though eminently fair-minded discussion in Ann Elizabeth Mayer, *Islam and Human Rights: Tradition and Politics*, 4th ed. (Boulder: Westview, 2006), pp. 105-11 and passim.

and formidable. An Afterword offers an interview with Darius Rejali, one of the world's leading authorities on the history of torture.

Finally, I would mention in conclusion that in my modest work against torture and for human rights two mentors have been ever before me. Robert McAfee Brown, one of my revered theological teachers, was tireless in his dedication to opposing the worst while striving for justice and peace. It was he who once introduced me to his friend William Sloane Coffin Jr., a larger-than-life peace activist, who taught me much when I served as his assistant for a year in the Riverside Church Disarmament Program. I dedicate this book, with affection, to their memories.

PART ONE

BACKGROUND

A time comes when silence is betrayal.

Martin Luther King Jr.

CHAPTER 1

Getting Away with Torture

Kenneth Roth

Who would have thought it still necessary to debate the merits of torture? Sure, there are always some governments that torture, but they do it clandestinely. Torture is inherently shameful — something that, if practiced, is done in the shadows. In the system of international human rights law and institutions that has been constructed since World War II, there is no more basic prohibition than the ban on torture. Even the right to life admits exceptions, such as the killing of combatants allowed in wartime. But torture is forbidden unconditionally, whether in time of peace or war, whether at the local police precinct or in the face of a major security threat.

Yet, suddenly, following the terrorist attacks of September 11, 2001, torture and related forms of mistreatment have become serious policy options for the United States. Academics are proposing ways to regulate the pain that can be inflicted on suspects in detention. Overly clever U.S. government lawyers have tried to define away laws against torture. The Bush administration claims latitude to abuse detainees that its predecessors would never have dared to contemplate.

Washington's new willingness to contemplate torture is not just theoretical. The abuse of prisoners has flourished in the gulag of offshore detention centers that the Bush administration now maintains in Guantánamo, Iraq, Afghanistan, and the secret dungeons where the U.S. government's "disappeared" prisoners are held. Hidden from public scrutiny, shielded from legal accountability, the interrogators in these facilities have been allowed to flout the most basic rules for the decent and humane treatment of detainees.

Yet torture remains the despicable practice it has always been. It dehumanizes people by treating them as pawns to be manipulated through their pain. It harnesses the awesome power of the state and applies it to human beings at their most vulnerable. Breaching any restraint of reciprocity, it subjects the victim to abuse that the perpetrator would never want to suffer.

Before looking at why Americans are suddenly confronting the torture option, it is useful to clarify what, exactly, torture is. The word *torture* has entered the vernacular to describe a host of irritants, but its formal meaning in international law is quite specific: the intentional infliction of severe pain or suffering, whether physical or mental, for whatever reason. Torture as defined in international law is not done by private actors but by government officials or those operating with their consent or acquiescence.[1]

Torture exists on a continuum of mistreatment. Abuse just short of torture is known in international law as cruel, inhuman, or degrading treatment. The lines between these different degrees of mistreatment are not crystal clear — lesser forms are often gateways to torture — which is one reason why international law prohibits all such forms of coercion.[2]

Torture — as well as cruel, inhuman, or degrading treatment — is flatly prohibited by such treaties as the International Covenant on Civil and Political Rights (ICCPR); the Convention Against Torture and Other Cruel, Inhuman or Degrading Treatment or Punishment (CAT); and the Geneva Conventions. All of these treaties are widely ratified, including by the United States. None permits any exception to these prohibitions, even in time of war or a serious security threat.

Indeed, these prohibitions are so fundamental that the Restatement of the Foreign Relations Law of the United States, the most authoritative U.S. treatise on the matter, lists them as peremptory jus cogens norms, meaning they bind governments as a matter of customary international law, even in the absence of a treaty. Breach of these prohibitions gives rise to a crime of universal jurisdiction, allowing the perpetrator to be prosecuted in any competent tribunal anywhere.

Yet it is precisely because of the fundamental character of the prohibition of torture and cruel, inhuman, or degrading treatment that the Bush

1. See United Nations Convention Against Torture and Other Cruel, Inhuman, or Degrading Treatment or Punishment, Art. 1. Available online at http://hrweb.org/legal/cat.html.

2. Convention Against Torture, Art. 16.

administration's deliberate disregard for it is so damaging. If this basic human rights protection can be cast aside, no right is secure.

Moreover, the Bush administration is not just any government. When most governments breach international human rights law, they commit a violation — the breach is condemned or prosecuted, but the rule remains firm. Yet when a government as dominant and influential as the United States openly defies that law and seeks to justify its defiance, it also undermines the law itself, and invites others to do the same. That shakes the very foundations of the international system for the protection of human rights that has been carefully constructed over the past sixty years.

This unlawful conduct has also damaged Washington's credibility as a proponent of human rights and a leader of the campaign against terrorism. The U.S. government's record of promoting human rights has always been mixed. For every offender it berated for human rights transgressions, there was another whose abuses it ignored, excused, or even supported. Yet despite this inconsistency, the United States historically has played a key role in defending human rights. Its embrace of coercive interrogation — part of a broader betrayal of human rights principles in the name of combating terrorism — has significantly impaired its ability to mount that defense.

As a result, governments facing human rights pressure from the United States now find it increasingly easy to turn the tables, to challenge Washington's standing to uphold principles that it violates itself.

Whether it is Egypt justifying torture by reference to U.S. practice, Malaysia defending administrative detention by invoking Guantánamo, Russia citing Abu Ghraib to blame abuses in Chechnya solely on low-level soldiers, Nepal explaining a coup by reference to America's post-September 11 excesses, or Cuba claiming the Bush administration had "no moral authority to accuse" it of human rights violations, repressive governments find it easier to deflect U.S. pressure because of Washington's own sorry counterterrorism record on human rights. Indeed, when Human Rights Watch asked State Department officials to protest administrative detention in Malaysia and prolonged incommunicado detention in Uganda, they demurred, explaining, in the words of one, "With what we are doing in Guantánamo, we're on thin ice to push this."[3]

---

3. See "Malaysia: P.M's Visit Puts Spotlight on Detainee Abuse," Human Rights Watch News, 19 July 2004, available online at http://hrw.org/english/docs/2004/07/19/malays9097.htm.

Washington's loss of credibility has not been for lack of rhetorical support for concepts that are closely related to human rights, but the embrace of explicit human rights language seems to have been calculatedly rare. In his January 2005 inauguration speech, President Bush spoke extensively of his devotion to "freedom" and "liberty," his opposition to "tyranny" and "terrorism," but hardly at all about his commitment to human rights.[4] The distinction has enormous significance. It is one thing to pronounce oneself on the side of the "free," quite another to be bound by the full array of human rights standards that are the foundation of freedom. It is one thing to declare oneself opposed to terrorism, quite another to embrace the body of international human rights and humanitarian law that enshrines the values rejecting terrorism. This linguistic sleight-of-hand — this refusal to accept the legal obligations embraced by rights-respecting states — has both reduced Washington's credibility and facilitated its use of coercive interrogation.

Because of this hypocrisy, many human rights defenders, particularly in the Middle East and North Africa, now cringe when the United States comes to their defense. Reformers in the Middle East speak of "the hug of death" — the ill effects of Washington's hypocritical embrace. They may crave a powerful ally, but identifying too closely with a government that so brazenly ignores international law, whether in its own abuses or its alliance with other abusers, has become a sure route to disrepute. At a time when the Bush administration is extolling itself as a champion of reform in the Middle East, as the catalyst behind recent democratic developments, however modest, in Iraq, Lebanon, Egypt, Saudi Arabia, and the Palestinian territories, it is a sad irony that so few reformers welcome its support.

That weakening of Washington's moral authority in the Middle East is particularly tragic, because that region is where effective counterterrorism efforts are most needed. Open and responsive political systems are the best way to encourage people to pursue their grievances peacefully. But when the most vocal governmental advocate of democracy deliberately violates human rights, it undermines democratically inclined reformers and strengthens the appeal of those who preach more radical visions. Instead, U.S. abuses have provided a new rallying cry for terrorist recruiters, and the pictures from Abu Ghraib have become the recruiting posters for what

---

4. Fifty-fifth Inaugural Ceremony, January 20, 2005; see http://www.whitehouse.gov/inaugural.

is becoming known as "Terrorism, Inc." Many militants need no additional incentive to attack civilians, but if a weakened human rights culture eases even a few fence-sitters toward the path of violence, the consequences can be dire.

Why is the United States taking this approach? To vent frustration, to exact revenge — possibly — but certainly not because torture and mistreatment are required for national security or protection. Respect for the Geneva Conventions does not preclude vigorously interrogating detainees about a limitless range of topics. The U.S. Army's field manual on intelligence interrogation makes clear that coercion undermines the quest for reliable information.[5] The U.S. military command in Iraq says that Iraqi detainees are providing more useful intelligence when they are not subjected to abuse. In the words of Craig Murray, the United Kingdom's former ambassador to Uzbekistan, who was speaking of the U.K.'s reliance on torture-extracted testimony, "We are selling our souls for dross."[6]

Moreover, coercive interrogation is making us less safe by effectively precluding criminal prosecution of its victims. Once a confession is coerced, it becomes extremely difficult to prove, as due process requires, that a subsequent prosecution of the suspect is free of the fruits of that coercion. As a result, the Bush administration finds itself holding some suspects who clearly have joined terrorist conspiracies and might have been criminally convicted and subjected to long prison terms, but against whom prosecution has become impossible. In February 2005, the Central Intelligence Agency (CIA) began openly fretting about the problem. What happens, it worried, when continuing to detain suspects without trial becomes politically untenable, but prosecuting them is legally impossible because of taint from coercive interrogation?[7]

None of this is to say that the United States is the worst human rights abuser. There are many more serious contenders for that notorious title, including governments that torture more frequently and more ruthlessly. But the United States is certainly the most influential abuser, making its

5. Headquarters, Department of the Army, Field Manual 34-52 Intelligence Interrogation, Washington, D.C., September 28, 1992, available online at http://atiam.train.army.mil/portal/atia/adlsc/view/public/302562-1/FM/34-52/FM34_52.pdf.

6. "'Torture Intelligence' Criticized," BBC News, October 11, 2004, available online at http://news.bbc.co.uk/1/hi/uk/3732488.stm.

7. Douglas Jehl, "C.I.A. Is Seen as Seeking New Role on Detainees," *New York Times*, February 16, 2005.

contribution to the degradation of human rights standards unique and the costs to global institutions for upholding human rights incalculable.

It is not enough to argue, as its defenders do, that the Bush administration is well intentioned — that they are the "good guys," in the words of the *Wall Street Journal*.[8] A society ordered on intentions rather than law is a lawless society. Nor does it excuse the administration's human rights record, as its defenders have tried to do, to note that it removed two tyrannical governments — the Taliban in Afghanistan and the Ba'ath Party in Iraq. Attacks on repressive regimes cannot justify attacks on the body of principles that makes their repression illegal.

So, how did we get here? How did the United States, historically perhaps the most vigorous governmental proponent of human rights, come to undermine through its own actions one of the most basic human rights there is? Several books, both new and old, provide insight into this sorry state of affairs.

Cover-Up and Self-Investigation

When the photos from Abu Ghraib became public, the Bush administration reacted like many abusive governments that are caught red-handed: it went into damage control mode. It agreed that the torture and abuse featured in the photographs were wrong but sought to minimize the problem. The abusers, it claimed, were a handful of errant soldiers, a few "bad apples" at the bottom of the barrel. The problem, it argued, was contained, both geographically (one section of Abu Ghraib prison) and structurally (only low-level soldiers, not more senior commanders). The abuse photographed at Abu Ghraib and broadcast around the world, it maintained, had nothing to do with the decisions and policies of more senior officials. President Bush vowed that "wrongdoers will be brought to justice,"[9] but as of March 2005, virtually all of those facing prosecution were of the rank of sergeant or below.

To some extent, the sheer outrageousness of the sexual and physical depravity featured in the Abu Ghraib photographs made it easier for the

8. "Red Double-Crossed Again," *Wall Street Journal*, 2 December 2004.

9. Remarks by President Bush and His Majesty King Abdullah II of the Hashemite Kingdom of Jordan in a Press Availability, 6 May 2004, available online at www.whitehouse.gov/news/releases/2004/05/20040506-9.html.

administration to disown responsibility. Few believe that President Bush or his senior officials would have ordered, for example, Lynndie England to parade about a naked detainee on a leash. Yet behind this particular mistreatment was an atmosphere of abuse to which the Bush administration, at the highest levels, did contribute.

The ingredients of that atmosphere are described in several new books. The most comprehensive compilation of the documentary record is contained in *The Torture Papers,* a book edited by Karen Greenberg and Joshua Dratel, which includes all of the administration's notorious "torture memos" available by late 2004. Mark Danner's book *Torture and Truth* includes many of these same documents, as well as his insightful analysis, drawn from his articles in the *New York Review of Books,* of the policy decisions that lay behind them. The Human Rights Watch report "The Road to Abu Ghraib" details how this atmosphere played out on the ground, as American interrogators deployed "stress and duress" interrogation techniques and then covered up the cruel and occasionally deadly consequences. *Torture: A Collection,* a new set of essays on torture edited by Sanford Levinson, contains thoughtful essays from a range of scholars, including a vigorous debate about how to limit torture in the post-September 11 environment.[10]

The key to the administration's strategy of damage control was a series of carefully limited investigations — at least ten so far. The reports of several of these are reprinted in the Greenberg and Dratel compilation. Most of the investigations, such as those conducted by Maj. Gen. George Fay and Lt. Gen. Anthony Jones, involved uniformed military officials examining the conduct of their subordinates; these officers lacked the authority to scrutinize senior Pentagon officials. Typical was the most recent investigation, conducted by Vice Admiral Albert T. Church III, who said he did not interview senior officials such as Secretary of Defense Donald Rumsfeld or draw conclusions about their individual responsibility.[11]

10. Karen Greenberg and Joshua Dratel, eds., *The Torture Papers: The Road to Abu Ghraib* (New York: Cambridge University Press, 2005); Mark Danner, *Torture and Truth: America, Abu Ghraib, and the War on Terror* (New York: New York Review Books, 2004); Human Rights Watch, "The Road to Abu Ghraib," available online at http://www.hrw.org/reports/2004/usa0604/; Sanford Levinson, ed., *Torture: A Collection* (New York: Oxford University Press, 2004).

11. Josh White and Bradley Graham, "Senators Question Absence of Blame in Abuse Report," *Washington Post,* 11 March 2005.

The one investigation with the theoretical capacity to examine the conduct of Secretary Rumsfeld and his top aides — the inquiry led by former secretary of defense James Schlesinger — was initiated by Rumsfeld himself and seemed to go out of its way to distance Rumsfeld from the problem. At the press conference releasing the investigative report, Schlesinger said that Rumsfeld's resignation "would be a boon to all America's enemies." The Schlesinger investigation lacked the independence of, for example, the September 11 Commission, which was established with the active involvement of the U.S. Congress.[12] As for the CIA — the branch of the U.S. government believed to hold the most important terrorist suspects — it has apparently escaped scrutiny by anyone other than its own inspector general. Meanwhile, no one seems to be looking at the role of President Bush and other senior administration officials.

As for criminal investigations, there has been none independent of the Bush administration. When an unidentified government official retaliated against a critic of the administration by revealing that his wife was a CIA agent — a serious crime because it could endanger her — the administration agreed, under pressure, to appoint a special prosecutor who has been promised independence from administration direction. Yet the administration has refused to appoint a special prosecutor to determine whether senior officials authorized torture and other coercive interrogation — a far more serious and systematic offense. So far, prosecutors under the direction of the administration have focused only on the "little guy."

The Policies Behind Abu Ghraib

What would a genuinely independent investigation find? It would reveal that the abusive interrogation seen at Abu Ghraib did not erupt spontaneously at the lowest levels of the military chain of command. It was not merely a "management" failure, as the Schlesinger investigation suggested. As shown in the collection of official documents organized by Greenberg and Dratel and Danner, Danner's analysis, and the Human Rights Watch study, these abuses were the direct product of an environment of lawless-

---

12. The 9/11 Commission Report; see http://a257.g.akamaitech.net/7/257/2422/05aug20041050/www.gpoaccess.gov/911/pdf/fullreport.pdf.

ness, an atmosphere created by policy decisions taken at the highest levels of the Bush administration, long before the start of the Iraq War. They reflect a determination to fight terrorism unconstrained by fundamental principles of international human rights and humanitarian law, despite commitments by the United States and governments around the world to respect those principles even in times of war and severe security threats. These policy decisions included:

- The decision not to grant the detainees in U.S. custody at Guantánamo their rights under the Geneva Conventions, even though the conventions apply to all people picked up on the battlefield of Afghanistan. Senior Bush officials vowed that all detainees would be treated "humanely," but that vow seems never to have been seriously implemented and at times was qualified (and arguably eviscerated) by a self-created exception for "military necessity." Meanwhile, the effective shredding of the Geneva Conventions — and the corresponding side-stepping of the U.S. Army's interrogation manual — sent U.S. interrogators the signal that, in the words of one leading counterterrorist official, "the gloves come off."[13]
- The decision not to clarify for nearly two years that, regardless of the applicability of the Geneva Conventions, all detainees in U.S. custody are protected by the parallel requirements of the International Covenant on Civil and Political Rights and the Convention Against Torture. Even when, at the urging of human rights groups, the Pentagon's general counsel belatedly reaffirmed, in June 2003, that the CAT prohibited not only torture but also other forms of ill treatment, that announcement was communicated to interrogators, if at all, in a way that had no discernible impact on their behavior.
- The decision to interpret the prohibition of cruel, inhumane, or degrading treatment narrowly, to permit certain forms of coercive interrogation — that is, certain efforts to ratchet up a suspect's pain, suffering, and humiliation to make him talk. At the time of ratifying the ICCPR in 1992 and the CAT in 1994, the U.S. government said it

13. Testimony of Cofer Black, former director of the CIA's Counterterrorism Center, before a joint session of the Senate and House Intelligence Committees, 26 September 2002, available online at www.fas.org/irp/congress/2002_hr/092602black.html. ("All I want to say is that there was 'before' 9/11 and 'after' 9/11. After 9/11 the gloves came off.")

would interpret this prohibition to mean the same thing as the requirements of the Fifth, Eighth, and Fourteenth Amendments to the U.S. Constitution. The clear intent was to require that if an interrogation technique would be unconstitutional if used in an American police station or jail, it would violate these treaties if used against suspects overseas. Yet U.S. interrogators under the Bush administration have routinely subjected overseas terrorist suspects to abusive techniques that would clearly have been prohibited if used in the United States. That the use of cruel, inhuman, or degrading treatment was intentional was suggested by Attorney General Alberto Gonzales during his confirmation process. In his written reply to Senate questions — after the administration had supposedly repudiated the worst aspects of its torture memos — he interpreted the U.S. reservation as permitting the use of cruel, inhumane, or degrading treatment so long as it was done against non-Americans outside the United States.[14] That makes the United States the only government in the world to claim openly as a matter of policy the power to use cruel, inhumane, or degrading treatment. Other governments obviously subject detainees to inhumane treatment or worse as a matter of clandestine policy, but the Bush administration is the only government to proclaim this policy publicly. Reflecting that policy, the Bush administration in late 2004 successfully stopped a congressional effort to proscribe the CIA's use of torture and inhumane treatment in interrogation.

- The decision to hold some suspects — eleven known[15] and reportedly some three dozen — in unacknowledged incommunicado detention, beyond the reach of even the International Committee of the Red Cross (ICRC). Many other suspects were apparently temporarily hidden from the ICRC. Victims of such "disappearances" are at the greatest risk of torture and other mistreatment. For example, U.S. forces continue to maintain closed detention sites in Afghanistan, where beatings, threats, and sexual humiliation are still reported. At least twenty-six prisoners have died in U.S. custody in Iraq and Afghanistan

14. "A Degrading Policy," *Washington Post,* 26 January 2005; "U.S. Justifying Abuse of Detainees," Human Rights Watch News, 25 January 2005.

15. Human Rights Watch, "The United States' 'Disappeared': The CIA's Long-Term 'Ghost Detainees' (New York: Human Rights Watch, 2004), available online at www.hrw .org/backgrounder/usa/us1004/index.htm.

since 2002 in what Army and Navy investigators have concluded or suspect were acts of criminal homicide.[16] One of those deaths was as recent as September 2004.

- The refusal for over two years to prosecute U.S. soldiers implicated in the December 2002 deaths of two suspects in U.S. custody in Afghanistan — deaths ruled "homicides" by U.S. Army pathologists. Instead, the interrogators were sent to Abu Ghraib, where some were allegedly involved in more abuse.

- The approval by Secretary of Defense Rumsfeld of some interrogation methods for Guantánamo that violated, at the very least, the prohibition of cruel, inhumane, or degrading treatment and possibly the ban on torture. These techniques included placing detainees in painful stress positions, hooding them, stripping them of their clothes, and scaring them with guard dogs. That approval was later rescinded, but it contributed to the environment in which the legal obligations of the United States were seen as dispensable.

- The reported approval by an unidentified senior Bush administration official, and use, of "waterboarding" — known as the "submarine" in Latin America — a torture technique in which the victim is made to believe he will drown, and in practice sometimes does. Remarkably, Porter Goss, the CIA director, defended waterboarding in March 2005 testimony before the Senate as a "professional interrogation technique."[17]

- The sending of suspects to governments such as Syria, Uzbekistan, and Egypt, which practice systematic torture. Sometimes diplomatic assurances have been sought that the suspects would not be mistreated, but if, as in these cases, the government receiving the suspect routinely flouts its legal obligation under the Convention Against Torture, it is wrong to expect better compliance with the nonbinding word of a diplomat. The administration claimed that it monitored prisoners' treatment, but a single prisoner, lacking the anonymity afforded by a larger group, would often be unable to report abuse for fear of reprisal. One U.S. official who visited foreign detention sites disparaged this

16. Douglas Jehl and Eric Schmitt, "U.S. Military Says 26 Inmate Deaths May Be Homicide," *New York Times*, 16 March 2005.

17. Douglas Jehl, "Questions Are Left by C.I.A. Chief on the Use of Torture," *New York Times*, 18 March 2005.

charade: "They say they are not abusing them, and that satisfies the legal requirement, but we all know they do."[18]

- The decision (adopted by the Bush administration from its earliest days) to oppose and undermine the International Criminal Court (ICC), in part out of fear that it might compel the United States to prosecute U.S. personnel implicated in war crimes or other comparable offenses that the administration would prefer to ignore. The administration spoke in terms of the ICC infringing U.S. sovereignty, but since the ICC could not have jurisdiction over offenses committed by Americans in the United States without Washington's consent, the sovereignty argument actually cuts the other way: it is a violation of the sovereignty of other governments on whose territory an atrocity might be committed not to be free to determine whether to prosecute the crime themselves or to send the matter to the ICC. The administration's position on the ICC was thus reduced to an assertion of exceptionalism — a claim that no international enforcement regime should regulate U.S. criminality overseas. That signaled the administration's determination to protect U.S. personnel from external accountability for any serious human rights offense that it might authorize. Since, in the absence of a special prosecutor, the administration itself controlled the prospects for domestic criminal accountability, its position offered an effective promise of impunity.
- The decision by the Justice Department, the Defense Department, and the White House counsel to concoct dubious legal theories to justify torture, despite objections from the State Department and professional military attorneys. Under the direction of politically appointed lawyers, the administration offered such absurd interpretations of the law as the claim that coercion is not torture unless the pain caused is "equivalent to the pain that would be associated with serious physical injury so severe that death, organ failure, or permanent damage resulting in a loss of significant body function will likely result." Similarly, the administration claimed that President Bush has "commander-in-chief authority" to order torture — a theory under which Slobodan Milosevic and Saddam Hussein may as well be given the keys to their jail cells, since they too presumably would have had "commander-in-chief authority"

18. Dana Priest, "CIA's Assurances on Transferred Suspects Doubted," *Washington Post,* 17 March 2005.

to authorize the atrocities that they directed. The Justice Department, in a December 2004 memorandum modifying the definition of torture, chose not to repudiate the claim about commander-in-chief authority to order torture but instead stated that repudiation was unnecessary because, it said, the president opposes torture as a matter of policy.

These policy decisions, made not by low-level soldiers but by senior officials of the Bush administration, created an "anything goes" atmosphere, an environment in which the ends were assumed to justify the means. Sometimes the mistreatment of detainees was merely tolerated, but at other times it was actively encouraged or even ordered. In that environment, when the demand came from on high for "actionable intelligence" — intelligence that might help stem the steady stream of U.S. casualties at the hands of Iraqi insurgents — it was hardly surprising that interrogators saw no obstacle in the legal prohibition of torture and mistreatment. Nor did these basic human rights rules limit the broader effort to protect Americans from the post-September 11 risks of terrorism.

To this day, the Bush administration has failed to repudiate many of these decisions. It continues to refuse to apply the Geneva Conventions to any of the more than 500 detainees held at Guantánamo (despite a U.S. court ruling rejecting its position) and to many others detained in Iraq and Afghanistan. It continues to "disappear" detainees, despite ample proof that these "ghost detainees" are extraordinarily vulnerable to torture. It continues to defend the practice of "rendering" suspects to governments that torture on the basis of unbelievable assurances and meaningless monitoring. It refuses to accept the duty never to use cruel, inhumane, or degrading treatment anywhere. It continues its vendetta against the ICC. It has only selectively repudiated the many specious arguments for torture contained in the administration lawyers' notorious "torture memos." And long after the abuses of Abu Ghraib became public — at least as late as June 2004 — the Bush administration reportedly continued to subject Guantánamo detainees to beatings, prolonged isolation, sexual humiliation, extreme temperatures, and painful stress positioning, all practices that the ICRC reportedly called "tantamount to torture."[19]

In selecting his cabinet for his second presidential term, President

19. Neil A. Lewis, "Red Cross Finds Detainee Abuse in Guantánamo," *New York Times,* 30 November 2004.

Bush seemed to rule out even informal accountability. Secretary of State Colin Powell, the cabinet official who most forcefully opposed the administration's disavowal of the Geneva Conventions, left his post. Secretary Donald Rumsfeld, who ordered abusive interrogation techniques in violation of international law, stayed on. White House Counsel Alberto Gonzales, who sought production of the memos justifying torture and who wrote that the fight against terrorism renders "obsolete" and "quaint" the Geneva Conventions' limitations on the interrogation and treatment of prisoners, was rewarded with appointment as attorney general.[20] As for the broader Bush administration, the November 2004 electoral victory seems to have reinforced its traditional disinclination to serious self-examination. It persists in its refusal to admit any policy-level misconduct in the treatment of detainees under interrogation.

The Twisted Logic of Torture

The Bush administration's policy of abusive interrogation has received important support in the United States from three Harvard professors: Alan Dershowitz and Phil Heymann of Harvard Law School and Juliette Kayyem of Harvard's Kennedy School. Rather than reinforce the absolute prohibitions of international law, each would seek to regulate exceptions to the prohibitions on mistreating detainees. Ostensibly their aim is to curtail that mistreatment but, by legitimizing it through regulation, they would have the opposite effect.

Dershowitz, in his book *Why Terrorism Works* and in his chapter in the Levinson compilation, typifies this regulatory approach.[21] In his view, torture is inevitable, so prohibiting it will only drive it underground, where low-level officials use it in their discretion. Instead, he would subject torture to judicial oversight by requiring investigators who want to use it to seek the approval of a judge — to procure a torture warrant, much like

20. Memorandum to the President from Alberto R. Gonzales, 25 January 2002, available online at http://www.msnbc.msn.com/id/4999148/site/newsweek. ("In my judgment, this new paradigm [the war against terrorism] renders obsolete Geneva's strict limitations on questioning of enemy prisoners and renders quaint some of its provisions requiring that captured enemy be afforded . . . [listed] privileges.")

21. *Why Terrorism Works: Understanding the Threat, Responding to the Challenge* (New Haven: Yale University Press, 2002); "Tortured Reasoning," in *Torture,* ed. Levinson.

they would seek a search warrant or an arrest warrant. This independent scrutiny, he posits, would reduce the incidence of torture.

Dershowitz's argument is built largely on the faith that forcing torture into the open would reduce its use. But he simply assumes that judges would have a less permissive attitude toward torture than do the senior members of the Bush administration. The available evidence is not encouraging. Since torture would presumably be sought in connection with investigations into serious criminal or national security matters, the information behind the request for a torture warrant would presumably be secret. As in the case of a search warrant or a wiretap, that would mean an ex parte application to a judge, with no notice to the would-be victim of torture and no independent counsel opposing the request.

How rigorous would judicial oversight be in such cases? We can derive some sense from the record of the courts used to approve foreign intelligence wiretaps, and the picture is not impressive. According to the Center for Democracy and Technology, between 1993 and 2003, courts operating under the Foreign Intelligence Surveillance Act (FISA) were asked to approve nearly 10,000 wiretaps of foreign sovereign agents. Of those, all but four were approved. When an intelligence agent claims that life-and-death matters of national security are at stake, there is no reason to believe that the scrutiny by Dershowitz's torture courts would be any more rigorous.

In the meantime, by signaling that torture is at least sometimes acceptable, Dershowitz would reduce the stigma associated with its use. Torture would no longer be a despicable practice never to be used, but merely one more tool in the law enforcement arsenal. Torture specialists eager to practice their trade would appear, international prohibitions of torture would be undermined, and America's credibility as an opponent of torture would be deeply tarnished. Dershowitz points out that accepting clandestine torture also legitimizes it, but he seems never seriously to consider the alternative: vigorously trying to stop, and prosecute, anyone who breaches the absolute ban on torture.

Heymann and Kayyem take a slightly different approach in their report "Preserving Security and Democratic Freedoms in the War on Terrorism."[22] They foreswear torture but would allow a U.S. president to order

---

22. "Preserving Security and Democratic Freedoms in the War on Terrorism," Final Report of the Long-Term Legal Strategy Project (Cambridge, Mass.: Belfer Center for Science and International Affairs, 2004).

cruel, inhumane, or degrading treatment so long as he or she certified to Congress that American lives were at stake. Again, the theory is that such treatment would be rare because the president would be reluctant to invoke that power. But since the president has already claimed "commander-in-chief authority" to order even torture, and since his attorney general claimed the power as recently as January 2005 to order cruel, inhuman, or degrading treatment so long as it is used against non-Americans overseas,[23] Heymann and Kayyem are probably overestimating presidential inhibitions. Making the defense against cruel, inhuman, or degrading treatment depend on the man who has made such treatment a central part of U.S. counterterrorism strategy truly is asking the fox to guard the chicken coop.

Heymann and Kayyem take a similar regulatory approach to coercive interrogation short of cruel, inhumane, or degrading treatment. The U.S. Army's field manual on intelligence interrogation makes clear that coercive interrogation is unnecessary, unreliable, and wrong. That's because, as most professional interrogators explain, coercive interrogation is far less likely to produce reliable information than the time-tested methods of careful questioning, probing, cross-checking, and gaining the confidence of the detainee. A person facing severe pain is likely to say whatever he thinks will stop the torture. But a skilled interrogator can often extract accurate information from the toughest suspect without resorting to coercion.

Yet Heymann and Kayyem would abandon that bright-line rule and permit coercive interrogation so long as the president notifies Congress of the techniques to be used. However, setting American interrogators free from the firm mooring of the U.S. Army field manual can be dangerous, as we have seen so painfully in Abu Ghraib, Guantánamo, Afghanistan, and elsewhere. If mere coercion (itself a violation of the Geneva Conventions in wartime) does not work — and, given that the suspect is supposedly a hardened terrorist, often it will not — interrogators will be all too tempted to ratchet up the pain, suffering, and humiliation until the suspect cracks, regardless of the dubious reliability of information provided in such circumstances. In this way, coercion predictably gives way to cruel, inhuman, or degrading treatment, which in turn gives rise to torture.

The proposals from Dershowitz and Heymann and Kayyem suffer from the same fundamental defect: they seek to regulate the mistreatment

---

23. "A Degrading Policy" and "U.S. Justifying Abuse of Detainees."

of detainees rather than reinforce the prohibition against such abuse. In the end, any effort to regulate mistreatment ends up legitimizing it and inviting repetition. "Never" cannot be redeemed if allowed to be read as "sometimes." Regulation too easily becomes license.

Behind the Dershowitz and Heymann and Kayyem proposals is some variation of the "ticking bomb" scenario, a situation in which interrogators are said to believe that a terrorist suspect in custody knows where a ticking bomb has been planted and must urgently force that information from him to save lives. Torture and inhumane treatment may be wrong, those who talk of ticking bombs would concede, but the mass murder of a terrorist attack is worse, so in these supposedly rare situations, the lesser evil must be tolerated to prevent the greater one.

The ticking bomb scenario makes for great philosophical discussion, but it rarely arises in real life, at least not in a way that avoids opening the door to pervasive torture. In fact, interrogators hardly ever learn that a suspect in custody knows of a particular, imminent terrorist bombing. Intelligence is rarely if ever good enough to demonstrate a particular suspect's knowledge of an imminent attack. Instead, interrogators tend to use circumstantial evidence to show such "knowledge," such as someone's association with or presumed membership in a terrorist group. Moreover, the ticking bomb scenario is a dangerously expansive metaphor capable of embracing anyone who might have knowledge not just of immediate attacks but also of attacks at unspecified future times. After all, why are the victims of only an imminent terrorist attack deserving of protection by torture and mistreatment? Why not also use such coercion to prevent a terrorist attack tomorrow or next week or next year? And once the taboo against torture and mistreatment is broken, why stop with the alleged terrorists themselves? Why not also torture and abuse their families or associates — or anyone who might provide lifesaving information? The slope is very slippery.

Israel's experience is instructive in showing how dangerously elastic the ticking bomb rationale can become, as described by the Israeli human rights group B'Tselem in its report on interrogations by Israel's intelligence agency, the General Security Services (GSS). In 1987, an official government commission, headed by former Israeli Supreme Court president Moshe Landau, recommended authorizing the use of "moderate physical pressure" in ticking bomb situations. As B'Tselem describes, a practice initially justified as rare and exceptional, taken only when necessary to save lives, gradually became standard GSS procedure. Soon, some 80 to 90 percent of Palestinian security detainees were being tortured, until 1999 when the Israeli Supreme Court curtailed the practice. Dershowitz cites the court's belated intervention as validation of his theory that regulating torture is the best way to defeat it, but he never asks whether the severe victimization of so many Palestinians could have been avoided with a prohibitory approach from the start. Notably, Israel's escalation in the use of torture took place even though a ministerial committee chaired by the prime minister was supervising interrogation practices — a regulatory procedure similar to the one proposed by Heymann and Kayyem. Indeed, in September 1994, following several suicide bombings, the ministerial committee even loosened the restrictions on interrogators by permitting "increased physical pressure." Heymann and Kayyem never explain why, especially in light of the abysmal record of the Bush administration, we should expect any better from high-level U.S. officials.

The Way Forward

Faced with substantial evidence showing that the abuses at Abu Ghraib and elsewhere were caused in large part by official government policies, the Bush administration must reaffirm the importance of making human rights a guiding force for U.S. conduct, even in fighting terrorism. That requires acknowledging and reversing the policy decisions behind the administration's torture and mistreatment of detainees, holding accountable those responsible at all levels of government for this abuse (not just a bunch of privates and sergeants), and publicly committing to ending all forms of coercive interrogation. These steps are necessary to reaffirm the prohibition of torture and ill treatment, to redeem Washington's voice as a credible proponent of human rights, and to restore the effectiveness of a U.S.-led campaign against terrorism.

Yet all that is easier said than done. How can President Bush and the U.S. Congress be convinced to establish a fully independent investigative commission — similar to the one created to examine the attacks of September 11, 2001 — to determine what went wrong in the administration's interrogation practices and to prescribe remedial steps? How can former Attorney General Gonzales, who as White House counsel played a central role in formulating the administration's interrogation policy, be persuaded to recognize his obvious conflict of interest and appoint a special prosecutor charged with investigating criminal misconduct independently of the Justice Department's direction? These are not steps that the administration or its congressional allies will take willingly. Pressure will be needed.

And that pressure cannot and should not come from only the usual suspects. The torture and abuse of prisoners is an affront to the most basic American values. It is antithetical to the core beliefs in the integrity of the individual, on which the United States was founded. And it violates one of the most basic prohibitions of international law.

This is not a partisan concern, not an issue limited to one part of the political spectrum. It is a matter that all Americans — and their friends around the world — should insist be meaningfully addressed and changed. It is an issue that should preoccupy governments, whether friend or foe, as well as such international organizations and actors as the UN Commission on Human Rights, Human Rights Committee, High Commissioner on Human Rights, and Special Rapporteur on Torture. Taking on the world's superpower is never easy, but it is essential if the basic architecture of international human rights law and institutions is not to be deeply compromised. As Secretary General Kofi Annan told the March 2005 International Summit on Democracy, Terrorism, and Security: "Upholding human rights is not merely compatible with successful counterterrorism strategy. It is an essential element."[24] There is no room for torture, even in fighting terrorism; it risks undermining the foundation on which all of our rights rest.

24. Keynote address to the Closing Plenary of the International Summit on Democracy, Terrorism, and Security, "A Global Strategy for Fighting Terrorism," Madrid, Spain, 10 March 2005, available online at www.un.org/apps/sg/sgstats.asp?nid=1345.

CHAPTER 2

A Survivor's View of Torture

Dianna Ortiz, OSU

Let me begin by saying that God and international law share at least one thing in common. Sometimes it is difficult to find either of them when you need them most. When the "Police Man," the first of the torturers to rape me, had finished his grisly work, he whispered in my ear, "Your God is dead." At the time, this seemed a reasonable conclusion. He made no mention of international law, because whatever that was, if it was, it was certainly irrelevant to my situation.

Over time, law has not gained much more relevance for me, personally. I sought justice both in Guatemala and the United States but found none. It is true that the Inter-American Human Rights Commission of the Organization of American States examined my case and found that I was telling the truth, but why was this important?

When I was being tortured by members of the Guatemalan security forces, they referred to their boss, Alejandro. I met Alejandro in that clandestine prison. He spoke perfect American English. His Spanish was spoken with a North American accent. He spoke of a friend at the American embassy and, referring to the death threats I had received, he said, "We tried to warn you."

After my escape, a friend of mine was told by a U.S. embassy official that I had better say nothing about the American, Alejandro. But I did. I believed that it was my moral responsibility to speak of what I had witnessed in that clandestine prison — of the others who were also being tortured and of the presence of an American. I foolishly believed that both my government and the American people would be outraged to know that an American was boss of a squad of torturers in another country.

Instead, I paid a price for that truth. The first story that was put out by my government was that I had not been tortured at all — that I was part of some political plot to deny the Guatemalan military funds from the U.S. Congress. The difficulty with this slander was that I had more than 111 cigarette burns on my back and elsewhere. And so the story changed. I still had not been tortured. The burns came from, and I quote, "kinky lesbian sex" that got out of hand.

For a number of years, I spent considerable time and energy asking my government about Alejandro and what an American was doing heading up a Guatemalan torture squad. George H. W. Bush, who was president when I was tortured, was of no help — unsurprisingly, since it was his ambassador to Guatemala who was involved in defaming me. Neither, I should emphasize, was his successor, Bill Clinton.

Finally, in some desperation, in 1996 I undertook a five-week vigil and fast in front of the White House asking for the truth. One hundred three members of Congress signed a letter to President Clinton asking him to release the requested information. He did not do so. I say this because it is important to note that in speaking of torture, we are not dealing with a partisan issue. When it comes to torture, both political parties have been involved, and both have protected those ordering these crimes against humanity.

I have told you that I was burned with cigarettes. I was gang raped. I was also lowered into an open pit filled with human bodies — bodies of children, women, and men — some decapitated, some caked with blood, some dead, some alive. Beyond this, I was forced to participate in the torture of another human being. I was also subjected to other forms of torture that I will not describe here. Worse than the physical torture was hearing the screams of the others being tortured. Can you hear the screams? I can.

Allow me to tell you this one thing more. When my first rapist, the Police Man, whispered to me, "Your God is dead," he was absolutely right. My God was dead. I sat naked in a cold, dark cell waiting for the next horror to befall me, and I prayed to God, "Please let me die. Free me from this hell." But God would not even do that for me. I was alone, utterly alone. No one listened to my begging prayer.

A Honduran torturer once said, "Eventually they all beg to die." The first words my friend Dr. Carmen Valenzuela heard when she was led blindfolded before her chief torturer were these: "Doctor, we are not going to kill you, but you are going to beg for us to kill you."

But whether they kill us or not, we all die in those secret cells. And so, for me, God died too in that clandestine prison, just as God has died in the concentration camps of Europe and at so many other places and times. It is true that I too died, but I was not to receive the mercy of permanent death. By some cruel irony the now-dead God still existed to force upon me a grotesque resurrection and return to unwanted life. And so began my dialogue with that dead God, who had not cared enough to save me. But the questions I asked continued to go unanswered.

I was sent back to a world where no one could be trusted, where betrayal was everywhere, where my torturers came to me nightly, even at times in broad daylight. I bathed for hours, even using Clorox, to try to cleanse myself of my torturers, but to no avail. The contamination was not on my skin; it was inside me. Anyone I touched I might contaminate as well. I drank cup after cup of coffee to keep awake, to try to keep my torturers away, those very men who would not leave me alone.

And I was asked questions. I was asked by others, friends as well as strangers, not whether I was receiving any justice from my government but whether I had forgiven my torturers. I wanted the truth. I wanted justice. They wanted me to forgive, so that they could move on. I suppose, once I forgave, all would be well — for them. Christianity, it seemed, was concerned with individual forgiveness, not social justice.

I found sanctuary in one way alone — with the only friend I had in this world, a friend who went with me everywhere. I still remember a conference in Washington in 1992 when I spoke publicly of my torture for the first time. It was there I introduced my friend. I held it up for all the world to see — the razor blade that was my protector. At any moment, I could save myself finally from an uncaring, dead God. I could use that blade to finish what the torturers had started.

I lived in a world created by my torturers. They had told me, as so many other tortured persons have been told, "Even if you survive what we have done to you and tell the world, no one will believe you. No one will care." That is the world I lived in: No one cared. No law, no God, no justice, no peace, no hope.

In one way, it is a world I continue to live in. I do so not by choice but because of the truth that "once tortured, always tortured." While I have found that God was not really dead, and I no longer carry the razor blade, still there are days, even weeks, when I long for its comfort. There are many days when I remember the words of the Austrian philosopher Jean Amery, who was tortured by the Nazis: "Anyone who has been tortured remains tortured. Anyone who has suffered torture will never again be at ease in the world, the abomination of the annihilation is never extinguished. Faith in humanity, already cracked with the first slap in the face, then demolished by torture, is never acquired again."[1]

Some twenty years later, Jean Amery took his own life. And he is not alone. Not long ago, one of our friends, a woman from Ethiopia, sat huddled in her closet as she made the decision that what her torturers had done was too much for her and she would finally escape their evil the only way she knew how — a young woman with two youthful children, dead by her own hand, or, perhaps better, dead finally by her torturers' hands. Torture's ghost walks with us every day of our lives, reminding us that the past is not gone, that the past will always be. We will never have the freedom to forget the past. At any moment, the smell of a cigarette, the jangling of keys, the sound of someone whistling, a gentle embrace, seeing someone in uniform, being alone in the dark, or even the simple act of making eye contact can transport us back to that horrible time.

My torturers still come to me from time to time. I can still smell them. But they are less and less the reason why that razor blade comes to mind — the reason why I need its protection. Increasingly it is because of the leaders of my own government and the torture they so arrogantly preside over, for I have not told you all that died with my torture and its aftermath.

The connection between my own government and justice was torn asunder, and remains so today. Certainly nothing the present administration is doing will alter this situation. Shall I, shall we, who have been tortured put our trust in the law when we are told the president is superior to law? Apparently the president can do what he wants in the name of protecting us from terrorism. He can torture to protect us from terrorism. But torture is a form of terrorism! Where is the law, international or otherwise, to protect us from our own government's practice of terrorism?

These past months have made one thing very clear. President George W. Bush bears direct responsibility for the torture practiced by the U.S. government. On June 26, 2003, on the U.N. International Day in Support of Torture Victims and Survivors, the president issued a statement de-

---

1. Quoted in Primo Levi, *The Drowned and the Saved* (New York: Vintage, 1988), p. 25.

claring in effect that the United States opposed torture by anyone at any time for any reason anywhere. He also pledged that the United States would lead the effort to eradicate torture from the world. Given all that we now know, there can be no doubt that Mr. Bush knew that what he was saying was untrue.

At this point, let me introduce a word into the discussion of whether the United States should torture, or engage in cruel, inhuman, or degrading treatment. The word is impunity. It is a word of considerable importance to survivors. Survivors wish to know the truth of our torture, and we seek justice, that is, accountability for its practice. We get neither from our government or any other. Therefore, this is one of the objectives of our organizing.

While I was being held in that clandestine prison, I made a promise to those I heard being tortured with me: "If I survive, I will tell the world what I have heard here." It is not a promise I have enjoyed keeping; instead, I am shackled to it. The God I believed was dead, the God I believed mocked me, this God may have made a mistake, or my torturers may have — but whatever the reason, I did not die in that clandestine prison. I'm still alive, and therefore I must continue to honor that promise made not only to the Guatemalans with whom I was tortured but to all those worldwide who suffer this horror.

Torture Abolition and Survivors Support Coalition (TASSC) is a result of that promise. It was created by survivors for the benefit of survivors. It was also created so that we might work to ensure that what happened to us will never happen to you or your children. Torture has plagued our past. It plagues our present, and it threatens our future — your future, your children's future, and that of their children as well.

Somehow we must find a way to convince the American people that to support torture, either actively or passively, repeats the brutality of the past. It puts us in the company of the Stalins, the Hitlers, the Pinochets, and the Argentine generals, who also found ethically comfortable reasons for torturing.

Together let us live by the words of Israeli historian Yehuda Bauer: "Thou shall not be a victim; Thou shall not be a perpetrator; and Thou shall never, but never, be a bystander."[2]

2. Yehuda Bauer, "Speech at the Ceremonial Opening of the Forum," Stockholm International Forum on the Holocaust, 2000. Available online at http://www.manskligarattigheter.gov.se/stockholmforum/2000/page898.html.

CHAPTER 3

Confessions of a Torturer

Tony Lagouranis as told to John Conroy

After interrogator's school, Tony Lagouranis spent 15 months learning Arabic at the Defense Language Institute in Monterey, California. In the summer of 2003, about four months after the invasion of Iraq, he was sent to Fort Gordon, Georgia, where he joined the 513th Military Intelligence Brigade, which contained soldiers who had already served in Afghanistan and Iraq. He got more training there, and he also began hearing stories from the veterans of more abusive approaches — though he figured some were boastful exaggeration.

"They were talking about using sexual humiliation on these guys, or certain stress positions they had used, or in Afghanistan they would make the guy sit in the snow naked for long periods of time. They said that the detainees that they had were not covered by the Geneva Conventions, which I continued to hear in Iraq too."

He arrived in Iraq in January 2004 and was stationed at Abu Ghraib, landing there ten days after Specialist Joseph Darby delivered the now infamous photographs of prisoner abuse to army investigators. "When we got

---

As a specialist in military intelligence, 37-year-old Tony Lagouranis interrogated prisoners in Iraq from January through December 2004. He was stationed in Abu Ghraib, Mosul, Fallujah, Al Assad, North Babil, and Baghdad. He is one of a handful of Iraq War veterans who have offered firsthand accounts of their experiences as interrogators. What follows is an abridged version of an article based on what Lagouranis told investigative reporter John Conroy of the *Chicago Reader*.

there we didn't know what had happened, but the Army knew, and they were making sure that things were cleaned up at Abu Ghraib."

Lagouranis says his own interrogations there were taken "right out of the Army field manual." Some of the older interrogators, however, were using harsher methods. Some detainees judged to be uncooperative were stripped of their mattress, blankets, and extra clothing to expose them to the cold in their cells. Others were kept in isolation for months at a time and hooded when they were taken to the interrogation booths, so that they'd see no one but their interrogators. Nevertheless, it seemed to Lagouranis that the administration of Abu Ghraib was getting progressively cleaner. Also, it was common knowledge that the CIA was torturing prisoners, he says, so anything the Army did paled by comparison.

Not long after his arrival, Lagouranis was assigned to a special projects team interrogating people who'd been involved with hiding Saddam Hussein, some of them just peripheral figures "who happened to brush up against Saddam Hussein and maybe they had information, but they weren't necessarily bad guys." A relative of a high-level Ba'athist complained to Lagouranis that he'd been tortured. "He told me that when he was arrested he was beaten and forced to stand against a wall and kneel for days, and he was kept from sleeping, and they'd come in occasionally and beat him up and kick him.

"He begged me to take the sandbag off his head so he could look at the sun, just walk around outside a little bit. I gave him the opportunity to do that. This guy was really a mess. Isolation is a really terrible thing for people.

"I filed an abuse report on this guy with the Criminal Investigation Division (CID). They had a standard form, like a memo someone had made up internally at Abu Ghraib, and so I asked my superior for that form, and I went in and did a specific interrogation to ask this guy about that abuse. The guy was really reluctant to talk about it, he said to forget it, he just didn't want any more trouble for himself. But I got it out of him. I wrote the abuse report and gave it to my superior. And that abuse report, as far as I know, has disappeared. It doesn't exist anymore."

After roughly a month at the prison, Lagouranis was transferred to a four-man mobile interrogation team. He had brief stints at Al Asad Air Force Base and again at Abu Ghraib, and then he was assigned to Mosul; it was there that he began to torture the men he was interrogating.

"We were working for this chief warrant officer who just wanted to go as far as he could. He handed us a piece of paper called an IROE — interrogation rules of engagement. It listed the things that the Pentagon said were okay to use during interrogations, but it was also sort of an open-ended document — it encouraged the interrogator to be creative.

"For instance, one technique that was approved was called environmental manipulation. It's really unclear what that means exactly. He took it to mean that we could leave them outside in the cold rain, or we could blast rock music and bombard them with strobe lights for days at a time, or use those things in combination. The document didn't really give us guidance, although that is what it was meant for.

"So when he would tell us to do things, we would go to this document in order to determine whether it was legal or illegal." Having been told that the detainees were not covered by the Geneva Conventions, Lagouranis thought his training in the law was not applicable. "We were in this murky area. They always tell you, if you're given an illegal order it's your duty to refuse to follow it, but we were in a place that we didn't know what the legal limit was, so we didn't know what to do." To protect himself, Lagouranis wrote up an interrogation plan for each detainee, had the warrant officer sign it, and put it in the detainee's file.

The site had been understaffed before Lagouranis's mobile interrogation team arrived. "Once we got there I think the chief warrant officer saw the opportunity to institute the things that he wanted to do. One of those things was a 24-hour operation. He was only running a 12-hour operation before that. He put us on shifts, and that way you could maintain the sleep deprivation, you could maintain stress positions all night. So within a week of our arriving there he started instituting these harsher tactics."

The warrant officer secured a shipping container that became the unit's interrogation booth. Stress positions became standard operating procedure. They included standing for long periods; kneeling on concrete, gravel, or plywood; and crawling across gravel. "Another one we'd use was where they would have their back against the wall and their knees bent at right angles. We used to do that as an exercise in basic training and it gets real painful after a few minutes, but we'd make the prisoners do that for a long time.

"We had three different strobe lights going at once, and the prisoner would be in a stress position, and it was cold, so he'd be freezing." At times the detainees were exposed directly to the strobe lighting, but at other times they wore goggles that obscured vision but allowed the pulsating light to enter. The music in the shipping container was applied by means of a boom box turned up to maximum volume.

"I didn't handle the dogs. We had professional dog handlers. They were MPs, military police, who lived right next to the compound where we were doing this, so I would just go and wake them up. We had a signal I would give him to cue the dog to lunge and bark at the prisoner. The prisoner would have blacked-out goggles on so he couldn't see that the dog was restrained, he couldn't see that the dog had a muzzle on, he just knew there was a dog in the room with him and that it was a big angry dog.

"What usually happened was the prisoner would be terrified the first time the dog became aggressive. But then that effect wore off — he figured out that the dog wasn't going to attack him. So maybe you'd get the prisoner totally terrified for like five seconds and he would wet his pants, literally. Then after that there was nothing. So it wasn't effective at all, but the chief warrant officer kept telling us to do this so we did it."

Though some prisoners complained, Lagouranis thinks others took the ill treatment for granted — "like this is what happens when you're detained. If you think about Iraq and what Iraqis would expect from being arrested under Saddam Hussein or whatever, I think they probably felt they were getting it pretty easy, especially because the treatment they had at our hands was a lot better than they got from the detainee unit. We were getting prisoners from the Navy SEALs who were using a lot of the same techniques we were using, except they were a little harsher. They would actually have the detainee stripped nude, lying on the floor, pouring ice water over his body. They were taking his temperature with a rectal thermometer. We had one guy who had been burned by the Navy SEALs. He looked like he had a lighter held up to his legs. One guy's feet were huge and black and blue, his toes were obviously all broken, and he couldn't walk."

Lagouranis says the MPs were "willing and enthusiastic participants in all this stuff. A lot of the guys that we worked with were former prison guards or they were reservists who were prison guards in their civilian life. They loved it."

Lagouranis says the MPs didn't know anything about individual detainees, most of whom, in Lagouranis's estimation, had nothing to do with the insurgency. "The MPs don't read the paperwork, they don't talk to the guy, they don't know anything about it, other than they think this is a guy who's been mortaring us and so they hate him. They'll abuse him if they can. They can do that in many ways. They can refuse his request for medical attention, refuse his request to go to the bathroom — that was really common — refuse his request for a blanket."

He says, "We had a lot of prisoners to deal with so most of the prisoners didn't get the full treatment for as long as the warrant officer would have liked. But there were two brothers in particular that we were going on pretty hard. We had some significant evidence on these guys, which was so rare — we almost never had evidence on anybody. We went on them hard for almost a month, I think, and these guys were just completely broken down, physically, mentally, by the end of it. One guy walked like a 90-year-old man when he was done. He was an ex-army guy, he was a healthy young man when he came in, and by the end he was a mess. Psychologically they couldn't focus on things. Their emotions would change all the time. They were obviously showing signs of deterioration."

If a man can't focus, can he answer questions? "It made interrogation harder, but we weren't getting information from these guys anyway. The person who was ordering all this stuff, the chief warrant officer, he never saw these prisoners, so there was no way for him to understand what was going on." The warrant officer's response to a lack of information, Lagouranis says, was simply to add another layer of abuse.

In April 2004 the *New Yorker* and *60 Minutes II* broke the story of detainee abuse at Abu Ghraib. Not long after those infamous photos were published, Lagouranis was transferred from Mosul back to Abu Ghraib. CNN broadcasts played constantly in the area where the interrogators wrote their reports, and it was there, while watching congressional hearings, that Lagouranis heard Defense Secretary Donald Rumsfeld say that the detainees in Iraq were being treated according to the Geneva Conventions. "I also heard Lieutenant General Ricardo Sanchez say that dogs were never authorized to be used in Iraq." This testimony flatly contradicted guidelines for interrogations that Sanchez, the military commander in Iraq, had issued in September and October of 2003.

Not long thereafter, the army's Criminal Investigation Division, investigating torture committed by the Abu Ghraib MPs, called in Lagouranis to answer questions about a prisoner who'd been abused by the MPs later charged in the scandal. Lagouranis says he wasn't able to help them with that case because he hadn't interrogated the detainee, but he did report everything he had done in the shipping container in Mosul and all that he had witnessed there. He also mentioned the earlier report he'd filed with CID on the high-level Ba'athist who'd been tortured at Abu Ghraib.

He heard nothing further before he was transferred to Kalsu, a base in Iskandariyah, about 25 miles south of Baghdad, where the Marines were in charge of a new detention facility. "When the scandal broke, it gave us the power to refuse to do any harsh tactics," Lagouranis recalls, "but at that base I saw the most egregious abuse. After the scandal broke, they stopped torturing people in prisons and they would torture them before they got to the prison. They would either torture them in their homes or they would take them to a remote location. The marines had a location — they called it the 'meat factory' — they would bring them there and they would torture them for 24 or 48 hours before they brought them to us, and they were using techniques like water boarding, mock execution, they were beating them up, breaking their bones, whatever. It was bad.

"And I was writing abuse reports during that time about these guys, and I was sending it up through the Marine chain of command. I was taking the prisoners' statements, I was making my own statements, I was taking photographs, and those photographs were put in the medical files of the detainees.

"No one ever came to look at those medical files, no one ever came to talk to the prisoners, no one ever came to interview me about this stuff. But they were assuring me that these things were going to be investigated."

Lagouranis left Iraq in December 2004. In January 2005 he was back at Fort Gordon in Georgia, angered and frustrated by what he'd seen and done.

"The idea with interrogation — you are taught this all the time — is that you are supposed to get a small piece of information and that piece is going to be synthesized into a big picture. And I don't think that is happening. I would get a prisoner whose brother was in another detention facility. I had no access to the interrogation reports for his brother. I would write intelligence reports, the prisoner would then be sent back to Abu Ghraib, and often my reports would not go with him. Information was being lost all over the place. Even though the Army had software set up for sharing information by interrogators and the entire intelligence community, commanders would set up their own. So we had these databases that couldn't communicate with each other. When I was in Abu Ghraib I couldn't even access the MP database to find out who was in Abu Ghraib. Everything was ridiculously difficult. It made no sense.

"I would write intelligence reports and someone would mention the name of somebody, a neighbor, with no incriminating information at all. And the analyst would get ahold of that and that person would become a target and I would be talking to that person the next week — and for what?

And I would call up the analyst and say, 'Why am I talking to this guy?' And he would quote my report out of context and tell me this was why. It just made no sense."

The vast majority of the men and women in Lagouranis's military intelligence brigade remained at Abu Ghraib and a nearby base for their entire tour, and at the end of that year they published an intelligence report he says was full of empty claims. "It was like, 'The top ten detainees and what we got out of them'?" Lagouranis says. "It was all bullshit. And that's for an entire year of interrogating thousands of prisoners at Abu Ghraib. They got nothing out of that place. That's not just my assessment — you can talk to anybody I worked with over there. The main reason for that is because 90 or 95 percent of the people we got had nothing to do with the insurgency. And if they did we didn't have any good evidence on them. And the detainees knew that and they knew they didn't have to talk to us." A February 2004 Red Cross report based on the estimates of coalition intelligence officers said that 70 to 90 percent of the prisoners were innocent.

"I got nothing in Iraq," says Lagouranis. "Zero."

Back at Fort Gordon, Lagouranis says, "I lost my mind a little bit. Panic attacks, anxiety, insomnia, nightmares. I was shaking all the time. Plus I was really angry. I was being pretty insubordinate. After you come back they do a lot of patting you on the back and calling you 'hero' and they are handing out medals to everybody.

"So they were saying, 'What are we going to do with this Lagouranis guy?' I was obviously a mess, too. So they got me out. They gave me an honorable discharge, which was good."

Lagouranis left the Army in mid-July of 2005, house-sat briefly in New Orleans for some friends, and returned to Chicago in August. "I think it was because I had been on Zoloft and Welbutrin and decided to stop taking that stuff, and I guess you're not supposed to just stop."

While the voices in his head were gone, his anger was not. Army press spokesman John Paul Boyce responded to Lagouranis's public statements by saying that the Army "has never given authority to any soldier throughout this war to abuse or torture detainees. We encourage Mr. Lagouranis to provide the Army any new information so that it may be investigated thoroughly."

Lagouranis didn't believe he had anything new to say to the Army aside from the abuse he'd reported in January 2004 in Abu Ghraib, in two CID interviews after he left Mosul that spring, three times to the marine

chain of command at Kalsu in September and October, and again in an interview he'd instigated with CID after his return to Georgia in January
2005. After his appearance on PBS's *Frontline* was aired in October 2005,
however, an investigator from the Army's CID came to Lagouranis's apartment and asked why he hadn't reported any of the abuse before going to
the media. "The guy said to me, 'We ran your name through the computer.
We don't have any reports from you.'"

And yet for all the courage Lagouranis has shown in coming forward,
taking on the Army and the Marines single-handedly, enduring denunciation from various partisans, and speaking at various human rights events, he
still has to face himself. He has tortured. The measure of that is his victims.

Asked what one might expect to see in a man who'd been held in a
shipping container, his vision obscured, bombarded with strobe lighting
and loud music, deprived of sleep, exposed to hypothermia, and threatened by a large dog, Rosa Garcia-Peltoniemi, senior consulting clinician
for the Center for Victims of Torture in Minneapolis, said she wouldn't be
surprised if the man suffered severe physical and psychological damage for
the rest of his life.

Asked how he explains himself, Lagouranis says, "It's tough. I can say I
was following orders, and that is partly true. But there are other answers.
You are in a war zone and things get blurred. We wanted intelligence. It
really became absolutely morally impossible for me to continue when I
realized that most of the people we were dealing with were innocent. And
that was tough. So it made it easier if I thought that I was actually dealing
with a real-life bad guy. Then, also, you're in an environment where everybody is telling you that this is okay, and it's hard to be the only person saying, 'This is wrong.' And I really was, even as I was doing it, I was the only
person saying, 'We've got to put the brakes on. What's going too far here?'

"You might think this is not a good defense either, but the things that I
did weren't really that horrible. I mean, I saw some really horrible torture.
And I'm sure every torturer would say this — 'Other people are doing
worse things.' I didn't carry the things that I was doing as far as I could
have. Like the guys that we were leaving out in the cold, I was always the
one who went out and checked on them all the time. Most of the other
people would just sit in the office and watch DVDs while these guys were
out in the cold. I was bringing them in and warming them up. So I didn't
go as far as I might have.

"I don't think people can imagine what it's like. In Mosul we were wide open. There was only concertina wire separating us from the town and we were getting mortared all the time. You'd be lying in bed and mortars were going off all over the place. The infantry brings you somebody and they tell you that this is the guy who's shooting mortars at you. Scaring him with a muzzled dog doesn't seem like the worst thing in that situation. I mean I was willing to try it. I didn't know that it wasn't going to work."

CHAPTER 4

Military Concerns about Torture:
Honor, Professionalism, Morale

Adm. John Hutson and Gen. Richard O'Meara

Admiral Hutson

I want to reflect on why the harsh interrogation of prisoners and terrorist suspects matters to the military, to military personnel, and ultimately to the national defense, which of course is what the military is about.

Let me start by saying that I believe it is absolutely critical that we win the global war on terror, and that we use whatever means are necessary to do so. The question is: what is winning the war on terror? What do we really mean when we say we want to win? I think what we don't mean is that we're going to lose our soul in the process. I think it doesn't mean that we are going to become like the enemy in an effort to defeat the enemy. Because if we become like the enemy — which is always a temptation in a war, to escalate, to act in blind vengeance, to respond in kind — we will have lost.

Worse than that, in some respects, we won't know whether we've won or lost. The effort will terminate and we will be significantly different than we were before. That's why the issue of our government's resort to torture is as important to the military as it is to everyone else. The military is charged with a responsibility of one thing, fighting and winning our nation's wars. But there are two elements to that responsibility, besides the fighting part there is also the winning part.

We are, and have been since World War II, the strongest nation on the face of the earth. I don't think we are as strong now as we were a few years ago, but we are still the strongest nation on earth. And why is that? I would say it's not because of our military strength, not because of our economy, not because of our natural resources or the essential island nature of our landmass, although all those factors are important. The reason we are the strongest nation on earth is because of what we have stood for since World War II. The United States of America has taken upon itself the responsibility to be a world leader, to stand tall for human rights, to support the rule of law, day in and day out. It is not the rule of law if it applies only when convenient. If that happens, then it's something else, but it's not the rule of law.

If the United States says that we stand for the rule of law, if the president and the Congress say that we stand for it, that means we stand for it all day, all night, all month, all the time. But we've nitpicked at our principles and applied them only when it was convenient. When it was inconvenient we said they were antiquated and quaint, that the rule of law didn't really apply anymore, because things have changed. That's not the kind of fluid structure that the military can deal with very well or very responsibly. There's a significant difference between a principled and a fluid commitment to the rule of law. I believe in the Constitution, in the civilian leadership of the military. That's why we have a president who is the commander-in-chief. That's why we have a secretary of defense, and service secretaries, and all those arrangements. But a different perspective is emerging about the rule of law, particularly in this administration. I say that as a lifelong Republican, as an increasingly troubled Republican.

But the military looks over the horizon. The military knows that this is not the last war we are ever going to fight, not even the next to last. If human history is any indication, we will be fighting wars, unfortunately, for generations to come. That means we have to keep things in perspective. We can't look at the 2006 or 2008 elections to determine what the end result is going to be. It may seem counterintuitive, but in certain respects the military has a better, more reasonable perspective than the civilians do. You can see it in war college scenarios when they set up war games. Civilians are brought in, religious leaders, business leaders, CEOs, all kinds of people, to take part. They play the president, the secretary of defense, the admirals, the generals, and so forth, in various scenarios. What I have seen happen is that the civilians will go nuclear before the military do, because the military understand the consequences and see the options. They see other ways to go forward while the civilians get stymied and impatient. They get scared and push the button. In the framework of the game, they do so quite literally.

So the military has its own perspective. Morale is high among their concerns. You want to be proud about what you've done. People aren't proud of Lynndie England. Or Graner. Or Pappas. And especially not Miller, hiding behind Article 31, invoking his Fifth Amendment rights, the other day. That is unheard of, a general invoking Article 31 rights, in this kind of situation. Not to stand tall, not to take responsibility for what happened, is antithetical to the entire military culture.

[Editor's note: Maj. Gen. Geoffrey Miller was at the center of the Abu Ghraib scandal. He became commander of Guantánamo Bay in November 2002. In August 2003 he was instructed by Secretary of Defense Rumsfeld to brief Army officers in Iraq on interrogation techniques. He favored methods that were outside the Geneva Conventions.

Adm. Hutson refers to the event in January 2006 when Gen. Miller refused to testify — invoking his Article 31 rights, similar to the Fifth Amendment — in court-martial proceedings against two soldiers accused of using dogs to terrorize prisoners at the Baghdad prison. Gen. Miller denied that he had recommended using dogs in interrogations, but was later contradicted under oath by Col. Thomas Pappas. Observers believed that Gen. Miller could have been a key to determining whether the Abu Ghraib abuses were the result of a few rogue soldiers ("bad apples") or whether responsibility lay higher up the chain of command. He eventually testified in May 2006 without being probed.

The fates of the others mentioned by Adm. Hutson may also be noted. Spc. Lynndie England, having received a dishonorable discharge, was sentenced to three years in prison. Spc. Charles Graner was sentenced to ten years, with a dishonorable discharge and the loss of all benefits. Col. Pappas, cited extensively in the Fay Report for oversight failures at Abu Ghraib, received many awards and decorations, including the Legion of Merit. Gen. Miller retired from the Army in July 2006, being awarded the Distinguished Service Medal at his ceremony and praised as an "innovator."]

I was once interviewed by Peter Jennings. It was long before Abu Graib, when I was arguing that the detainees in Guantánamo had a right to what are called "competent tribunals" in the Geneva Conventions to determine their status and decide whether they should be detained or released. I said to Mr. Jennings: "Now don't misunderstand me. I'm not suggesting that any of these people have been mistreated. I'm just saying they have a right to a hearing and that we are denying them this basic right."

Whereupon Peter Jennings smiled, looked at me quizzically, and said: "Well, how do you know that?" I pulled myself up tall and retorted: "Well, I spent twenty-eight years in the United States Navy. I know military personnel, and I know that that wouldn't happen." I've often wondered about that interview. After we saw those horrific pictures from Abu Ghraib, it was one of my very first thoughts. I wonder if Peter Jennings remembers how wrong I was. For me it felt as if a family member had died. To see people like Lynndie England — whoever thought she was going to be a good soldier, I'm not sure — but people like that have been tremendously let down. They've been let down by their superiors. A tragedy like that is very personal with the military. It's not an abstract question. It's not just a matter of following rules. It's personal. It's your friends. It's the troops under your care. It's you who are involved, you who are responsible for them. A debacle like Abu Ghraib makes a huge impact on morale.

There's also a military aspect to this kind of failure, which is that it imperils troops. It imperils them now and in the future, in those future wars we are going to confront. We are going to need coalition allies in the future for other wars. We are having a heck of a time getting them now, and we won't be able to get them in the future if they can't trust us to not be abusive. If they can't trust us to comply with the Geneva Conventions, we're going to have a problem. I say this from a military point of view, from the point of view of prosecuting a war.

There is, of course, personal morality, and everybody's got their own sort of personal morality, and this runs counter to that sense of ethics and right and wrong of military people who when told to do something, most of them will do it. And you want them to do it, you want the chain of command to work so that they are sort of mindlessly following their orders. We don't want them to have to think every time they are given an order to do something, "Gee, I wonder if that's the way to go. Because if it's not legal up the chain of command, the accountability part of the chain of command isn't working and I'm going to take the fall for it because Gen. Miller is going to take Article 31." So it negatively — significantly negatively — impacts the effectiveness of the chain of command when that sort of thing happens, and the Lynndie Englands of the world are left holding the bag.

So the military, I'll say in closing, ends up with a very personal and also a very professional need in all this. I would suggest that at some point the leadership, whether civilian or military, has to face a decision of honor. At some point you have to put your stars on the table. You have to say I'm not going to be complicit in this; I'm not going to participate in this anymore. If those are the interrogation tactics that you want to use, then I have to count the cost and say no. And by the way, those abusive techniques are not effective. What really gets information out of people is sex, money, and pride. What works is breaking down the barriers, not reminding the detainees every moment of the day and night that you're their enemy.

For all these reasons I think the military has a significant interest in this scandal. Individually and professionally, they have been significantly let down by their leadership. It's a great tragedy.

General O'Meara

How can we assure that established legal norms regarding torture, cruel, inhuman, and degrading treatment are honored by military combatants?

Consider the following story as recounted by Stephen Ambrose, a World War II historian. On the date of June 10, 1944, a certain captain in the 101st Airborne Division handed out cigarettes to twelve German POWs, and gave the men a light. He then pulled out his carbine and killed all twelve prisoners in cold blood.[1] The Captain went on to complete his mission for the day, ultimately got promoted, and completed a career in the Army. The Law of Land Warfare has been articulated on numerous occasions both before and after that day, and yet war crimes, crimes against humanity, torture, and cruel, inhuman, and degrading treatment of detainees have continued to trouble the conduct of military operations to the present.[2]

1. Stephen E. Ambrose, "Atrocities in Historical Prspective," in *Facing My Lai: Moving Beyond the Massacre,* ed. David L. Anderson (Lawrence, Kans.: University Press of Kansas, 1998), pp. 107-20, on p. 115.

2. Military personnel are generally tried for violations of the Uniform Code of Military Justice rather than for violations of international law. During World War II, for example, in the United States and in Europe, the United States Army tried, convicted, and executed 146

A number of issues are relevant to this discussion.

First, What does the American public expect of its military force? It is important to remember that U.S. military forces, CIA operatives, interrogators, and independent contractors — the individuals most likely to be involved in walking the definitional lines discussed herein — are American citizens themselves. Arguably, they reflect the legal and moral values of the American public. To the extent that the public follows these issues at all, there appears to be at best a tepid concern.[3] Indeed, regarding Vietnam, according to an ABC News/*Washington Post* poll conducted in 1985, 57% of the public did not have a "clear idea" what the war was all about and 33% did not even know which side the U.S. supported. It is a legitimate question whether the American public is any more interested in the treatment of Iraqi detainees than it was in the fate of Vietnamese civilians, especially in a post-9/11 environment.

Second, is the law of land warfare as clear as it sounds? Certainly there appears to be some disagreement regarding the definition of terms, the authority of the executive branch regarding its response to terrorism, and, finally, the ability of the U.S. government to conduct warfare consistent with international law and treaty obligations.

There is a good deal of disagreement in academic and legal circles regarding the ability of contemporary international law to respond to situations which are created by non-state actors bent on terrorizing and destroying the civilian populations of nation-states such as the United States.[4] Indeed, there has been considerable disagreement even within the

---

United States Army soldiers for rape or murder. See Walter E. Boomer et al., "The Law of War," in *Facing My Lai*, pp. 121-38, on p. 128.

3. The chief prosecutor regarding the My Lai case characterized the public's response as follows: "After President Nixon commuted Calley's sentence, the final message of the justice system was 'politics reigns.' Never forget that there are two sides. There is one group that says: 'These sorts of things happen. This is routine: the military does this all the time.' Then you have the other group over here that says: 'Kill, kids, kill. They're Communists, go ahead, kill them.' After all, that's what the military is supposed to do, isn't it? It's awful, and to both of them, a pox on both their houses. That's why we talk about noncombatants and deal with just war tradition, international law, and all of those things. There's the middle." William G. Ekhardt et al., "Experiencing the Darkness," in *Facing My Lai*, pp. 27-52, on p. 49.

4. See for example John Yoo, "Terrorists Have No Geneva Rights," *Wall Street Journal*, May 26, 2004; Bruce Hoffman, "A Nasty Business," *The Atlantic Monthly*, January 2002; Jimmy Carter, *Our Endangered Values* (New York: Simon & Schuster, 2005), pp. 1-6; Derek Jinks and David Sloss, "Is the President Bound by the Geneva Conventions?" *Cornell Law*

government regarding the use of "torture" itself as a methodology for the treatment of detainees who may have actionable intelligence.[5] The McCain Amendment was an attempt to put to rest at least one of these issues, that being the use of torture. The myriad issues that remain, however, abide decisions in the courts, in Congress, and in the political process — hardly the bright-line guidance necessary to insure that future generations comply with clear and unambiguous articulations regarding these issues.

Third, given the environment in which this generation of soldiers and civilians are required to operate, are they capable of understanding and honoring the moral and legal commitments to which the United States has bound them?

There is no doubt that U.S. military forces are provided with a wide range of training opportunities regarding the general principles of the Law of Land Warfare. Commentators looking at the military's Law of War Training Program instituted in 1972 note that it was "command-driven," that is, emphasis for its success came from commanders in the field. They further relate that the program bore fruit during the Gulf War, wherein the International Red Cross applauded the manner in which massive numbers of Iraqi prisoners of war were detained and treated.[6]

And yet, within less than a year after the inception of hostilities in Iraq, the massive violations of the law of war at Abu Ghraib began leaking out and the conditions at Guantánamo and in Afghanistan became public.[7] Subsequent investigations have revealed problems with definitions re-

---

Review 97 (2004): 108-20; Michael Hoffman, "Rescuing the Law of War: A Way Forward in an Era of Global Terrorism," *Parameters* 18 (2005): 18-35; and Wayne McCormack, "Emergency Powers and Terrorism," *Military Law Review* 185 (2005): 65-148.

5. See for example the Memorandum of August 1, 2002, from Jay S. Bybee, Assistant Attorney General, Office of Legal Counsel to Alberto R. Gonzalez, Counsel to the President, *Regarding Standards of Conduct for Interrogation under 18 U.S.C. sec. 2340-2340A* (August 1, 2002) [hereafter 'Bybee Opinion']; Memorandum for Deputy Attorney General James B. Coney, from Daniel Levin, Acting Assistant Attorney General, *Re: Legal Standards Applicable Under 18 U.S.C. 2340-2340A* (December 30, 2004) (supersedes August 1, 2002 memo); Harold Hongju Koh, "A World Without Torture," *Columbia Journal of Transnational Law* 43 (2005); and McCormack, "Emergency Powers and Terrorism," on p. 120.

6. David L. Anderson, "What Really Happened?" in *Facing My Lai*, pp. 1-18, on p. 4.

7. See, for example, Mark Bowden, "The Dark Art of Interrogation," *The Atlantic Monthly*, October 1, 2003; Daniel Byman, "Reject the Abuses, Retain the Tactic," *Washington Post*, April 17, 2005.

garding treatment,[8] flawed and confusing policy,[9] and the inadequacy of the training.[10]

Ironically, the above-cited recommendations are eerily similar to those which formed the basis of the revamped Law of War Training Program in 1972. American citizens — military and civilian — tend to perform difficult tasks in a competent and professional, moral and legal manner. Yet it appears clear that when leadership, military and civilian, public and private, provides mixed messages, cloudy definitions, and sloppy guidance, some may wander.

A captain from the 82nd Airborne Division reported his concerns to Senator John McCain in September, 2005:

> Others argue that clear standards will limit the President's ability to wage the War on Terror. Since clear standards only limit interrogation techniques, it is reasonable for me to assume that supporters of this argument desire to use coercion to acquire information from detainees. This is morally inconsistent with the Constitution and justice in war. It is unacceptable.[11]

8. Army Regulation 15-6 Investigation into FBI Allegations of Detainee Abuse at Guantánamo Bay, Cuba Detention Facility, April 1, 2005. Recommendations included new focus on the definitions of humane treatment, military necessity and proper employment of interrogation techniques as well as a "reevaluation of the DOD inter-agency interrogation training consistent with the new realities of the requirements of the global war on terror."

9. Human Rights First, *Getting to Ground Truth: Investigating U.S. Abuses in the 'War on Terror'* (September 2004).

10. Department of the Army, Inspector General, *Detainee Operations Inspection* (July 21, 2004).

11. Captain Ian Fishback, "A Matter of Honor," Letter to Senator McCain, *Washington Post*, September 28, 2005.

PART TWO

CHRISTIANS SPEAK OUT

Remember those who are in prison,
as though you were in prison with them;
those who are being tortured,
as though you yourselves were being tortured.

Hebrews 13:3

CHAPTER 5

Beyond Numbness: A Personal Meditation

Marilyn McEntyre

Last semester in one of my courses for pre-meds I assigned Susan Sontag's last book, *Regarding the Pain of Others*. It offers a penetrating reflection on the ambiguous effects of war photography — how it affects our imaginations and our capacity to empathize with other people's suffering.

Sontag suggests that when we become accustomed to seeing stark scenes of human suffering, often inflicted by other humans, day after day with our morning coffee, and — because we must go on with our day — turn the page and toss the paper, we condition ourselves, willfully or not, to "take in" that suffering as a neutral fact, and come to regard engagement with it as optional. Pain and suffering, framed and cropped and confined to the innocuous two-dimensional space of the newspaper or newscast, may, she argues, numb rather than activate our moral sensibilities and our motivation to alleviate or prevent others' pain. Since reading that book, with its finely nuanced warnings about the neutralization and even commodification of human suffering, I have looked at the daily paper differently.

Torture is not something most of us want to hear about, but the issue of how I regard the pain of others was raised again for me when my husband and I attended a January 2006 conference at Princeton Seminary on "Theology, International Law, and Torture," organized by our friend George Hunsinger. Included among those who attended were survivors of torture, international lawyers, theologians, and representatives from a wide variety of human rights organizations and churches.

The first speaker was Sr. Dianna Ortiz, now director of Torture Abolition and Survivors Coalition International, the only organization founded by torture survivors. Its mission is to abolish torture wherever it occurs. Sr. Dianna, a missionary, was tortured in a Guatemalan prison where she was incarcerated on suspicion of helping local farmers with plans for insurrection. (She was, as many imprisoned in such situations are, innocent.) In the midst of her almost unthinkable suffering, she promised to God, herself, and fellow sufferers that if she survived and returned to the U.S., she would tell her story. She found, upon her return, that very few wanted to hear what she had to say. Church and state alike met her readily demonstrable testimony largely with indifference, evasion, or denial. Her story was hard to hear even for those of us who quite deliberately gathered to listen, there in a comfortably heated, nicely accommodated room in Eerdman Hall. But it is a story that deserves to be told, along with many other stories of suffering that, whatever legitimations might be offered, no human being should undergo at the hands of another.

Every generation has its own reckonings to make with abuses of power and gross violations of basic human rights. Every generation of Christians has to consider once again how to be the Body of Christ in a world where human beings inflict suffering on each other by means of war, resource abuse, economic abuse, or more immediate forms of cruel, inhuman, and degrading treatment. Many of us manage to postpone that reckoning by one of three common strategies: denial, legitimation, or personal exculpation.

But perhaps the most insidious way in which we may sidestep this and other pressing instances of injustice toward and abuse of our fellow human beings is to reduce such matters to partisan politics. So much of American public discourse has been co-opted for partisan purposes, it is hard, I think, for people of faith to retrieve language that allows them to gather and reason together about matters that are first of all moral, ethical, and theological, not political or partisan.

One of the conference participants, a woman from Amnesty International, raised a convicting question that drove to the heart of the purposes for which we were gathered. She said, "Our teams have gone all over the country trying to raise public awareness of the rising incidence of torture, now practiced both openly and secretly in over 150 countries. Very few churches are willing to speak out on this issue. Why? Where are those whose mandate is to care for the powerless, to do justice and love mercy?" George Hunsinger replied, "I have no answer. That's my question, too.

That's why we're here." Gary Haugen, president of International Justice Mission and a significant voice in evangelical efforts to address global injustices, including torture, also spoke eloquently about the need for Christians on both sides of the aisle, as they say on Capitol Hill, to recognize the scope of human rights abuses that continue to be ignored and so, tolerated. He personally knows many torture victims; his organization seeks them out and rescues them.

Some of the other organizations represented were the Presbyterian Peacemaking Program, the Episcopal Church, the Churches' Center for Theology and Public Policy, the Friends Committee on National Legislation, Rabbis for Human Rights, the Islamic Society of North America, Human Rights First, and the U.S. Army and Navy (retired officers from both branches came to add their voices to the call to end all practices of torture in and outside of the military, and to reflect on the dishonor and manifold consequences of incidents like those so shockingly documented at Abu Ghraib).

It is hard to come away from a conference like that without deep discomfort and a refocused sense of how to direct both my prayers and my political energies. A question that kept coming back to me in the course of the weekend is this: what am I willing to know about? How do I protect myself from knowing what threatens my complacencies? To what extent am I willing to take responsibility not only for my personal moral behavior, but for the wrongs I may be in some position to help right? To what extent am I willing to disturb my peace for the sake of seeking ways to promote peace and safety for others?

I don't believe we're called to live in a state of chronic guilt or depression over the enormities of global injustice. I do, however, believe we are accountable collectively as well as individually for the kinds of behavior Jesus enumerated in the Sermon on the Mount and Matthew 25, including visiting the imprisoned, caring for the vulnerable, and loving our enemies. Jesus, himself a victim of state-sanctioned torture, reminds us of the high stakes of our behavior toward each other when he says both, "Inasmuch as you have done it to one of the least of these, you have done it to me," and, "Inasmuch as you have not done it to one of the least of these, you have not done it to me." Sins of both commission and negligence are included.

I say these things here because they're on my heart, and because I think our call to be citizens of this world as well as of God's kingdom impels us to look at the world's sorrows with eyes wide open, and to reach out to those who suffer, not only in individual and personal ways, but collectively, forcefully, and vocally, to use the privileges we enjoy as members of a powerful nation and of a divinely empowered church in the defense and service of those most vulnerable to abuse — the poor, the easily exploited, and even, and perhaps especially, the "enemies" for whom Jesus urged us specifically and without reservations, to pray.

So let us pray: Father of us all, we do pray that you will hold in your powerful embrace those who even now live in fear or pain or darkness. Help us learn how to act in this world as members of Christ's body, dealing gently with one another, but forcefully in the service of justice, mercy, and lovingkindness. Amen.

CHAPTER 6

Torture Is the Ticking Time Bomb:
Why the Necessity Defense Fails

George Hunsinger

> *Q: Thank you, sir. A simple question.*
> *THE PRESIDENT: Yes. It may require a simple answer.*
> *Q: What's your definition of the word "torture"?*
> *THE PRESIDENT: Of what?*
> *Q: The word "torture." What's your definition?*
> *THE PRESIDENT: That's defined in U.S. law,*
> *and we don't torture.*
> *Q: Can you give me your version of it, sir?*
> *THE PRESIDENT: Whatever the law says.*[1]

The Current Crisis

Of all the scandals that currently beset us, there is one that history is likely to judge most harshly, namely, the Bush administration's authorization of torture and abuse. Haunting Abu Ghraib photographs have seared into our minds that grievous violations of international law have occurred. There is every reason to believe that such violations continue to this day in secret CIA prisons and detention centers around the world. No one up the

---

1. Press Conference by President George W. Bush, October 18, 2007; available online at http://www.whitehouse.gov/news/releases/2007/10/print/20071017.html. The precise legal definition is "severe mental or physical pain or suffering" to elicit information.

chain of command has been held accountable while, significantly, many of those associated with authorizing torture have been promoted or politically rewarded.

The terror detainee bill passed by Congress in the fall of 2006 — the Military Commissions Act (MCA) — has implicitly condoned torture and effectively rendered it lawful. The MCA would seem to ensure that the resort to criminal means will define the Bush era for posterity. As if to confirm this grim prognosis, in July 2007 the administration then issued an executive order restarting a discontinued CIA program in which gulag techniques[2] — including waterboarding, extreme temperatures, stress positions, and sleep deprivation — have reportedly been authorized and used. Legalizing torture marks a milestone in the disintegration of American democracy.

Having passed the Senate by a 65-34 margin, with twelve Democrats voting in concert with the Republican majority, the MCA has not since been repealed. One hopeful sign is the June 12, 2008, Supreme Court ruling that Guantanamo detainees indeed have a right to habeas corpus and may challenge their detentions in federal court, thus overturning as unconstitutional a contrary provision in the MCA. But even many of its lesser evils are far from minor. Christopher Anders, legislative counsel for the American Civil Liberties Union, comments:

> Nothing could be less American than a government that can indefinitely hold people in secret torture cells, take away their protections against horrific and cruel abuse, put them on trial based on evidence they cannot see, sentence them to death based on testimony literally beaten out of witnesses, and then slam shut the courthouse door for any habeas corpus petition. But that's exactly what Congress just approved.[3]

The administration claims to be against torture, and yet it refuses to renounce, without equivocation, the cruel, inhuman, and degrading treatment of detainees. In the authoritative documents of international law — as represented by the Geneva Conventions (especially Geneva Common Article 3), the U.N. Universal Declaration on Human Rights, the Conven-

2. See Andrew Sullivan, "Torture by any other name is just as vile," *The Sunday Times* (London), September 26, 2006.

3. ACLU press release, "Senate Passes Dangerous Bush Military Commissions Bill, ACLU Says Legislation Upends the Rule of Law," September 28, 2006. Available online at http://www.aclu.org/safefree/detention/26947prs20060928.html.

tion Against Torture, and other treaties binding on our government — the ban against cruel, inhuman, and degrading treatment is not separated from the ban against torture. The two proscriptions are one, a point to which we shall return.

The disquieting innovation of this administration has been to produce documents disrupting that unity. Extreme forms of abuse are disconnected from what counts as "torture" in order to make them permissible. When the president proclaims, as he often does, that "we do not torture," he is being less than straightforward. He has kept the word, but changed the dictionary.

The policy that results is radically inconsistent. Officially, our government opposes torture and advocates a universal standard for human rights. Yet at the same time, it has adopted methods that violate these standards. The methods include waterboarding (or simulated drowning), sleep deprivation, induced hypothermia, mock burials, stress positions, sexual humiliation, and the desecration of religious objects. The president calls these extreme methods "alternative means of interrogation," a phrase reminiscent of Orwell. The vice president is more candid. He calls them "working the dark side."

"Enhanced interrogation techniques," Bush's euphemism for working the dark side, is a term with an interesting history. *Verschärfte Vernehmung*, the exact translation in German, was in fact a phrase invented by the Gestapo. It was used to describe what became known as the "third degree." It left no marks. It included hypothermia, stress positions, long-time standing, and sleep deprivation.[4] "Our country for the first time in my life time has abandoned the basic principle of human rights," Jimmy Carter stated in the fall of 2007. "We've said that the Geneva Conventions do not apply to those people in Abu Ghraib prison and Guantánamo, and we've said we can torture prisoners and deprive them of an accusation of a crime." Carter indicated that the interrogation methods cited by the *New York Times,* including "head-slapping, simulated drowning, and frigid temperatures," constitute torture "if you use the international norms of torture as has always been honored — certainly in the last sixty years since the Universal Declaration of Human Rights was promulgated."[5]

But Bush's nominee to the post of attorney general, Judge Michael Mukasey, who was questioned in Congressional hearings, was evasive on

---

4. Frank Rich, "The 'Good Germans' Among Us," *New York Times,* October 14, 2007.
5. "Jimmy Carter: US Tortures Prisoners," Associated Press, October 11, 2007.

this very point. He refused to state when pressed that waterboarding or simulated drowning was indeed a crime under international and domestic law.

> "Is waterboarding constitutional?" he was asked by Senator Sheldon Whitehouse, a Rhode Island Democrat, in one of today's sharpest exchanges.
> "I don't know what is involved in the technique," Mr. Mukasey replied. "If waterboarding is torture, torture is not constitutional."[6]

Mukasey was sending a clear signal that nothing would change regarding the tolerance of torture in the Department of Justice, and that no higher-ups need fear being prosecuted for such crimes under his watch.

In 2005 the PBS program *Frontline* televised a report about how Secretary of Defense Donald Rumsfeld and General Geoffrey Miller "Gitmoized" the interrogations of detainees in Iraq. The program included many interviews, including the story of U.S. Army interrogator Spc. Tony Lagouranis (Ret.). The former military interrogator stated:

> Well, hypothermia was a widespread technique. I haven't heard a lot of people talking about that, and I never saw anything in writing prohibiting it or making it illegal. But almost everyone was using it when they had a chance, when the weather permitted. Or some people, the Navy SEALs, for instance, were using just ice water to lower the body temperature of the prisoner. They would take his rectal temperature to make sure he didn't die; they would keep him hovering on hypothermia. That was a pretty common technique.
>
> A lot of other, you know, not as common techniques, and certainly not sanctioned, were just beating people or burning them. Not within the prisons, usually. But when the units would go out into people's homes and do these raids, they would just stay in the house and torture them. Because after the scandal, they couldn't trust that, you know, the interrogators were going to do "as good a job," in their words, as they wanted to.[7]

---

6. Philip Shenon, "Mukasey Faces Tough Questions on Interrogations," *New York Times*, October 18, 2007.

7. Interview, PBS *Frontline*, September 25, 2005. Available online at http://www.pbs.org/wgbh/pages/frontline/torture/interviews/lagouranis.html.

How to Test Torture's Rationale

Most of the recent scholarly writing on torture has been done by international lawyers and legal scholars. Some of them defend interrogational torture while others do not. Moreover, highly trained philosophers writing about torture are also divided in their opinions. As far as I can see, however, no Christian ethicist of any standing has endorsed the resort to torture. For example, David Gushee, a leading evangelical scholar, wrote a cover story for *Christianity Today* entitled "Five Reasons Why Torture Is Always Wrong."[8]

As a way of sorting out the existing range of scholarly disagreement, I propose to adopt a new modification of an old analytical scheme. The scheme comes from the just war tradition. Just as there are traditional criteria for determining whether a war can be justified, so similar criteria can be developed for assessing the justifiability of torture. Can something as intuitively repugnant as torture ever reasonably be justified? Is the resort to torture in an emergency situation anything like killing in a justified war? Proponents of torture seem to think that it is. I will follow the lead of others, however, in arguing that torture is uniquely different from killing in war. I will also argue that when just war criteria are modified to fit the case, torture comes to light as uniquely monstrous, and so beyond rational justification. When real-world contingencies are taken into account, the prohibition against torture emerges as a practical absolute or an exceptionless moral rule.[9]

In the just war tradition, as is well known, the criteria fall into two parts. *Ius ad bellum* assesses justifiable reasons for going to war, while *ius in bello* examines justifiable means by which a war may be conducted. The criteria in both parts must be met. A war conducted by criminal means, for example, would still be unjust even if going to war had been justified. On the other hand, even a war conducted in a permissible way would be unjust if the reasons for going to war were illegitimate to begin with. According to just war criteria, only a war undertaken for legitimate reasons and conducted in a tolerable way can be justified.

Can the resort to torture be analyzed according to a similar scheme?

8. David Gushee, "Five Reasons Why Torture Is Always Wrong," *Christianity Today* (February 2006). A longer version of this essay appears as Chapter 7 in this volume.

9. See Jeremy Waldron, "Torture and Positive Law," *Columbia Law Review* 105 (2005): 1681-1750; esp. pp. 1717, 1735.

Might there be justifiable reasons for resorting to torture, *ius ad tormentum?* Since some thoughtful people suppose that there are, can the second step also be taken? Can torture be conducted in a justifiable manner, *ius in tormento?* Proponents of torture rarely confront this question, which prima facie seems to be absurd. As will be argued here, the unique practical differences between killing in war and torturing are very largely why torture fails of justification. The failure is compounded, however, because the warrants for resorting to torture in the first place will also not bear scrutiny. For good reason, there is no such thing in our history as a just torture tradition.

Ius Ad Tormentum

Among the standard criteria for deciding whether it is justifiable to resort to war, three will be examined here. The tradition teaches that going to war is justified (1) to defend against aggression, (2) if carried out by legitimate authority, and (3) when there is a reasonable chance of success. When these criteria are modified to fit the case of torture, none of them can reasonably be met.

The so-called "ticking time bomb scenario" is analogous to the just war case of defending against aggression. It prompts some to invoke the maxim that "necessity makes that lawful which is otherwise unlawful." A recent example can be found in the *Stanford Encyclopedia of Philosophy*.[10] The scenario goes like this: A small nuclear device has been planted in a major city and is about to go off. One of the terrorists has been captured, and a lot is known about him. He is a known terrorist, has been involved in past terrorist incidents, and knows where the device is hidden. He is even the leader of the group. The police also know that he will probably talk if tortured. All other sources of information have dried up. No time exists to evacuate the city. Torture is the means of last resort. The article sums up:

> In this case torture . . . seems to be justifiable. Consider the following points: (1) The police reasonably believe that torturing the terrorist will probably save thousands of innocent lives; (2) the police know that there is no other way to save those lives; (3) the threat to life is imminent; (4) the thousands about to be murdered are innocent — the ter-

10. Seumas Miller, "Torture," *The Stanford Encyclopedia of Philosophy* (Winter 2006 edition), ed. Edward N. Zalta. Available online at http://plato.stanford.edu/entries/torture/.

rorist has no good, let alone decisive, justificatory moral reason to murder them; the terrorist is known to be (jointly with the other terrorists) morally responsible for planning, transporting, and arming the nuclear device and, if it explodes, he will be (jointly with the other terrorists) morally responsible for the murder of thousands.

Indeed, given the way the case is set up by this article, it would seem that an even stronger conclusion cannot be avoided. Knowing everything the police know, and having no other recourse, they would be morally irresponsible themselves if they did not torture the terrorist until he talked. All those murders would be on their conscience.

Scenarios like this fail, however, for two main reasons. First, they are extremely hypothetical. In any actually existing situation, not all the conditions posited by the scenario are likely to be met. Indeed it is not unlikely that few if any of them would be met. The defenders of hypothetical torture never seem to ask about the justifiability of torture under real-life conditions.

Even more important, however, is the use to which this argument is commonly put. It is a hypothetical argument with real-life implications. Hypothetically, the scenario posits an abnormal situation, one that is said to be highly exceptional. It is suffused with all the pressure of an extreme emergency. The argument is used, however, to interpret the necessity defense so broadly as to justify the normalizing of torture.[11] The abnormal is normalized, the exceptional is regularized, and the state of emergency turns out to be endless. Declaring a permanent state of emergency in order to justify a systematic resort to criminal means is the well-known hallmark of dictatorship.[12]

This point is amply confirmed by revelations about the destruction of CIA videotapes depicting harsh interrogation. One terrorist suspect whose tapes were destroyed was Abu Zubaydah. According to the *Washington Post*,

Officials said harsh tactics used on him at a secret detention facility in Thailand went on *for weeks or, depending on the account, even months.* The videotaping of Abu Zubaydah in 2002 went on day and night

11. See especially David Luban, "Liberalism, Torture, and the Ticking Bomb," *Virginia Law Review* 91 (2005): 1425-61.

12. See Giorgio Agamben, *State of Exception* (Chicago: University of Chicago Press, 2005).

throughout his interrogation, including waterboarding, and while he was sleeping in his cell, intelligence officials said. "Several hundred hours" of videotapes were destroyed in November 2005, a senior intelligence officer said. The CIA has said it ceased waterboarding in 2003.[13]

Andrew Sullivan comments:

> Notice what the Zubaydah case tells us about the key argument of torture advocates: that torture should only be used when we already know that someone has actionable information about an imminent catastrophic threat. We're five years into the Bush torture regime and despite hundreds — and possibly thousands — of torture sessions, this was never, ever the case. [The ticking bomb] argument has been rendered completely moot by the evidence of the past five years.
>
> The United States made the decision to torture Zubaydah after he had already given helpful information — solely because they suspected he had more — and not in response to any knowledge of any imminent, catastrophic threat. In the beginning — not even in the end — torture became its own rationale, creating a need for torturers to justify their war crimes by finding more information through more torture, and unleashing the sadism and evil that exists in every human heart — even the most trained and professional. And then the war crimes created a need to destroy the evidence of war crimes, and so the criminality of the government deepened, cloaked in the secrecy of national security.[14]

The question is not whether torture might work in some extremely hypothetical situation. The question is how hypothetical justifications end up normalizing torture, and how torture once normalized inevitably spreads — as shown by history and recent experience — like wildfire. "Once torture begins," writes Alfred McCoy, "it seems to spread uncontrollably, particularly during times of crisis, in a downward spiral of fear and self-empowerment."[15]

13. Dan Eggen and Walter Pincus, "FBI, CIA Debate Significance of Terror Suspect," *Washington Post,* December 18, 2007. Italics added.

14. Andrew Sullivan, "The Torture Of Abu Zubaydah," *The Daily Dish/The Atlantic online,* December 18, 2007. Available online at http://andrewsullivan.theatlantic.com/the_daily_dish/2007/12/the-torture-of.html.

15. Alfred McCoy, *A Question of Torture* (New York: Metropolitan Books, 2006), p. 209.

Many commentators have noted how the ticking bomb scenario becomes dubious when real-life circumstances are admitted. There are at least five reasons for skepticism.

- The first is the reliability factor. How likely is it that the desired information would actually be obtained? Is not torture notoriously ineffective under any circumstances in obtaining reliable information? While the clock ticks on, what is to prevent the hardened terrorist simply from holding out, or at least from providing false leads until it is too late?
- Second is the uncertainty factor. Suppose the police know less about the captured person than is built into the scenario. How certain would they have to be in an emergency to justify resorting to torture? The larger the permissible range of uncertainty, the greater the warrant for normalizing torture.
- Closely related is the slippery slope factor. Torturing the suspect is thought to be justifiable because he might have knowledge of a ticking bomb. Would there not be hundreds or even thousands of suspects who might have dangerous knowledge? To justify torturing them, how immediate would the emergency need to be? Again we are on the slide toward normalization.
- Then, fourthly, there is the accountability factor. Suppose the police are wrong about key matters of fact? What happens to a society when torture can be carried out with impunity? When there is no accountability, there is no bright line that in practice will not be crossed. When there is no accountability, the legitimacy of the torturing authority is very much in doubt.
- Finally, there is the corruptibility factor. The ticking bomb scenario assumes a case that is confined, and that can be kept confined. However, as the philosophers Bufacchi and Arrigo point out: "The accuracy and speed of virtuoso torture interrogation dictate long advance preparation and coordination, and ultimately corruption, of many key social institutions." This observation is relevant, because just war stipulations require a reasonable chance of success. The preparations needed for success in a ticking time bomb emergency would profoundly corrupt the culture of medical, scientific, police, military. and legal institutions.[16] The real choice is not between an isolated case and

16. For a detailed discussion of this corruptibility factor, see Vittorio Bufacci and Jean

catastrophe, but between refraining from criminal means and corrupting the society. In this sense Elaine Scarry is correct: "Torture is itself a ticking bomb."[17]

In short, the ticking time bomb scenario would appear to meet *ius ad tormentum* conditions only under rarified circumstances that are highly unlikely in the real world.[18] The *Stanford Encyclopedia* posits a scenario which is highly unusual, as it admits, and which is said to include prior structures of accountability. The discussion fails to consider how unlikely those circumstances actually are, and how contrary to fact are the posited structures. More precisely, it fails adequately to consider the great likelihood of unreliable confessions, the real-world uncertainties surrounding a detainee's actual innocence, the slippery slope of permitting persons to be tortured on mere suspicion, the lack of real-world accountability commensurate to the enormity of the deed, and, finally, the moral certainty that any attempt to institutionalize torture would corrupt the very society it intends to defend.

Ius In Tormento

The failings of *ius ad tormentum* only metastasize when we turn our attention to torture as a practice in itself *(ius in tormento)*. Torture is not like killing in war. The relationship of the torturer to the tortured is, in important respects, unlike that between military combatants. From an ethical standpoint, it is uniquely abhorrent.[19]

- In a military conflict, a form of reciprocity exists among the combatants; both sides subject themselves to more or less equal risks. Torture, by contrast, is more like killing the defenseless.
- In combat honor can be a motive for making sacrifices, and military

---

Marie Arriga, "Torture, Terrorism and the State: A Refutation of the Ticking Bomb Argument," *Journal of Applied Philosophy* 23 (2006): 355-73, esp. pp. 363-67.

17. Elaine Scarry, "Five Errors in the Reasoning of Alan Dershowitz," in *Torture: A Collection*, ed. Sanford Levinson (New York: Oxford University Press, 2004), p. 288.

18. Among many discussions, see Kim Lane Schepple, "Hypothetical Torture in the War on Terrorism," *Journal of National Security Law and Policy* 1 (2005): 285-331.

19. See David Sussman, "What's Wrong with Torture?" *Philosophy and Public Affairs* 33 (2005): 1-33.

discipline is important to prevent atrocities.[20] But there is no honor in the practice of torture, no courage in the infliction of pain, no discipline not undercut by inducements to escalate.

- In combat both sides have room to maneuver and to outwit the adversary's strategies. The torturer, by contrast, has unchecked power to inflict degrees of pain that are utterly indescribable upon a victim who is totally helpless.

- The *in bello* condition implies that in military combat acts of cruelty, though possible, are not necessary, and in any case are impermissible. Torture, by contrast, is based on extreme cruelty and humiliation. It is less like combat and more like mutilation or rape. It systematically violates what should be most intimate to a person.

- The *in bello* condition also requires a measure of restraint in the conduct of hostilities. It assumes that a primary purpose of the war is to preserve certain cherished values and institutions. By contrast, torture undermines legitimate values and institutions. It involves a relationship of extreme domination, in which the tortured is tyrannized by the torturer. The victim lies completely exposed, while the power of the torturer is absolute.

- The *in bello* condition also requires an irreducible measure of respect for life in the conduct of hostilities. Respect for life is entailed in the requirements of proportionality and noncombatant immunity. Torture, by contrast, systematically dehumanizes its victim by attacking the center of her personality. It uses pain, deprivation, and humiliation to shatter a person, forcing her to act against felt loyalties, against conviction, and against conscience. Torture violates a person's body, and terrorizes her mind, in order to destroy her will. Torture survivors, who afterwards will never be the same, are psychologically and emotionally maimed. They suffer from an inability to establish bonds of trust, from deadened emotional lives, and from the urge to commit suicide, to which many of them tragically succumb.[21]

---

20. See Peter Olsthoorn, "Honor as a Motive in Making Sacrifices," *Journal of Military Ethics* 4 (2005): 183-97.

21. The name of Jean Amery, a torture victim at the hands of the Nazis, may be mentioned here along with that of Primo Levi, who described torture by the Nazis as he had witnessed it. Both Amery and Levi committed suicide. See Amery, "Torture," in *Art from the Ashes*, ed. Lawrence L. Langer (New York: Oxford University Press, 1995); Levi, *The Drowned and the Saved* (New York: Vintage, 1989).

In short, traditional *in bello* stipulations cannot meaningfully be translated into the torture chamber. They cannot be adapted to fit conditions *in tormento.* The very enormity of torture prevents it. In the torture chamber there is, comparatively speaking, no reciprocity of risks, no possibility of honor for the torturer, no self-defense for the victim, no meaningful constraints upon cruelty, no preservation of the values supposedly being defended, and no minimal respect for the inalienable personhood of the victim.

At least one point needs to be stressed before moving on. The difference between military conflict and torture is of course merely relative. Military conflict also produces dishonor, trauma, abuse, violation, and atrocity. Nevertheless, the paradoxes of war differ from those of torture. War can call forth courageous behavior in the defense against aggression in a way that torture cannot. It is not for nothing that like the pirate and the slave trader before him, the torturer is called *hostis humani generis,* the enemy of all humankind.[22]

Torture: What Is It Good For?

To understand further why torture should not be made lawful, its purposes need to be examined. It is not self-evident that torture is always merely about interrogation. The purposes of torture are relevant to an assessment of its legal and ethical legitimacy. Although it is common to distinguish interrogational torture from terroristic torture,[23] this distinction is arguably insufficient to capture the full spectrum of torture's purposes. For the sake of completeness, and for lack of a better term, the interrogational and the terroristic forms of torture need to be seen in relation to torture under the aspect of the demonic.[24]

22. For a classic discussion of the paradoxes of war see J. Glenn Gray, *The Warriors: Reflections on Men in Battle* (New York: Harper & Row, 1970).

23. Henry Shue, "Torture," in *Torture,* ed. Levinson, pp. 47-60; on p. 53.

24. A fourth form of torture would be "confessional," in which the purpose is to coerce the victim into pleading guilty to a past event. See Darius Rejali, *Torture and Democracy* (Princeton: Princeton University Press, 2007), p. 531.

Interrogational Torture

The deepest puzzle about interrogational torture is that it is notoriously ineffective.[25] Aristotle already knew in the fourth century B.C., for example, that no trust can be placed in evidence obtained by torture. Under the compulsion of torture, he observed, people "tell lies quite as often as they tell the truth — sometimes persistently refusing to tell the truth, sometimes recklessly making a false charge in order to be let off sooner." Evidence under torture, he concluded, is unreliable. Shrewdly, he also observed that contending parties will often accept or reject such evidence for merely cynical reasons, depending on whether it suits their case.[26]

Aristotle's viewpoint has not disappeared in the current climate of concern about how to treat terror suspects. Let me give an example from Great Britain. In 2004 a Court of Appeals laid down a controversial ruling. Evidence obtained under torture abroad, it was decided, would be admissible under certain circumstances in court. Some months later a panel of Law Lords voted unanimously against this decision. Lord Bingham of Cornhill, the former Lord Chief Justice who headed the panel, explained their reasoning in words that Aristotle himself could have written. Lord Bingham stated:

> First of all, it is clear that a statement made under torture is often an unreliable statement, and it could therefore be contrary to the principle of fair trial to invoke such a statement as evidence before a court. Even in countries whose court procedures are based on a free evaluation of all evidence, it is hardly acceptable that a statement made under torture should be allowed to play any part in court proceedings.
>
> Consequently, if a statement made under torture cannot be invoked as evidence, an important reason for using torture is removed and the prohibition against the use of such statements as evidence before a court can therefore have the indirect effect of preventing torture.[27]

25. That torture is indeed ineffective as a means of interrogation is confirmed by Rejali's defintive study. See *Torture and Democracy*, pp. 446-79, 576-77.

26. Aristotle, *Rhetoric*, Book I, chapter 15, 1376b-1377a.

27. Opinions of the Lords of Appeal for Judgment in the Case A (FC) and others (FC) (Appellants) v. Secretary of State for the Home Department (Respondent), *UKHL* 71, no. 39 (December 8, 2005). Available online at http://hei.unige.ch/clapham/hrdoc/docs/Aandothers 2005HoL.htm.

Relying on evidence obtained by torture not only can be unfair and misguided but sometimes even catastrophic. In his widely acclaimed address to the U.N. on February 5, 2003 — the speech that took the U.S. into war — Colin Powell cited evidence that turned out to be acquired under torture. Ibn al-Libi has been identified as the primary source of the flawed prewar intelligence that al-Qaeda was being trained by Iraq in the making of bombs and poisonous gases. Al-Libi, who had been captured in the aftermath of September 11 and flown by extraordinary rendition to Egypt — where he was severely tortured — was the high-value source of much of the false intelligence that Powell invoked.[28]

Here are Powell's exact words: "My colleagues, every statement I make today is backed up by sources, solid sources. These are not assertions. What we are giving you are facts and conclusions based on solid intelligence. I will cite some examples, and these are from human sources."[29]

A former top aide to Colin Powell, Col. Lawrence Wilkerson, describes his participation in this fiasco. "I wish I had never been involved in it," he says. "I look back on it, and say it was the lowest point in my life."[30] Al-Libi's statements, he explained, "were obtained through interrogation techniques other than those authorized by the Geneva conventions."[31]

Terroristic Torture

The dubious value of information obtained by interrogational torture raises disturbing questions. If low-grade intelligence is all that can be extracted from high-value detainees, why is torture used at all?[32]

---

28. Michael Isikoff, "Iraq and Al Qaeda: Forget the 'Poisons and Deadly Gases,'" *Newsweek*, July 5, 2005.

29. Secretary of State Colin L. Powell, "Remarks to the United Nations Security Council," New York City, February 5, 2003. Available online at http://www.state.gov/secretary/former/powell/remarks/2003/17300.htm.

30. "Former aide: Powell WMD speech 'lowest point in my life,'" CNN.com, August 23, 2005. Available online at http://www.cnn.com/2005/WORLD/meast/08/19/powell.un/.

31. Simon Jeffery, "Prewar claims 'sourced from rendition detainee,'" *Guardian Unlimited*, December 9, 2005. Available online at http://www.guardian.co.uk/Iraq/Story/0,2763,1663743,00.html.

32. There is at least one important exception to the maxim that torture produces only unreliable results. Historical examples show that torture on a massive scale can be effective. "Torture of the few yields little useful information," writes Alfred McCoy. ". . . But mass torture of thousands of suspects, some guilty, most innocent, can produce some useful intelli-

The first to admit that torture is an ineffective tool of interrogation are professional interrogators themselves. Consider a few statements.

- Any professional interrogator you speak with, uniformed or otherwise, will tell you that torture doesn't work. . . . I don't even like putting "interrogation" and "torture" in the same line. (Mark Jacobson, former planning officer for Guantánamo in the Department of Defense)[33]
- I, and everyone I know with any experience in the field, am disgusted. It is illegal to torture or humiliate. Illegal, immoral, dishonorable, and ineffective. It is not why we're there. (Philip Gold, writing in the wake of the Abu Ghraib revelations. From 1977 to 1979, he commanded a Marine Corps interrogation team.)[34]
- No one has yet offered any validated evidence that torture produces reliable intelligence. . . . While torture apologists frequently make the claim that torture saves lives, that assertion is directly contradicted by many Army, FBI, and CIA professionals who have actually interrogated al-Qaeda captives. (Brigadier General David R. Irvine, retired Army Reserve strategic intelligence officer. For 18 years he taught prisoner interrogation and military law at the Sixth Army Intelligence School.)[35]

The point is confirmed, from another perspective, by Douglas A. Johnson, executive director of the Center for Victims of Torture. In testimony before the Senate Judiciary Committee, he stated:

Torture does not yield reliable information. Well-trained interrogators, within the military, the FBI, and the police have testified that torture does not work, is unreliable and distracting from the hard work of interrogation. Nearly every client at the Center for Victims of Torture, when

---

gence"; yet it does so only at "a prohibitively high political cost." See McCoy, *A Question of Torture*, pp. 196, 198; cf. pp. 190-206.

33. Mark Jacobson, PBS Frontline Interview, July 13, 2005. Available online at http://www.pbs.org/wgbh/pages/frontline/torture/interviews/jacobson.html.

34. Philip Gold, "The ABCs of Interrogation," *The Seattle Post-Intelligencer*, May 12, 2004. Available online at http://seattlepi.nwsource.com/opinion/172852_interogate12.html.

35. Brig. Gen. David R. Irvine, "Why Torture Doesn't Work," AlterNet, November 22, 2005. Available online at http://www.alternet.org/rights/28585/.

subjected to torture, confessed to a crime they did not commit, gave up extraneous information, or supplied names of innocent friends or colleagues to their torturers.[36]

The question becomes acute. If torture is as futile as professional interrogators testify, what is it really about?

Perhaps one clue lies in the nature of state power. The logic of torture is the logic of domination. It is a logic that begins in the torture chamber and extends to the outside world. When torture is practiced on an administrative basis, the victim is shattered, but the society is terrorized. Torture is a means of communication. It sends a terrifying message that the state will stop at nothing to secure its perceived interests and ensure its own survival. Torture functions as an instrument of general intimidation. It demonstrates that those in power are above the law and cannot be held to account.

Terroristic torture usually includes a punitive element. It retaliates against the hated enemy, whom it does not regard as truly human. Because the enemy is less than human, subjecting even mere suspects to excruciating forms of pain, degradation, and abuse is thought to be permissible. The punitive aspect becomes a part of the message. No due process, to say nothing of mercy, will be shown to enemies of the state.[37]

Terroristic torture becomes increasingly hard to distinguish from what it purports to hate. To fight terrorism by resorting to torture, for example, is finally to fight terrorism by terrorism, because torture with no interrogational value is little more than terrorism. The state that fights terrorism by torture continually generates new enemies. It takes on the features of a protection racket, producing precisely the enemies it needs to justify itself as the defender of society against the threat that it has itself created.[38]

At the same time, its strategy becomes self-defeating. Torture without interrogational value, when practiced on an administrative basis, inevitably leads at some point to a legitimation crisis. Iran under the Shah, the

36. Testimony of Douglas A. Johnson before Judiciary Hearing on the Nomination of the Honorable Alberto R. Gonzales to be the Attorney General of the United States (January 6, 2005). Available online at http://Judiciary.senate.gov/testimony.cfm?id=1345&wit_id =3939.

37. As Luban points out, punishment has sometimes been the sole purpose of torture. See Luban, "Torture," pp. 1433-35.

38. This theme is developed at length by William T. Cavanaugh, *Torture and Eucharist* (Oxford: Blackwell, 1998).

Philippines under Marcos, and Chile under Pinochet are only a few examples of states whose terroristic torture contributed to their demise.[39]

Terroristic torture would seem to be a noxious amalgam compounded of ruthlessness, hubris, resentment, and fear. It is as shortsighted as it is virulent. It grossly underestimates the corrupting power that torture effects upon everything with which it comes into contact. This uncanny power of corruption needs to be looked at in its own right. The conclusion of this section, however, pertains to the failure of the necessity defense.

The necessity defense consistently underestimates the costs of resorting to torture while tragically exaggerating any supposed benefits. Although interrogational torture and terroristic torture both appeal to necessity as a sufficient justification, the justification fails. It fails, because torture has no interrogational value, and because terrorism has no possible legitimacy. Interrogational torture is always tinged with the tincture of terror, and terroristic torture is usually wrapped in the mantle of intelligence gathering. Torture is a crime — an internationally recognized crime — which cannot be made lawful by necessity. Whether in its interrogational or its terroristic form, it is a crime without a defense.

Demonic Torture

Just as the persistence of torture is unnerving, so the costs of torture are incalculable. Torture corrupts. It corrupts everything and everyone it touches. It corrupts them profoundly and often irreversibly. There is a political level to this corruption, but the category of the political is not sufficient. Likewise, there is a moral level to it, but neither does the moral suffice to capture what is at stake. At its deepest level the corruption represented by torture is spiritual.

The category of the spiritual is descriptively required, because, as many have observed, torture tends toward becoming an end in itself. That is the deepest horror. As if by some invisible yet inexorable force, torture seeks and creates domination for its own sake, even as it also seeks and creates cruelty for its own sake. It seeks and creates cruel dominion and wanton cruelty toward another in disregard of the other's inherent dignity as a human being.

In its lust for absolute domination — what St. Augustine called *libido*

39. See McCoy, *Question of Torture*, pp. 74, 85, 91; cf. 190, 199.

dominandi — as joined with a corresponding lust for unrestrained cruelty as expressed by the infliction of excruciating humiliation, deprivation, and pain — which might in turn be called *libido crudelitatis* — torture assumes the spiritual form of the demonic. There seems to be, as is often remarked, an erotic aspect to torture. Cruelty and subjugation become forms of pleasure for the perpetrator. But even this perverse eroticism — which can be seen in the explicitly sexual aspects of many Abu Ghraib photographs — has tendrils sunk deeply in the soul.[40]

For something to become an absolute end in itself means that it has usurped a status that does not belong to it. The place belonging to God and God alone can be only seized by the human creature in the form of a monstrous caricature. The power of love is replaced by loveless power, compassion for the weak by sadistic cruelty, fair treatment by demonic subjugation, respect for life by the meanest contempt. Demonic torture is essentially destructive in its brutal self-elevation and self-justification. It proceeds at the expense of all legitimate obligations and norms. Its needs, its pleasures, and its purposes are carried out by shattering the essential humanity of another.

When Christians appeal to the image of God in their arguments against torture, they are not, properly speaking, merely adding a religious patina to the concept of human dignity. They are pointing to the ultimate meaning of human life. From Bonhoeffer through Barth to recent Catholic theology, the doctrine of the imago Dei has been reconceived in terms of relationality instead of the traditional rationality. It is human relationality as such that stands in analogy to the Holy Trinity, and therefore to the ultimacy of community. For the Trinity is itself a holy communion of love and freedom, joy and peace. Human creatures receive the vocation and the gift of living with God and one another on these terms.

When torture is conducted as an end in itself, and is therefore become demonic — when the purpose of power is power, and the purpose of cruelty is cruelty, when torture's purpose is tyrannical subjugation and sadistic degradation — then the divinely given meaning of life is unspeakably distorted and destroyed. The relation of the torturer to the tortured, and of the tortured to the torturer, makes a travesty of the most basic relations given by heaven to earth. In so degrading the human being and human community, torture blasphemes against God, neighbor, and self.

40. Cf. Susan Sontag, "Regarding the Torture of Others," *New York Times Magazine,* May 23, 2004, pp. 24-29, 42.

The mystery of torture is the mystery of this demonic aspect. The urge to humiliate, torment, and degrade lurks deep within the human breast.[41] Under conducive circumstances no one can entirely withstand it.[42] Sadism is not born but made. That is why torture, once chosen, cannot readily be contained, and is soon preferred. Torture, once chosen, both proliferates and corrupts. Proliferation is its dimension of breadth, and corruption its dimension of depth. Torture undermines victim and torturer alike.[43] It corrodes the society that permits it. It overthrows the rule of law, and then destroys the tyrannies that it spawns. Corrupting the soul, it eventually corrupts everything in its path. Torture is itself the ticking bomb.

The Military Commissions Act represents this very corruption. It does not come out of the blue. It has its roots in the fifty-year history of CIA and military involvement in torture. It brings to fruition a sinister past that includes CIA funding for academic research in torture techniques, military torture training programs for Latin American regimes and other dictatorships around the globe, the publishing of torture manuals, on-site U.S. supervision of client-state torture chambers, the outsourcing of torture to private contractors, and more.[44] What was once condoned in the shadows

41. Cf. Jonathan Glover, *Humanity: A Moral History of the Twentieth Century* (New Haven: Yale University Press, 2001). Jane Mayer quotes a former CIA officer: "When you cross over that line of darkness, it's hard to come back. You lose your soul. You can do your best to justify it, but . . . you can't go back to that dark a place without it changing you." See "The Black Sites," *The New Yorker*, August 13, 2007. A French interrogator during the Algerian conflict commented: "I realized that torture could become like a drug. I understood then that it was useless to claim to establish limits and forbidden practices. . . . In this domain too, it was all or nothing." Quoted by Rejali, *Torture and Democracy*, p. 485.

42. Philip Zimbardo, *The Lucifer Effect: Understanding How Good People Turn Evil* (New York: Random House, 2007); C. Haney, W. C. Banks, and P. G. Zimbardo, "Interpersonal dynamics in a simulated prison," *International Journal of Criminology and Penology* 1 (1973): 69-97.

43. For the effects of torture on the torturers, see Rejali, *Torture and Democracy*, pp. 524-26.

44. See McCoy, *Question of Torture*; Jennifer Harbury, *Truth, Torture, and the American Way: The History and Consequences of U.S. Involvement in Torture* (Boston: Beacon Press, 2005); Lesley Gill, *The School of the Americas: Military Training and Political Violence in the Americas* (Durham, N.C.: Duke University Press, 2004); Michael McClintock, *Instruments of Statecraft: U.S. Guerrilla Warfare, Counterinsurgency, and Counterterrorism, 1940-1990* (New York: Pantheon, 1992); Noam Chomsky and Edward S. Herman, *The Political Economy of Human Rights*, 2 vols. (Boston: South End Press, 1979).

is now made lawful at home. The stripping of habeas corpus, the establishment of secret prisons, the arbitrary power to declare U.S. citizens as "unlawful enemy combatants," the legalizing of indefinite detention, the admission of evidence obtained by abuse, the immunization of human rights violators from prosecution — these and other provisions of the Military Commissions Act compromise our commitment to the basic dignity of all human beings.[45]

The Military Commissions Act demonstrates that a government which takes off its gloves will not soon put them on again. It demonstrates that torture is not just one issue among others, but that, as Jeremy Waldron contends, the prohibition against torture is archetypal, containing the rule of law within itself, being an "icon of the whole," so that it marks the line between civilization and barbarism, between constitutional government and dictatorship.[46] Above all, the Military Commissions Act, along with similar policies and legislation, demonstrates the uncanny corruption that is torture; for torture, once tolerated, is not easily contained, and has today become the bomb ticking at the heart of our democracy.

As a postscript to this comment, it is worth noting that President Bush has now, openly, invoked the Military Commissions Act to justify torture. On March 8, 2008, he vetoed the 2008 Intelligence Authorization Act. By bringing the CIA under the jurisdiction of the Army Field Manual, this legislation, as passed by Congress, would have banned sleep deprivation, waterboarding, long-time standing, sensory deprivation, and other gulag tactics from interrogation practices as conducted by intelligence agencies. In his public statement Bush claimed, for the first time, that the Congress had already "authorized" the CIA program by adopting the Military Commissions Act.[47] In claiming the power to torture, the president of the United States not only displayed a callous disregard for human rights. More than ever before, he placed the authority of his office above the rule of law. Torture is the measure and definition of authority with dictatorial pretense.

A second postscript has also become necessary. According to an explo-

---

45. See Joan Mariner, "The Military Commissions Act of 2006: A Short Primer," FindLaw, October 6, 2006. Available online at http://writ.news.findlaw.com.mariner/20061009.hmtl.

46. Waldron, "Torture and Positive Law," pp. 1718-30, 1734-39 (quoted phrase, p. 1722).

47. "President's Radio Address," March 8, 2008. Available online at http://www.whitehouse.gov/news/releases/2008/03/20080308.html.

sive ABC News report on April 9, 2008,[48] dozens of top-secret meetings took place in the White House, beginning in 2002, in which the president's top advisors approved the use of torture. Those involved were members of the National Security Council's "Principals Committee" — Dick Cheney, Condoleezza Rice, Donald Rumsfeld, Colin Powell, George Tenet, and John Ashcroft. When the history of our era is written, their decisions will surely go down in infamy. Because of these senior officials — and not just *Animal House* on the night shift — America is widely regarded around the world as a Torture Nation.

The techniques that the advisors not only approved but also reportedly even choreographed amount to torture by any reasonable standard. Near drowning (waterboarding), sleep deprivation, subjection to temperatures of extreme cold (hypothermia), physical assault, and stress positions are proscribed by international and domestic law. They are tactics that have no place in a democratic society. John Ashcroft rightly asked at one point: "Why are we talking about this in the White House? History will not judge this kindly." But according to the report, Condoleezza Rice prevailed, telling the CIA: "This is your baby. Go do it."

Nor does it seem that the president was insulated from these decisions. As the head of the National Security Council, he signed a decision memo in which torture was effectively authorized (February 7, 2002).[49] He has also admitted that the new report is accurate: "And, yes," he told a reporter, "I'm aware our national security team met on this issue. And I approved."[50] Commenting on these developments, George Washington University law professor Jonathan Turley stated bluntly: "This was a torture program . . . and it goes right to the President's desk." He added: "I

48. Jan Crawford Greenburg et al., "Sources: Top Bush Advisors Approved 'Enhanced Interrogation,'" ABC News (April 9, 2008). See also Lara Jakes Jordan and Pamela Hess, "Cheney, Others OK'd Harsh Interrogations," Associated Press (April 10, 2008). http://ap.google.com/article/ALeqM5iA8mY9rbbDdKUe1Y9KObwHhqr9YgD8VVCEG80; "The Torture Sessions," New York Times Editorial (April 20, 2008). http://www.nytimes.com/2008/04/20/opinion/20sun1.html?ref=opinion; http://abcnews.go.com/TheLaw/LawPolitics/story?id=4583256&page=1

49. National Security Council Action Memorandum (February 7, 2002). http://www.gwu.edu/~nsarchiv/NSAEBB/NSAEBB127/02.02.07.pdf. The pivotal role of this Memorandum in sanctioning torture is carefully noted by Philippe Sands, *Torture Team* (New York: Palgrave Macmillan, 2008).

50. Jan Crawford Greenburg et al., "Bush Aware of Advisers' Interrogation Talks," ABC News (April 11, 2008). http://abcnews.go.com/TheLaw/LawPolitics/story?id=4635175&page=1.

don't think there's any doubt that [the president] was aware of this. The only doubt is simply whether anybody cares enough to do something about it."[51]

The Military Commissions Act pertains directly to these disclosures, because it amended the 1997 War Crimes Act in order to grant retroactive immunity for any abuses authorized by the Bush administration that would otherwise be in defiance of that Act and related covenants like Geneva Common Article 3.[52] Whether those who may have violated these laws can so easily be rendered immune from prosecution has been questioned. "I predict that there will be calls for top administration officials to be prosecuted in an international court for war crimes," said Erwin Chemerinsky, a civil liberties expert who teaches at Duke University Law School. "This meeting [of the Principals Committee] supports the involvement of top officials — including the president — in approving torture."[53]

Conclusion

Torture is a form of lawlessness that cannot rightfully be made lawful. It cannot be made lawful, because it tends toward wanton cruelty, lawless power, and dictatorship. It is morally wrong, because cruelty, degradation, and bondage are morally wrong. Torture is a subcategory under cruelty, as its most extreme form, not an independent category alongside it. It is an international crime without defense, because cruel, inhuman, and degrading treatment is a crime without defense. To reject torture while permitting cruel, inhuman, and degrading treatment is either disingenuous or incoherent — the work of a knave or a fool.

Interrogational torture is a delusion, terroristic torture is an abomination, and demonic torture devours its children. Torture admits no necessity by which it can be justified.

51. "War Crimes Trial Warranted," WordPress (April 11, 2008). http://writechic .wordpress.com/2008/04/11/war-crimes-trial-warranted/.

52. See Human Rights First, "Questions and Answers About the Military Commissions Act of 2006." http://www.humanrightsfirst.org/us_law/etn/ca3/hrf-ca3-102406.html.

53. Quoted in Spencer Ackerman, "Torture and the Law," *The Washington Independent* (April 18, 2008). http://www.washingtonindependent.com/view/torture-and-the-law.

CHAPTER 7

Six Reasons Why Torture Is Always Wrong

David P. Gushee

Perhaps the best way to engage a moral issue realistically is first to view it in concrete rather than abstract terms. To that end, consider the following vignettes:

- "Three marines in Mahmudiya shocked a detainee with an electric transformer, forcing him to 'dance' as the electricity hit him."[1]
- "On another occasion DETAINEE-07 was forced to lie down while MPs jumped on his back and legs. He was beaten with a broom and a chemical light was broken and poured over his body. . . . During this abuse a police stick was used to sodomize DETAINEE-07 and two female MPs were hitting him, throwing a ball at his penis, and taking photographs."[2]
- "A dog was allowed in the cell of two male juveniles and allowed to go 'nuts.' Both juveniles were screaming and crying, with the younger and smaller trying to hide behind the other juvenile."[3]

1. Thomas E. Ricks, "Detainee Abuse by Marines Is Detailed," *Washington Post,* December 15, 2004, p. A01. Information from Defense Department documents.

2. Mark Danner, "Abu Ghraib: The Hidden Story," Part II, *New York Review of Books,* October 7, 2004. Available online at http://www.ccmep.org/2004_articles/general/100704_abu_ghraib.htm. Information from Fay-Jones Report for Defense Department.

3. Major General George R. Fay, "Investigation of the Abu Ghraib Detention Facility and 205th Military Intelligence Brigade," p. 68. Available online at http://files.findlaw.com/news.findlaw.com/hdocs/docs/dod/fay82504rpt.pdf.

- "They threw pepper on my face and the beating started. This went on for a half hour. And then he started beating me with the chair until the chair was broken. After that they started choking me. . . . And then they started beating me again. They concentrated on beating me in my heart until they got tired from beating me."[4]
- A detainee "had been hooded, handcuffed in the back, and made to lie down, on a hot surface during transportation. This had caused severe skin burns that required three months' hospitalization. . . ."[5]
- "In November 2002, an inexperienced CIA case officer allegedly ordered guards to strip naked an uncooperative young detainee, chain him to the concrete floor, and leave him there overnight without blankets. He froze to death, according to four U.S. government officials."[6]
- "al-Qatani was forced to perform dog tricks on a leash, was straddled by a female interrogator, forced to dance with a male interrogator, told that his mother and sister were whores, forced to wear a woman's bra and thong on his head during interrogation, and subjected to an unmuzzled dog to scare him."[7]
- A former Iraqi general "died of asphyxiation after being stuffed headfirst into a sleeping bag . . . at an American base in Al Asad."[8]
- Over 83,000 people have been detained in the "War on Terror." Roughly 14,500 are currently in custody. Over two hundred have been detained for more than two years. One hundred eight have died in U.S. custody as of March 2005. Twenty-six of these deaths are being investigated as criminal homicides.[9]

4. Karen J. Greenberg and Joshua Dratel, *The Torture Papers: The Road to Abu Ghraib* (Cambridge: Cambridge University Press, 2005), p. 505.

5. Report of the International Committee of the Red Cross, February 2004, quoted in Mark Danner, *Torture and Truth* (New York: New York Review Books, 2004), pp. 259-60.

6. Dana Priest, "CIA Holds Terror Suspects in Secret Prisons," *Washington Post,* November 2, 2005, p. A01.

7. Evan Thomas and Michael Hirsh, "The Debate Over Torture," *Newsweek,* November 21, 2005, p. 31.

8. Douglas Jehl and Tim Golden, "C.I.A. Is Likely to Avoid Charges in Most Prisoner Deaths," *New York Times,* October 23, 2005, p. 6.

9. Katherine Shrader, "U.S. Has Detained 83,000 in War on Terror," Associated Press, November 16, 2005. Available online at http://www.sunherald.com.

Understanding Torture

The word "torture," tellingly, comes from the Latin *torquere*, to twist. According to international law scholar Lisa Hajjar, the governmental context is the key to understanding torture, at least as we are discussing it in this context. Torture involves "purposefully harming someone who is in custody — unfree to fight back or protect himself or herself and imperiled by that incapacitation."[10] For Hajjar, the definition of torture hinges not so much on the specific details of various tortuous acts, but on the fact that the tortured are prisoners in the custody of a government. They are persons upon whom suffering is inflicted for some public purpose.

The question that our nation has not yet fully resolved concerns whether various specific kinds of harm can or should be inflicted by those serving our government upon prisoners who are in our custody. Most particularly (though misleadingly), the debate has focused on what kinds of measures legitimately can be taken in the attempt to extract information from prisoners held by us in the "war on terror" and the wars in Afghanistan and Iraq. In this sense it is a debate about the proper use of government power. In our context, it has also become a debate about decision-making and accountability in a liberal democracy.

To focus exclusively here on the use of torture or torture-like activities by agents of the United States government could be misunderstood. In offering such a focus I am not saying or implying that the United States is the only nation whose representatives have sometimes engaged in torture or who should be censured for torture. I am not saying or implying that the United States has a history of routinized torture. I am not saying or implying that the United States military or intelligence services are a bastion of torturers. I am not saying or implying that the United States is the world's new evil empire, like Nazi Germany or the Soviet Union or ancient Rome. I am not saying or implying that the policies of the United States are morally equivalent to the policies of such tyrannical states. What I *am* saying is that the United States has edged near and at times across the line into torture during the last five years. And what I am *doing* by saying this, and by morally evaluating it, is exercising my responsibilities as a citizen, and particularly as a Christian citizen, and most particularly as a Protestant evangeli-

---

10. Lisa Hajjar, "Torture and the Future," *Middle East Report Online*. Available online at http://www.merip.org/mero/interventions/hajjar_interv.html.

cal Christian. That is all I am doing, and that is quite enough to try to do in one article.

Torture in International Law and Recent U.S. Practice

There is no single precise definition concerning the exact kinds of actions that constitute torture — such acts seem to fall along on a continuum. But this does not signify that the meaning of the term is infinitely elastic. International agreements that deal with torture provide some clues. Article Five of the 1948 Universal Declaration of Human Rights simply states that "no one shall be subjected to torture or to cruel, inhuman, or degrading treatment."[11] Article 17 of the Third Geneva Convention (1949) asserts that "no physical or mental torture, nor any other form of coercion, may be inflicted on prisoners of war," but instead, "Prisoners of war must at all times be humanely treated."[12] The 1985 U.N. Convention Against Torture defines torture as "any act by which severe pain or suffering, whether physical or mental, is intentionally inflicted on a person."[13] The United States is a signatory to all of these international declarations and historically has incorporated their principles into military doctrine. For example, the U.S. Army Field Manual tells military interrogators that "the use of force, mental torture, threats, insults or exposure to unpleasant and inhumane treatment of any kind is prohibited by law."[14]

Mark Bowden, a military scholar and author of *Black Hawk Down*, reminds us that torture is "a crude and ancient tool of political oppression,"[15] practiced by governments for various reasons through the centuries and by many still in our own time. The kinds of acts most often classified as torture make for a dreary catalog of pain. They include physical mutilation, beatings, electric shocks, employment of mind-altering drugs, and other forms

11. "Universal Declaration of Human Rights." Available online at http://www.un.org/Overview/rights.html, 3/16/06.

12. "Geneva Convention Relative to the Treatment of Prisoners of War," Article 17, Article 13. Available online at www.unhch.ch/html/menu3/b/91.htm.

13. U.N. Convention Against Torture, Article 1. Available online at http://www.hrweb.org/legal/cat.html.

14. U.S. Army Field Manual 34-52. Available online at http://www.globalsecurity.org/intell/library/policy/army/fm/fm34-52/chapter1.htm.

15. Mark Bowden, "The Dark Art of Interrogation," *Atlantic Monthly*, October 2003, p. 53.

of unimaginably sadistic violence. There is no end to inventive ways of harming the bodies and minds of other human beings.

When President George W. Bush says of the United States that "we do not torture," perhaps these kinds of acts are what he has in mind. But it is now clear that since September 11, 2001, the Bush administration, chafing under the perceived constraints of the longstanding ban against torture, has attempted to carve out room for acts that brush up against the boundary line separating aggressive interrogation from torture — without, they believe, crossing over it. Called in internal administration documents by such names as "enhanced interrogation techniques," "professional interrogation," "moderate physical pressure," or even (by outside analysts) "torture lite," these have included a variety of measures, some approved as policy by our government and others not publicly acknowledged or approved but found by both independent and government investigators to have occurred in our detention facilities.

Among the sometimes approved measures have been prolonged standing, forced nakedness, withdrawal of food and water, sensory deprivation, hooding (often with intentionally foul-smelling hoods), prolonged interrogations, assaults with extremely loud noise, use of threatening dogs, grabbing, poking or pushing, sleep adjustment/deprivation, and waterboarding (dripping water onto a wet cloth over the detainee's face, which feels like drowning).

Among the (apparently) unapproved but sometimes practiced measures, some of which were mentioned at the beginning of this article, have been punching, slapping, beating, and kicking detainees; religious and sexual humiliation; prolonged shackling; exposure to severe heat or cold; food and/or toilet deprivation; mock or threatened executions; letting dogs in some cases bite and severely injure detainees; and the taking of humiliating photographs of such acts as well as of dead detainees. Other acts, such as the electric shock and sodomizing instances detailed at the beginning of this article, seem to be described best as neither approved nor regularly practiced measures but as occasional "abuses" that extended beyond the already questionable acts which were either officially approved or unofficially permitted.

Such abuses appear to have been particularly prevalent in military intelligence interrogations, among private U.S. contractors serving the military, and among the underprepared and poorly trained military police at places like Abu Ghraib from 2002 until 2003. There are also profound worries and disturbing allegations about events at Bagram in Afghanistan, about what is being done to "high value" detainees in CIA interrogations at undisclosed locations, and certainly about what is happening to prisoners "rendered" to other countries (many known to practice torture) by our government. Lack of any access to such sites or prisoners makes it impossible to know what is happening in these cases.

Internal Bush administration documents reveal various efforts to define either acts or prisoners in such a way as to permit at least the approved measures just described. Techniques that many reasonably construe as torture, or tantamount to torture, perhaps most obviously the practice of waterboarding, have been renamed as "enhanced interrogation." Meanwhile, though "torture" has been officially rejected, the administration has balked at any legal restriction on "cruel, inhuman, or degrading" (CID) treatment of detainees, thereby drawing a distinction between forms of mistreatment that can at least reasonably be construed as indistinguishable. When Congress passed legislation in late 2005 banning CID, the president's signing statement continued to indicate his reservations about such restrictions on interrogation techniques, and late revisions in the law leave questions about who, if anyone, would be held accountable if the line were to be crossed.

Prisoners held in the War on Terror generally have been viewed as "unlawful combatants" and thus beyond the reach of American criminal, civil, or most military law protections or of international law. Those held on foreign soil or by foreign governments at our request have become essentially invisible. The extension of the most minimal protections to those prisoners held by the United States even on our soil or in areas directly under our control (such as Guantánamo Bay) has occurred gradually, unevenly, and generally only when the courts have demanded such protections. By defining torture and the applicability of civil liberties narrowly — and "military necessity" in the War on Terror broadly — the U.S. government has made official room for deeply questionable acts against legally defenseless detainees. The question before us is whether, as citizens, and especially as Christians, we can support our government in this movement into the neighborhood of torture and sometimes across the border into torture. I believe the answer is a clear no.

Why Torture Is Banned

The ban on torture in international law, as Lisa Hajjar notes, "is stronger than almost any other human right because the prohibition of torture is absolutely non-derogable and because the law recognizes no exceptions. What this means is that no one — ever, anywhere — has a 'right' to torture, and that everyone — always, everywhere — has a right not to be tortured. It also means that anyone who engages in or abets torture is committing a crime."[16]

The prohibition on torture has been understood since the late 1940s as both a matter of fundamental human rights and a right accorded to prisoners of war. In other words, no *human being* may be tortured, simply because they are human. And no *prisoner of war* may be tortured, not just because they are human but particularly because they are prisoners of war and as such are covered by various protections in international law, especially the Geneva Conventions. Both kinds of legal protections were deeply affected by the atrocities that occurred against civilians and prisoners of war during World War II.

The ban on torture also has roots deep in the emergence of liberal democracy, because, as Michael Ignatieff has written, "liberal democracy stands against any unlimited use of public authority against human beings, and torture is the most unlimited, most unbridled form of power that one person can exercise against another."[17] It is one of the strongest international legal prohibitions in existence; once ratified and codified by states it becomes part of each nation's law as well. Hajjar points out that at least in legal terms the right not to be tortured is actually stronger than the right to life: "There are many circumstances in which people legally can be killed, but none under which people legally can be tortured."[18] For example, it is perfectly legal (however tragic) to kill an enemy combatant in wartime, but not at all legal to take that same person into custody, disarm him, and then torture him.

This prohibition on torture in international law quite explicitly admits no exceptions. The U.N. Convention Against Torture puts it this way: "No

16. Hajjar, "Torture and the Future," pp. 3-4.
17. Michael Ignatieff, "Evil Under Interrogation," *Financial Times* (London, England), May 15, 2004.
18. Hajjar, "Torture and the Future," p. 5.

exceptional circumstances whatsoever, whether a state of war or a threat of war, internal political instability or any other public emergency, may be invoked as a justification for torture."[19]

The U.S. ratified this convention in 1994, before 9/11, before our launch of the War on Terror. Now some in our government and in our nation believe that acts at least tantamount to torture are indeed morally permissible in the exceptional case posed by Islamist terrorism. As State Department official Cofer Black famously put it: "All I want to say is that there was before 9/11 and after 9/11. After 9/11 the gloves came off."[20] I believe that, regardless of 9/11, the absolute prohibition of torture remains a moral and legal norm that should not be weakened.

A Christian Moral Analysis of Torture

Let me begin by granting the obligation of government to preserve public order and protect the security of its population. This principle is recognized in international law, moral thought, and public opinion. For Christians, it is clearly stated in Romans 13:1-7. Government deters violations of peace and order, punishes wrongdoers, and does all it can to advance the common good within the limits of its mandate. This work of government does involve the "sword"; that is, coercion, and in necessary cases, violence. Various legal and moral restrictions are placed on government as it exercises this fearsome power. It is generally understood that government officials must use the minimum force necessary to accomplish their missions. Thoughtful moral theorists recognize that governments easily abuse this power of the sword and must be watched carefully.

Let me also grant that the terrorist attacks of September 11, 2001, were one of the most heinous acts ever visited upon this nation and a clear violation of the laws of war and of any kind of civilized moral code. Terrorist acts around the world since then remind us that our nation, along with many others, faces the threat of enemies who do not adhere to the kinds of moral scruples that we are considering in this essay.

Finally, I also grant the point that Mark Bowden makes in arguing that

---

19. Convention Against Torture, Article 2.

20. Quoted in "The Roots of Torture," *Newsweek,* May 24, 2004. Available online at http://www.msnbc.msn.com/id/4989422/.

there is a built-in tension between what he calls the "warrior" ethic and the "civilian" ethic.[21] For the warrior, the goal is to accomplish the mission. For the civilian, the goal is to preserve the rule of law. Even if we grant that well-intentioned warriors also recognize the importance of the rule of law, and that well-intentioned civilians recognize the importance of accomplishing the mission, their passions and priorities tend to differ. Managing this tension is a major challenge in any civilized society. I acknowledge that I write from the civilian side.

I do not write to demonize those who believe that protecting our nation's security, and preventing the horror of another September 11, requires the use of interrogation techniques that could be classified as at least borderline torture. But I do believe that the case against this move is far stronger than the case for it. Here is why:

1. Torture Violates the Intrinsic Dignity of the Human Being, Made in the Image of God

The human person is a creation of God. Every inch of the human body and every aspect of the human spirit come from God and bear witness to his handiwork. We are made in the image of God (Gen. 1:26-28). Human dignity (value, worth) comes as a permanent and ineradicable endowment of the Creator, to every person.

Recognition of the intrinsic dignity of the human being requires a corresponding restraint in our behavior toward all human beings. Christians, at least, should be trained to see in every person the imprint of God's grandeur. This should create in us a sense of reverence or even sacredness. Here, we say — and we say it even of detainees in the war on terror — is a human being sacred in God's sight, made in God's image, someone for whom Christ died. No one is *ever* "subhuman" or "human debris," as Rush Limbaugh has described some of our adversaries in Iraq.[22] An inchoate sense of the proper reverence due to every human person makes its way even into "secular" and public codes, such as international legal documents. These texts may not be able to say why human beings should be treated with respect but they know that this is in fact a binding obligation.

21. Bowden, "Dark Art of Interrogation," p. 70.

22. A widely quoted remark from his radio show. Available online at http://www.smithersmpls.com/2004/05/more-rush-limbaugh-from-yesterday-it_13.html.

Christians can say why: because this "detainee," even this "terrorist," if he is one, is a child of God, made in God's image.

A moral commitment to the dignity of the human person is sometimes fleshed out in terms of human rights. Just because they are human, on this view, people have rights to many things, including the right not to be tortured. Christians sometimes debate the legitimacy of "rights-talk," partly because it is a language often overused and misused in modern debate and partly because we think about how Jesus gave up all of his "rights." Just because someone claims a "right" does not mean that it is a right. But I believe that at least an implication of a biblical understanding of human dignity is the existence of a set of human rights. Among the most widely recognized of these in both legal and moral theory is the right to bodily integrity; that is, the right not to have intentional physical and psychological harm inflicted upon oneself by others. The ban on torture is one expression of the right to bodily integrity.

The absoluteness of such human rights can be debated. Following the categories of Catholic moral reasoning, Robert G. Kennedy has argued that even the most widely recognized human rights, such as the right to life or the right not to be tortured, are absolute in *existence* but not *extent*.[23] What this means is that while the right not to be tortured applies to all persons, like all rights it can, at least in theory, be qualified by other rights and by the requirements of justice. Kennedy argues that "defensive interrogatory torture" (and only this kind of torture, intended strictly to defend the nation against an urgent and immediate threat to its security) may be morally legitimate under very carefully qualified conditions. And yet he goes on to argue that "it is quite likely that most instances in which interrogatory torture is employed would not conform to these principles and so would be immoral."[24]

Whether we open the door to torture just a crack, as Kennedy suggests, or keep it firmly shut as an absolute ban, as I believe, the principle of human dignity and its correlated rights remains a transcendently important reason to resist the turn toward torture. And because rights correspond with obligations, all of us who recognize the human right not to be tortured have an obligation to protect those rights.

---

23. Robert G. Kennedy, "Can Interrogatory Torture Be Morally Legitimate?" Paper presented to the 2003 Joint Services Conference on Professional Ethics. Available online at www.usafa.af.mil/jscope/JSCOPE03/Kennedy03.html.

24. Kennedy, "Can Interrogatory Torture Be Morally Legitimate?" p. 9.

2. Torture Mistreats the Vulnerable and Thus Violates the Demands of Public Justice

Lisa Hajjar points out that torture, by definition, is something that a government does to a person in its custody.[25] Imprisoned people are vulnerable people. Whatever they did, or may be suspected of having done, once in our hands they are completely vulnerable to us. The fact that many thousands of those held in U.S. custody have been released as neither having committed a crime nor posed any terrorist threat ought to be remembered here as well.

Justice has many dimensions and can be defined in many ways. But it is clear in the Scriptures that God's understanding of justice tilts in the direction of the vulnerable. Justice is quite often treated as *the use of power to protect the vulnerable and powerless.* "Do not mistreat an alien or oppress him, for you were aliens in Egypt. Do not take advantage of a widow or an orphan. If you do and they cry out to me, I will certainly hear their cry" (Exod. 22:21-23). As this text suggests, primary forms of injustice include the violent abuse and domination of the powerless by the powerful and their exclusion from participation in a community that cares about their rights and needs.

One reason why there are so many layers of procedures and protections given to accused and imprisoned persons in our legal system (and to prisoners of war in international law) is precisely their powerlessness at the hands of government authority. Justice requires attempting to balance the scales so that defenseless people are not overpowered or abused by governments. This is especially important in any legal system, which has the power to deprive people of their liberty, and sometimes their lives.

The tens of thousands who have been detained by our government and military in the last four years are, by definition, as prisoners, vulnerable to injustice. Those of them who have been abused or mistreated by representatives of our nation — as in the examples cited in this essay — are victims of injustice, however carefully we may define or excuse the treatment that we have meted out to them. They were in our hands and we abused our power over them. They were dominated, harmed, abused, and sometimes violated physically, even murdered, whether negligently or intentionally. Christians must learn to care about justice — more, we must

25. Hajjar, "Torture and the Future," p. 6.

develop a deep passion for justice, the kind of passion for justice that God has, the one who hears the cries of the oppressed and dominated and acts on their behalf (Exod. 2:23-25). Torture is an injustice and must be protested as such.

3. Authorizing Any Form of Torture Trusts Government Too Much

Human beings are sinful through and through (Rom. 3:10-18). We are not to be trusted. We are especially dangerous when unchecked power is concentrated in our hands. This applies to all of us.

Therefore it is certainly likely that authorizing even the "lightest" forms of torture risks much abuse. As Richard John Neuhaus puts it, "We dare not trust ourselves to torture."[26] Or as evangelical human rights activist Gary Haugen writes, "Because the power of the state over detainees is exercised by fallen human beings, that power must be limited by clear boundaries, and individuals exercising such power must be transparently accountable."[27]

Haugen rightly emphasizes both the procedural and substantive regulation of detainee interrogation. Given human sinfulness, it is not just that people should be told not to torture, but also that structures of due process, accountability, and transparency must buttress those standards to make them less likely to be violated — and subject to redress if violated. This is what is so dangerous about the discovery of secret CIA prisons in Europe and "ghost detainees" who are located no one knows where. As Manfred Nowak, U.N. special rapporteur on torture, said at the time the CIA's secret prisons were revealed, "Every secret place of detention is usually a higher risk for ill treatment, that's the danger of secrecy."[28] Just because U.S. government officials say that we can be trusted to act "in keeping with our values" — without due process, accountability, and transparency — does not make it so. No government is so virtuous as to be able to overturn the too often verified laws of human nature, or to be be-

26. Richard John Neuhaus, "Speaking About the Unspeakable," *First Things,* March 2005, pp. 61-62.

27. Gary A. Haugen, "Silence on Suffering," *Christianity Today Online,* October 17, 2005. Available online at www.christianitytoday.com/ct/2005/142/12.0.html.

28. Dana Priest and Josh White, "Policies on Terrorism Suspects Come Under Fire," *Washington Post,* November 3, 2005.

yond the need for democratic checks and balances. To believe that our nation is somehow that virtuous is to subscribe to a dangerous and, frankly, heretical form of American exceptionalism.

4. Torture Invites the Dehumanization of the Torturer

In reflecting on torture, Mark Bowden concludes that sometimes it is the right choice. But even so, he worries, "How does one allow it yet still control it? Sadism is deeply rooted in the human psyche. Every army has its share of soldiers who delight in kicking and beating bound captives. Men in authority tend to abuse it — not all men, but many. As a mass, they should be assumed to lean toward abuse."[29] And there is plenty of evidence that many who do not begin their military careers delighting in sadism can drift into such a delight once having tasted the experience.

Loosening longstanding restrictions on physical and mental cruelty toward prisoners risks the dehumanization not just of the tortured but the torturers. What may be intended as carefully calibrated interrogation techniques easily tempt their implementers in the direction of sadism — pain infliction for the sheer fun of it, especially in the heat of military conflict, in a climate of fear and loathing of the enemy, and in the context of an endless War on Terror. How many of us could be trusted to draw the line consistently between the permitted "grabbing, poking, and pushing," on the one hand, and the banned "punching, slapping, and kicking" (or worse) on the other? How much self-control can we reasonably expect people to exercise? And once the line has been crossed to torture, as Michael Ignatieff claims, it "inflicts irremediable harm on both the torturer and the prisoner."[30]

Frederick Douglass commented famously on how holding a slave slowly ruined the character of the woman who owned him. Martin Luther King Jr. frequently talked about how in a sense the greatest victims of segregation were the white racists whose souls were deformed by their own hatred. Aleksandr Solzhenitsyn, reflecting on the Soviet Gulag, said that "our torturers have been punished most horribly of all: they are turning into swine, they are departing downward from humanity."[31]

29. Bowden, "Dark Art of Interrogation," p. 74.
30. Ignatieff, "Evil Under Interrogation," p. 3.
31. Aleksandr Solzhenitsyn, "What I Learned in the Gulag." Available online at http://www.freerepublic.com/forum/a3798e53e4620.htm.

War threatens the dehumanization of all sides and all parties. This is why there are so many limits placed on how wars may be fought — and why they are so frequently violated. The ban on torture is one of those limits, and for good reason.

5. Torture Erodes the Character of the Nation that Tortures

A nation is a collective moral entity with a character, an identity across time. Causes come and go, threats come and go, but the enduring question for any social entity is who "we" are as a people. This is true of a family, a church, a school, a civic club, or a town. It is certainly true of a nation.

Senator John McCain, who has courageously led the Republican charge against the drift toward torture, has said, "This isn't about who they are. This is about who we are. These are the values that distinguish us from our enemies." In a November *Newsweek* article, he put it this way: "What I . . . mourn is what we lose when . . . we allow, confuse, or encourage our soldiers to forget that best sense of ourselves, that which is our greatest strength — that we are different and better than our enemies, that we fight for an idea, not a tribe, not a land, not a king . . . but for an idea that all men are created equal and endowed by their Creator with inalienable rights."[32]

Regardless of whether we agree with this articulation of American exceptionalism and moral superiority, McCain is saying something very important here. His worry is that any move toward torture threatens our national character, our shared values, and our morality as a nation. He rightly acknowledges that our Islamist terrorist enemies do not share our commitment to the rule of law, to human rights, to procedural justice, to limits on what can be done for the cause, however holy. This is tragic, even evil, and it makes them a particularly lethal and insidious threat, but it does not somehow settle the question of how we as a nation should respond. To say this is not to be naïve about our enemies, but instead to express an unshakable commitment to our own moral identity.

We often say in Christian circles that people of integrity respond to life on the basis of scriptural principles, not preferences, feelings, or circumstances. We act on the basis of who we are, not who others are. If someone is ruthless to us at work, for example, this does not authorize persons of

---

32. Sen. John McCain, "Torture's Terrible Toll," *Newsweek*, November 21, 2005, p. 35.

faith to be equally ruthless in return. If someone violates their covenant with us it does not authorize us to do the same to them. Mature persons, and nations, know what their core values are and seek to act in every circumstance in a manner consistent with those values. If they abandon those values when severely tested, it raises real questions as to how deeply such values were ever held.

6. Torture Risks Negative Consequences at Many Levels

Those who know anything about moral theory know that the argument for torture is essentially a utilitarian one. Some are willing to torture because they believe it is the best means available to protect the 300 million people who live in this country. Hundreds or perhaps thousands of (foreign) detainees suffer as the price of protecting millions of us. Thus we achieve the greater good for the greater number of people.

Yet utilitarianism is a deeply flawed moral theory, as many philosophers, ethicists, and other thinkers have shown over the years. In emphasizing intrinsic human dignity, and concerns about both personal and national character, I have implicitly rejected any purely utilitarian argument for (or against) torture. Indeed, because I believe that torture is intrinsically wrong, it poses a risk to the very argument I am making even to entertain utilitarian considerations. But because many policymakers and citizens at least implicitly operate from a utilitarian framework, it must be addressed here.

The greatest gain promised by the resort to torture is that it might extract information from suspects that would otherwise be unavailable. In the most sensational and widely discussed scenario — the so-called ticking bomb case — utilitarians argue strongly that the torture of one terrorist at a pivotal moment could in turn save thousands of lives, and thus it must be permitted.

In a brilliant utilitarian analysis of what an institutionalized torture regime might look like, and what its consequences might be, Jean Marie Arriga has suggested a number of difficulties even for a utilitarian approach to torture.[33]

For example, and as many others have noted, there is abundant evi-

---

33. Jean Marie Arriga, "A Utilitarian Argument Against Torture Interrogation of Terrorists," *Science and Engineering Ethics* 10, no. 3 (June 3, 2004): 543-72.

dence that people will say anything under torture, just to stop the pain. It is not just that they will be deceptive intentionally, but even more that after sufficient torture they may lack the mental ability to distinguish between truth and falsehood, or the ability to convey the truth. If the goal of torture is to extract critical information, these problems are obviously profound. Several news agencies have reported that information apparently gained from torture has proven false — after being announced as an important intelligence score by the U.S. government. The overall reliability of intelligence gained from torture remains the subject of great controversy.

The ultimate goal in gaining this information is to protect national security. However, there is good reason to wonder whether the use of torture more deeply motivates extant terrorists, and turns more people from concerned bystanders into hardened terrorists, than any intelligence benefit that might be gained. An editorial in the *Vancouver Sun* put it well: "Those subjected to physical torture usually conceive undying hatred for their torturers."[34] One must therefore also consider the greater likelihood that American civilians (here or especially abroad) and American troops overseas will be subject to torture (or terror) by aggrieved enemies.

Further, as has already happened, sometimes the consequences of torture are worse than intended, as when victims die prematurely due to the physical or mental toll. From a utilitarian perspective the main problem here is that a dead person cannot give you any information whatsoever. And, of course, as news of deaths trickle out, moral outrage scandalizes the torturer's own people, the families and communities of the persons who have died in custody, and general world opinion.

Arriga's most original insights concern the unintended but likely institutional consequences that can and often do flow from a torture regime. For example, medical and psychological practitioners become involved in enhancing and medically managing torture techniques, thereby risking the corruption of these professions which are supposed to serve as agents of healing — or evoking their opposition. Biomedical specialists are recruited to study and develop torture, and torture resistance, techniques. Special torture interrogation units are established, with training in especially sophisticated methods of torture, and consequently other governmental and security institutions are demoralized and experience other negative consequences. Further, the use of rogue torture interrogation services, such as

---

34. Douglas Todd, "The Case Against Torture," *Vancouver Sun*, June 4, 2005, p. 3.

organized crime, covert U.S. torture agencies, and brutal foreign intelligence services, also poses severe problems in terms of command and control of torture operations and the empowerment of rogue elements here and abroad.[35] Arriga's article was published in 2004; one wonders how many of her concerns already are uncomfortably close to hitting their mark in our own case.

The "ticking bomb" case is theoretically important but in actuality a red herring. It has been wisely said that "bad cases make bad law" and this is true here. The percentage of such ticking bomb cases among the 83,000 people we have detained must be less than infinitesimal. It is just as foolish to legitimize the practice of torture because of this rare possible exception as it would be, say, to legitimize the practice of adultery because of the possibility that someone might have to commit adultery to save their child's life from a criminal who demands sex in exchange for the child's survival.

Much ink has been spilled considering how to handle these very rare ticking bomb cases. Perhaps the most widely discussed proposal has been Alan Dershowitz's suggestion that we permit torture only through a "torture warrant" signed by a judge or a very high government official, such as the president himself, who would therefore bear full legal, political, and moral responsibility.[36]

This would certainly be better than the drift into torture without such accountability. But I think that any potential resort to torture in rare, ticking bomb cases would be better handled within the context of an outright ban. The grand moral tradition of civil disobedience, for example, specifies that there are instances in which obedience to laws must be overridden by loyalty to a higher moral obligation. These are usually unjust laws but this is not always the case. Dietrich Bonhoeffer participated in an assassination plot against Hitler but did not argue for the rewriting of moral prohibitions of political assassinations. He was prepared to let God be his judge. If a one-in-a-million instance were to emerge in which a responsible official believed that the ban on torture must be overridden as a matter of emergency response, let him do so knowing fully that he would have to an-

---

35. Arriga, "A Utilitarian Argument Against Torture Interrogation of Terrorists," pp. 551-60.

36. Among other sources, see Alan Dershowitz, "Let America Take Its Cues from Israel Regarding Torture," *Jewish World Review*, January 30, 2002, p. 2. Available online at www.jewishworldreview.com/0102/torture.asp.

swer for his action before God, law, and neighbor. This is a long way from an authorized torture regime.

Resisting the Temptation to Torture

Long ago, German philosopher Immanuel Kant wrote about the perennial human tendency to find exceptions to binding moral rules when those obligations bind just a bit too tightly on *us*. "Hence there arises a natural . . . disposition to argue against these strict laws of duty and to question their validity, or at least their purity and strictness; and, if possible, to make them more accordant with our wishes and inclinations, that is to say, to corrupt them at their very source, and entirely to destroy their worth."[37]

I believe that this is the best explanation for what is happening on the issue of torture in our nation. Since 9/11 we have felt ourselves to be under siege. The extent to which we actually are under siege is of course impossible to determine; we are dependent on the information our government gives us, and we have had reasons in recent years to doubt the reliability of some of this information. But in any case, given the sense of siege, we have faced the temptation to abandon both legal and moral norms related to actions permissible for national self-defense. Our current crisis represents our succumbing to the temptation to waive moral rules that we have every reason to know are applicable to us. Bans on torture are part of international law, military law, and moral law. We could not wish to universalize such actions. We would not want our troops or our "detainees" or we ourselves to be tortured were the shoe on the other foot. We know that torture is wrong, but just not now, not in our exceptional case, not in this global War on Terror. We are tempted to follow the logic of a *Time* magazine article when it says, "In the war on terrorism, the personal dignity of a fanatic trained for mass murder may be an inevitable casualty."[38]

And yet we are queasy enough about even this "inevitable casualty" that we do not want to call torture torture. We do not want to expose our policies, or our prisons, or our prisoners, to public view, even to the pub-

37. Immanuel Kant, *Groundwork of the Metaphysic of Morals* (New York: Harper and Row, 1964), p. 73.

38. Adam Zagorin and Michael Duffy, "Inside the Interrogation of Detainee 063," *Time*, June 20, 2005, p. 33.

licity associated with our own legal processes. We deny that we are torturing, or we deny that our prisoners are really prisoners, or when pushed to the wall we remind one another of how evil the enemy is and how much worse other countries or ideologies are. We give every evidence of the kind of self-deception so characteristic of the descent into sin.

It is past time for American citizens, and especially evangelical Christians who have provided such reliable support to this president, to remind both government and society of perennial moral values that also just happen to be international and domestic laws. We must shake free from sluggish inattention to this issue, and in some cases must also shake free from our overall tendency toward comfortable partnership with (Republican) American government. We must speak truth to power. We say we care about moral values and that we vote on the basis of such values. Many of us say that we care deeply about human rights violations around the world. Now it is time to raise our voice about human rights violations directed and permitted by our own government.

This is a call to say a clear and unequivocal *No* to torture, ultimately on religious grounds, but not on the basis of any kind of idealistic withdrawal from realistic engagement with the world. It is time that we raise our voices and make ourselves heard in our churches, in Congress, in the judiciary, in the executive branch, in the military, and in public opinion.

Christians have dual loyalties that do not always easily cohere. We are loyal to our nation but also, and always more fundamentally, loyal to Jesus Christ. Sometimes these loyalties conflict. In this case, though, rightly understood, they do not.

We serve a tortured, crucified Savior. In the politics of a long-ago empire, reasons of state appeared to require his torture and death. "It is better for you that one man die for the people than that the whole nation perish" (John 11:50).

I have sought to show that a proper understanding of our national well-being requires the rejection of torture. Now I want to close by saying that for Christians a proper understanding of our ultimate loyalty — to Jesus the tortured one — makes any support of torture unthinkable.

CHAPTER 8

Torture and Eucharist: A Regretful Update

William T. Cavanaugh

The Imagination of Torture in Chile and the United States

Carlos Rueda, a director of children's theater, is the central character in Lawrence Thornton's novel *Imagining Argentina*. Carlos's wife and daughter are disappeared under the military dictatorship, leaving him to undertake a fruitless search for those he loves. In the course of his search, he meets many others similarly engaged. As he shares their grief and anguish, Carlos is visited with a miraculous gift. Carlos finds himself telling a boy whose father has been disappeared and tortured for several days that that very night a colonel will visit his father in his cell. The colonel will bring food and wine and tell his father, a university professor, that he must be more careful in what he says to his students. Two soldiers will come, allow him to shave, and release him. Even as Carlos tells the boy this story, he fears that it is a cruel lie. But it happens exactly as he says. People begin coming to Carlos every evening hoping to learn the fate of their loved ones.

Carlos's gift is not just that of seeing, for his stories can actually alter reality. Men appear in the middle of the night to give back babies snatched with their mothers. Holes open in solid concrete walls, and tortured prisoners walk through to freedom. Carlos's imagination can actually bring back people who have been disappeared, though he cannot control it. Sometimes his stories end in torture and death with no escape. His imagination is a shared one, larger than himself.

Carlos's friends are skeptical, convinced that one cannot confront tanks and helicopters with imagination and stories. They can see the conflict only in terms of fantasy versus reality. Carlos, on the other hand, rightly grasps that the contest is not between imagination and the real but between two types of imagination: that of the generals and that of their opponents. Carlos realizes that "he was being dreamed by [General] Guzman and the others, that he had been living inside their imagination."[1] A Ford Falcon driven by security agents drives slowly by. Carlos tells his friend Silvio what he thinks the men in the car see:

> They see sheep and terrorists because they imagine us that way. But look at the people, Silvio, that old woman, the man in shirt sleeves. They remember a time before the regime, but they do not take their imaginations beyond memory because hoping is too painful. So long as we accept what the men in the car imagine, we're finished. All I've been trying to tell you is that there are two Argentinas, Silvio, the regime's travesty of it, and the one we have in our hearts. We have to believe in the power of imagination because it is all we have, and ours is stronger than theirs.[2]

In my book *Torture and Eucharist* I describe the regime of torture and disappearance in Argentina's neighbor, Chile, under General Augusto Pinochet's regime. I refer to torture as the "imagination of the state," not, of course, to deny the reality of torture but to call attention to the fact that torture is part of a drama of inscribing bodies to perform certain roles in the imaginative project that is the nation-state. The state is not a tangible thing that exists somewhere. The state is rather conjured up in a group of people's sense of who it is, its memory of where it came from, its fears and hopes, and its sense of friends and enemies. There are tangible things — armies, prisons, tax forms, and the like — but they take on their peculiar power only when harnessed to the imaginative idea of the state. The imagination of the state can evoke compassion and solidarity for people we have never met, as in the case of a rural Minnesota town that donated a fire truck to distant New York City in the aftermath of 9/11. The imagination of the state can also convince Minnesota farm kids to travel to the other side

---

1. Lawrence Thornton, *Imagining Argentina* (New York: Doubleday, 1987), p. 131.
2. Thornton, *Imagining Argentina*, p. 65.

of the world as soldiers and kill people they know nothing about. It is not just the physical force of the state but *belief in* the state that, as Philip Abrams writes, "silences protest, excuses force, and convinces almost all of us that the fate of the victims is just and necessary."[3] This is what it means, as Carlos Rueda puts it, to live inside the generals' imagination.

The state is imaginary in the precise sense of the phrase "make believe." French Jesuit Michel de Certeau uses this phrase *(faire croire)* in describing torture's effects: "Torture is the technical procedure by which the tyrannical power acquires for itself this impalpable primary matter which it itself destroyed and which it lacks: authority, or, if one prefers, a capacity to make believe."[4] Torture, in other words, is the most acute example of the ability of the state to impose its narrative on an individual. But the effects go far beyond the body of the tortured individual. Torture is a social, one might say "liturgical," enactment of the imaginative power of the state. Torture is both a product and a reinforcement of a certain story about who "we" are and who "our" enemies are. The state is not just the agent of torture but the effect of torture as well.

In my book I also describe the Eucharist as the Christian antidote to torture. The Eucharist is the imagination of the body of Christ, the liturgical enactment of the redemptive power of God in the bodies of believers. To participate in the Eucharist is to live inside God's imagination. As a result, it makes possible resistance to the state's attempt to define what is real through the mechanism of torture.

In this essay I touch on the experience of torture in Chile under the Pinochet regime and explore some of the lessons of the Chilean experience for the United States, which has both significant differences and distressing similarities with Chile. I begin by arguing that torture is a way of imagining who our enemies are. I then explore the nature of American exceptionalism, which is used both to justify and oppose torture. Finally, I conclude with some suggestions for how faith communities can promote the kind of solidarity needed to resist the imagination of torture.

---

3. Philip Abrams, "Notes on the Difficulty of Studying the State," *Journal of Historical Sociology* 1, no. 1 (March 1988), p. 77.

4. Michel de Certeau, "Corps torturés, paroles capturées," in *Michel de Certeau,* ed. Luce Giard (Paris: Centre Georges Pompidou, 1987); my translation.

Making Enemies

Silence, disappearance, and fear were the primary media in which the Chilean secret police worked. Victims of torture were silenced, their voices and their very identities disarticulated by the trauma of intense pain and humiliation. The intended target of torture, however, was not so much individual bodies but social bodies that would rival the state's power. Torture spread fear in the body politic, and people learned to keep to themselves and avoid contact with others. Parties, unions, cooperatives, women's groups, and base communities were dismantled and "disappeared." At the same time, the secret police apparatus itself remained invisible, making people disappear off the street without a trace, taking them to clandestine torture centers, causing horrific pain but leaving no marks on the bodies of victims. The overall effect in society at large was that of Michel Foucault's Panopticon: People were cut off from each other but perfectly visible to the secret police, which could see but was not seen.[5]

Consider the following two reports:

I was arrested at about midnight. . . . Around eight civilians arrived at my house, all armed with machine guns and small arms; after searching the house . . . they handcuffed me together with my wife, put tape over our eyes and dark glasses over that. The whole operation was carried out without them identifying themselves at any moment, nor did they show any arrest or search warrant. We were put into a private car and . . . taken to the [secret prison].[6]

Arresting authorities entered houses usually after dark, breaking down doors, waking up residents roughly, yelling orders, forcing family members into one room under military guard while searching the rest of the house and further breaking doors, cabinets and other property. They arrested suspects, tying their hands in the back with flexi-cuffs, hooding them, and taking them away. . . . In almost all instances. . . , arresting authorities provided no information about who they were, where their base was located, nor did they explain the cause of arrest. Similarly, they

---

5. Michel Foucault, *Discipline and Punish: The Birth of the Prison* (New York: Vintage, 1977), pp. 195-228.

6. Case D.O. 178-1176, archives of the *Vicaría de la Solidaridad*, Santiago; my translation.

rarely informed the arrestee or his family where he was being taken and for how long, resulting in the de facto "disappearance" of the arrestee. Many [families] were left without news for months, often fearing that their relatives were dead.[7]

The first report is from a man temporarily disappeared by the Chilean secret police in 1975. The second is from the 2004 Red Cross report on the treatment of detainees by U.S. forces in Iraq. The striking similarities do not end with nighttime disappearances and secret prisons. Once in custody, the techniques used by the Chilean secret police and U.S. forces in Iraq to break down detainees are also similar: hooding and blindfolding, beating with fists and hard objects, sexual humiliation, hanging by handcuffs, sleep deprivation, confinement in stress positions for long periods, and near drowning (called "waterboarding" by U.S. forces and "*submarino*" by Chilean agents).[8] Many in both cases have been tortured to death. As of March 2005 the latest official count was 108 confirmed cases of death in U.S. custody in Iraq, Afghanistan, and Guantánamo Bay.[9] We should not be surprised by the similarities in techniques between Chile and the United States. In the second half of the twentieth century, torture developed into a carefully refined skill, honed through the experiences of state operatives throughout the world and shared both informally and through more formal "police training programs" and other kinds of interstate security cooperation. One Argentine woman reported her torturer telling her that, although she undoubtedly considered him a sadist, he was in fact a scientist, plying an art based on a mastery of human physiology.[10] Torture techniques are carefully designed to dismantle the sources of a person's security and strength, to strip away markers of identity so that

---

7. *Report of the International Committee of the Red Cross (ICRC) on the Treatment by the Coalition Forces of Prisoners of War and Other Protected Persons by the Geneva Convention in Iraq during Arrest, Internment, and Interrogation,* February 2004, quoted in Mark Danner, *Torture and Truth: America, Abu Ghraib, and the War on Terror* (New York: New York Review Books, 2004), p. 2. The complete report is found in Danner, pp. 251-75.

8. The main difference is in the use of electricity in torture. Chilean agents used it extensively, whereas U.S. forces do not seem to have used it directly.

9. "Report: 108 died in U.S. custody," Associated Press, March 16, 2005. Available online at http://www.cbsnews .com/stories/2005/03/16/terror/main680658.shtml.

10. Ricardo Rodríguez Molas, *Historia de la Tortura y el Orden Represivo en la Argentina* (Buenos Aires: Editorial Universitaria de Buenos Aires, 1984), p. 149.

there is nothing to hold inside any information that the person may be trying to hide from the interrogators.

That torture is about the extraction of information tends to be the accepted story among both those who defend "aggressive interrogations" and those who oppose them. Defenders — though seldom using the taboo word "torture" — commonly use the "ticking bomb" scenario: For example, a terrorist is compelled to reveal the location of a nuclear device set to go off in New York City.[11] Opponents argue that information should be obtained only without compromising our shared moral principles. What tends to go unnoticed, however, is how few cases of torture actually involve the extraction of information previously unknown to the interrogators. In Chile, despite the form of interrogation, information was rarely at stake. Torture victims tell of finally relinquishing a piece of information after withstanding days of brutal treatment, only to be told by their interrogators, "We already knew." People were commonly forced to sign false confessions fabricated by the security forces. People said anything to stop the torture. According to one prisoner, "If they wanted you to reply that you had seen San Martin on horseback the previous day, they succeeded."[12] Thousands of people were arrested and tortured who had no connection to resistance against the regime. A post-Pinochet report by the Chilean government states that of the permanently disappeared, 46 percent were not known to be politically active.[13] Similarly, the Red Cross report on Iraq states, "Military intelligence officers told the ICRC that in their estimate between 70 and 90 percent of the persons deprived of their liberty in Iraq had been arrested by mistake."[14] Top U.S. commanders confirmed to the *New York Times* that they had learned "little about the insurgency" from all the interrogations.[15] Former secretary of defense James Schlesinger's re-

11. See, e.g., Alan Dershowitz, *Why Terrorism Works: Understanding the Threat, Responding to the Challenge* (New Haven: Yale University Press, 2002). Dershowitz recommends the institutionalization of "torture warrants" to pry information out of terrorists who have information on imminent acts of destruction.

12. Daniel Eduardo Fernández, quoted in *Nunca Más: A Report by Argentina's National Commission on Disappeared People* (London: Faber & Faber, 1986), p. 43. The reference is to José de San Martín, nineteenth-century hero of Argentina's war for independence from Spain.

13. *Report of the Chilean National Commission on Truth and Reconciliation,* trans. Phillip E. Berryman (Notre Dame: University of Notre Dame Press, 1993), p. 902.

14. *Red Cross Report,* in Danner, *Torture and Truth,* p. 257.

15. Danner, *Torture and Truth,* p. 23.

port states that the Abu Ghraib abuses were not "even directed at intelligence targets."[16]

It seems, then, that gathering information is only part — maybe even a small part — of the story behind the use of torture by the modern state. What is the rest of the story? The rest of the story has to do, I think, with fostering a certain kind of collective imagination. One significant part of that imagination is fear, not just among the detainees themselves but in the subject population as a whole. A joke that made the rounds in Chile following the military coup went like this: "A terrified bunny rabbit runs off to the border. The guard who stops him on the other side asks, 'What are you running away from?' He answers, 'They're killing all the elephants in Chile.' The border guard soothes him, saying, 'That's OK, you're a bunny.' The bunny answers, 'And how am I supposed to prove that?'"[17] The joke reflects the popular knowledge that seemingly random victims were arrested and tortured. If "mistakes" were made, then no one could feel entirely secure, and anxiety could spread throughout the entire society like a virus. The security of the state was made to depend on the insecurity of its citizens. The citizens then became self-disciplining, avoiding organized groups and taking refuge in private life.

A related effect of torture on the collective imagination in Chile was to produce enemies for the regime. This may seem like a counterintuitive claim. But in fact the lack of resistance following the coup in 1973 was a problem for the Pinochet regime. The ideologues of the new regime saw themselves as saving the nation from a diabolical Marxist conspiracy to destroy the liberty of Chileans. However, the Marxists did not play their part in the drama with sufficient enthusiasm; only fifteen Chilean soldiers were killed on the day of the coup and only ten more over the next four months. A month after the coup, General Sergio Arellano was dispatched on an infamous helicopter trip to visit military installations throughout Chile. Upon General Arellano's arrival in Talca, he asked Colonel Efraim Jana how many casualties his troops had sustained in subduing the area. When the colonel replied that the region had been secured peacefully, the general grew furious. "Later I understood," Jana explained, that "[my attitude] did

16. James R. Schlesinger et al., "Final Report of the Independent Panel to Review DoD Detention Operations," in Danner, *Torture and Truth*, p. 331.

17. Manuel Antonio Garretón, "Fear in Military Regimes: An Overview," in *Fear at the Edge: State Terror and Resistance in Latin America*, ed. Juan E. Corradi, Patricia Weiss Fagen, and Manuel Antonio Garretón (Berkeley: University of California Press, 1992), p. 25, n. 5.

not square with the superior plans, which called for exacerbating military fury against the left."[18] General Arellano had prisoners in Talca taken out and shot, with dozens more such executions everywhere his Helicopter of Death, as it became known, touched down. Most of the prisoners shot were awaiting trial or serving light sentences for minor charges. Arellano's trip, and the whole apparatus of torture and disappearance that swung into high gear following it, *simulated* the atmosphere of war that the regime needed to justify its policies. Violence was used not merely as a response to threats to the state but rather to create the threats from which the state offered itself as protector. At issue was not "repression" as such, since there was little to repress, but rather *production* of enemies and the scripting of people into a drama of fear.

The regime desperately needed the monstrous enemies its propaganda spoke of, and such enemies were produced largely in the torture chamber. As de Certeau remarks, "The goal of torture, in effect, is to produce acceptance of a State discourse, through the confession of putrescence."[19] The omnipotence of the state depends on the manifestation of its other — the Marxist, the terrorist — as filth. The victim does not take on the voice of the regime but rather its opposite, the voice of corruption — under conditions guaranteed to produce the degradation of the victim to his or her required place in the drama.[20] Torturers humiliate the victim, exploit his human weakness through the mechanism of pain, render him ashamed, passive, and broken until he does take on the role of filth, confessing his lowliness and saying what his tormentors want him to say. Such filth assumed an important role in the mythos of the regime; witness one of the members of the Chilean junta, Admiral Merino, publicly justifying the actions of the regime by referring to Marxists as "humanoids."[21]

What does this have to do with U.S. torture of detainees? We must cer-

---

18. Efraim Jana, quoted in Pamela Constable and Arturo Valenzuela, *A Nation of Enemies: Chile under Pinochet* (New York: W. W. Norton & Co., 1991), pp. 37-38. Jana was imprisoned for three years for his lack of rigor. During this period other officers were killed or imprisoned and tortured for being too "soft" on political prisoners; see pp. 54-55; and Eugenio Ahumada and Rodrigo Atria, *Chile: La Memoria Prohibida* (Santiago: Pehuén Editores, 1989), vol. 1, p. 369, n. 39.

19. Michel de Certeau, "The Institution of Rot," in *Heterologies: Discourse on the Other* (Minneapolis: University of Minnesota Press, 1986), pp. 40-41.

20. de Certeau, "Institution of Rot," p. 42.

21. Quoted in Constable and Valenzuela, *Nation of Enemies*, p. 83.

tainly recognize that despite the troubling increase of government surveillance under the current administration, neither the United States nor U.S.-occupied Iraq is the same kind of authoritarian regime imposed in Chile under Pinochet. In general, people in the United States do not fear to speak out. Fear of direct government reprisal is not yet a significant concern for most. Nevertheless, fear is an important dynamic in the War on Terror. Fear is constantly stoked, but it is not the fear of the state but of the enemies of the state against whom the state protects us. The tragedy of 9/11 is incessantly invoked, not so that history will not be repeated but so that — to the contrary — it will continually recur in our imagination. The fear of 9/11 and terrorism in general is kept ever before us and used to justify everything from the war in Iraq to domestic surveillance to deficit spending.

Torture is part of this theater of fear. Terrorists are our humanoids. It is not simply that the demonization of people as terrorists allows us to justify their maltreatment (why should we bother with human rights when the enemy is subhuman?). Torture also helps to *create* the enemies that we need. Torture is a kind of theater in which people are made to play roles and thereby reinforce a certain kind of social imagination. The Abu Ghraib photos lay this dynamic out for all to see. The detainees in the photos are made to play the role of deviant, of the filth that the terrorist is in the morality play that we call the War on Terror. Hooded, contorted, stacked naked, chained to cages, cowering before snarling dogs, covered with excrement, dragged around on leashes, made to masturbate and howl in pain, the prisoners become what terrorists are in our imagination: depraved subhumans. The imagination of the War on Terror is inscribed on their bodies in a kind of ritual drama, or antiliturgy.

Torture reinforces an imaginative distancing between us and the tortured. Not only the actual torturer but the rest of society must guard against identifying with the tortured body. The sympathy we might feel toward another body in pain is cut off by the beastly extremity of torture. The tortured person is not like us. As Ariel Dorfman says, if we felt their pain, we could not go on living.[22] So we make believe it is not happening, or call it an aberration, or think darkly, "They must have done something to deserve it."

22. Ariel Dorfman, "The Tyranny of Terror: Is Torture Inevitable in Our Century and Beyond?" in *Torture: A Collection*, ed. Sanford Levinson (Oxford: Oxford University Press, 2004), p. 9.

Once the Abu Ghraib photos made it out into the world media, many people saw the episode as a public relations gaffe of epic proportions. On the one hand, here we are trying, in the Bush administration's words, to "transform the Middle East" so that "it will no longer produce ideologies of hatred that lead men to fly airplanes into buildings in New York and Washington."[23] Meanwhile, on the other hand, we are systematically brutalizing the civilian population of Iraq and thereby instilling in them a fierce hatred of the United States. Commentators across the board wrung their hands over the senselessness of it, the waste of turning potential friends into permanent enemies. It would not be so puzzling if it were indeed just a few lower ranking bad apples who perpetrated the violence. As the Red Cross, Mark Danner, and others have conclusively shown, however, the policy of brutalization was and is systematic, approved and justified all the way up to the highest levels of the administration.[24] How could they be so stupid?

It is inexplicable unless one sees how necessary enemies are to the global War on Terror. The Bush administration may be sincere in wanting to make friends of the Iraqi people. But we simply cannot have a global war on terror without enemies. Despite the rhetoric, wars are never simply about making friends. Wars are about the imaginary dividing of the world into friends and enemies. And enemies must exist in sufficient abundance and sufficient monstrosity if a war is to be sustained. Nothing effects such an imaginative division better than torture, what General Fay in his report on Abu Ghraib called the "escalating de-humanization of the detainees."[25] The global War on Terror would not exist without such dehumanization. In other words, this war is not simply about *response*, but *production*. It is not simply about responding to enemies who attacked us while we were minding our own business. The global War on Terror is part of a larger social production.

This war is not simply about oil or weapons of mass destruction or regime change. It is about a much larger imagination of a clash of civilizations, of progress and democracy versus archaic oppression, of the beacon of freedom and light versus those who hate our freedoms, of all that is

23. Quoted in Danner, *Torture and Truth*, p. 23.

24. For complete documentation, see Karen J. Greenberg and Joshua L. Dratel, *The Torture Papers: The Road to Abu Ghraib* (Cambridge: Cambridge University Press, 2005).

25. Quoted in Danner, *Torture and Truth*, p. 45.

good versus an implacable evil, of Captain America versus the humanoids. Torture is this drama of friend and enemy brought to its most heightened realization.

It is not that the United States has a deliberate plan to make others hate it. The point is more about *our* imagination. If we did not think of opponents of U.S. policy in the Middle East as enemies and backward fanatics, if we thought of them as rational beings, we would have to reconsider our own policies and consider the possibility that our opponents might have some legitimate grievances. The extremity of torture helps to erase such gray areas, not only by reducing the tortured to subhuman status but also by identifying all righteousness with the torturer. This too may seem counterintuitive, given the moral condemnation with which torture meets in civilized discourse, but those who torture tend to think of their work in extremely high moral terms. Torture helps guard the nation against diabolical threats. Torturers sometimes imagine their acts as a kind of self-sacrifice on their part: "What terrible things I must do in order to defend my beloved people!"[26] It is a dirty business, and those who "take the gloves off" and "get their hands dirty" do so for a higher moral purpose. Indeed, and this is the crucial point, the moral purpose is made *more righteous,* is pushed to the extreme of righteousness, by the extremity of the act of torture itself. The threat against the nation must be extremely severe if such an extreme procedure as torture is used, and therefore the defense against such threats is invested with the highest moral seriousness. Only the most morally righteous nation could be trusted with the capacity to use torture for a good purpose.

American Exceptionalism

There are two different stories being told here about America, and the American political imagination tends to oscillate between the two. On the one hand, we believe that we do not torture. What we are really about is the spread of freedom throughout the world and an end to hate and enmity. If torture has occurred, it is so obviously contrary to our own best in-

26. The private motto of the DINA, the Chilean secret police, was, "We will fight in the shadows so that our children can live in the sunlight"; quoted in Constable and Valenzuela, *Nation of Enemies,* p. 90.

terests in spreading freedom that it must be a temporary aberration, an isolated instance, a few bad apples. Or, if it is more systematic, it is a recent deviation from our most sacred commitments as a nation. On the other hand, we believe that we must reserve the right to use extreme measures in extreme circumstances. We are faced with a diabolical enemy who has no qualms about the taking of innocent life. Because of our unique position as bearer of freedom to the world, our hands must not be tied in dealing with a monstrous enemy.

We could perhaps take John McCain and Alberto Gonzales as representing these two positions in contemporary debate. They appear as contradictory positions; one says we don't torture, and the other implies that we must. Nevertheless, George W. Bush has managed to take both sides at different times. The positions might not be so different after all, because they both depend upon a larger common story, what is commonly called American exceptionalism. The first position says, as McCain does, that of all the nations of the world, America holds a unique place in safeguarding humanizing principles. We must stand firm as an exception to the usual run of amoral politics and consequentialist thinking and never deviate from the principles that made our nation great. The second position is also based on American exceptionalism. It believes that because of its position as the bearer of freedom to the world, America is confronted by a unique coalition of enemies that have singled America out for harm. This exceptional responsibility means that, of all nations, America must not be bound by external rules such as the Geneva Convention. America must decide for itself what measures are required. But because of our exceptional goodness, America above all nations can be trusted to use such power prudently, for good not evil.

Chile had its own version of exceptionalism. Scholars and others within Chile and without have long puzzled about how a nation with the longest tradition of democracy in Latin America, a nation with a large middle class and a long record of respect for human rights, could lurch so quickly into a brutal military regime. Most Chileans expected a relatively brief and benign military intervention into Chilean politics, just long enough to restore order and set up new elections. Chilean exceptionalism also had a dark side, however. The ideologues of the new junta saw Chile, with its long tradition of freedom, as the great hope for the salvation of Latin America from the evils of Marxism. September 11, the day of the coup in 1973, would begin the vindication of Chile's historical destiny. Precisely because of Chile's tradition of freedom, Marxism was inherently contradictory to *el chilenismo*. Marxism needed to be stamped out by any means necessary in Chile. At the same time, Chile would serve as an example and as a material aid to other regimes in Latin America seeking to extirpate the Marxist menace. In Chile, free-market economics and other structural reforms were imposed by a brutal regime in which torture was routine. When Milton Friedman told the junta in March 1975 that the Chilean economy needed "shock treatment," they took him literally. The "grill," that is, torture by electricity, was their favored method. All the while, the junta used Chile's exceptional position as bastion of freedom in Latin America to justify seventeen years of brutality.

American arguments in favor of using "enhanced interrogation techniques," as the euphemism would have it, trade heavily on the imagination of American exceptionalism. The Justice Department memos written under Alberto Gonzales's direction appeal to a reservation made by the United States as a condition for its ratification of the U.N. Convention against Torture. The reservation stated that as the United States understood it, the intent covered by the Convention must be a *specific* intent to torture, and mental suffering must rise to the level of physical torture in order to be considered torture. The United States also refused to accept the jurisdiction of the International Court of Justice to decide such cases.[27] The architects of the Bush administration's legal justifications for "enhanced interrogation techniques" also appeal to the exceptional nature of the war and the enemy America is fighting. Alberto Gonzales wrote that "the war against terrorism is a new kind of war" that involves "a new paradigm [that] renders obsolete Geneva's strict limitations on questioning of enemy prisoners and renders quaint some of its provisions."[28] In an op-ed piece, Deputy Assistant Attorney General John Yoo argued that McCain's anti-torture amendment would prevent the president from taking "necessary measures" against a "terrible and unprecedented enemy."[29] In short, an exceptional nation fighting an exceptional war against an exceptional enemy must be allowed to use exceptional means.

John McCain's version of American exceptionalism is certainly more

27. "Letter: John C. Yoo to Alberto Gonzales, August 1, 2002," in Danner, *Torture and Truth,* pp. 108-13; and "Memo: Jay S. Bybee to Alberto Gonzales, August 1, 2002," in Danner, *Torture and Truth,* pp. 115-66.

28. Quoted in Danner, *Torture and Truth,* p. 42.

29. John Yoo, "Terrorists are not POWs," *USA Today,* November 1, 2005.

palatable, but it has its own perils. McCain claims that what is lost when we resort to torture is "the best sense of ourselves, that which is our greatest strength — that we are different and better than our enemies, that we fight for an idea, not a tribe, not a land, not a king, not a twisted interpretation of an ancient religion, but for an idea that all men are created equal and endowed by their Creator with inalienable rights."[30] Ironically, our convictions about the equality of all people lead us to regard ourselves as "different and better." In his defense of American virtue, McCain strips the enemy of normal human sensibilities, stating, "Al Qaeda will never be influenced by international sensibilities or open to moral suasion. If ever the term 'sociopath' applied to anyone, it applies to them."[31]

Yet McCain's narrative of American virtue also relies on a sanitized version of American history. According to McCain, when he was abused as a prisoner in Hanoi, he could count on the fact "that we were different from our enemies, that we were better than them, that we, if the roles were reversed, would not disgrace ourselves by committing or approving such mistreatment of them."[32] As Naomi Klein points out, "By the time McCain was taken captive, the CIA had already launched the Phoenix program and . . . 'its agents were operating forty interrogation centers in South Vietnam that killed more than twenty thousand suspects and tortured thousands more.'"[33] This claim is supported by press reports and congressional probes.[34] The truth is that the United States has been involved in torture through proxies for decades. After years of denials, the Pentagon was forced on September 20, 1996, to admit officially that Army intelligence manuals used at the School of the Americas to train Latin American military officers contained instructions on torture techniques.[35]

The case of Brazil provides well-documented evidence that the United States has been instrumental in introducing the science of torture into its client states. American official Dan Mitrione was one of the first to provide

30. John McCain, "Torture's Terrible Toll," *Newsweek*, November 21, 2005.

31. McCain, "Torture's Terrible Toll."

32. McCain, "Torture's Terrible Toll."

33. Naomi Klein, "'Never Before!' Our Amnesiac Torture Debate," *Nation*, December 9, 2005. The internal quote is from Alfred McCoy, A *Question of Torture: CIA Interrogation from the Cold War to the War on Terror* (New York: Metropolitan Books, 2006).

34. See McCoy, *Question of Torture.*

35. See "Pentagon Admits Use of Torture Manuals," *National Catholic Reporter,* October 4, 1996.

systematic instruction on torture methods to the military regime in Brazil. Mitrione provided classes for the police in Belo Horizonte, using beggars taken off the streets as his subjects. Mitrione was later killed by guerrillas after being transferred to Uruguay, but the Brazilian military continued to conduct classes in torture using live subjects.[36] The history of Latin America in the twentieth century is a deeply disturbing tale of torture and other atrocities being committed with the full knowledge, encouragement, and support of the United States. In the Middle East, Saudi Arabia, Egypt, Israel, and the Shah's Iran are examples of U.S. client states that have tortured with full U.S. support. Many Middle Eastern Muslims do not see the slightest inconsistency between Abu Ghraib and U.S. intentions in the Middle East; the United States has *always* been about abusing them and treating them as enemies.

McCain's version of exceptionalism is dangerous because it perpetuates a collective amnesia about our own history with torture. McCain does not simply argue that we should not torture but that we do not and never have. He not only buys into the same narrative of American righteousness that the more malignant strand of American exceptionalism accepts, but he also encourages an unrealistic view of the nation-state as guardian of sacred moral values. We must face the fact that torture is not an exceptional measure. Walter Benjamin's words are as relevant now as when he wrote them in Europe in the 1930s: "The tradition of the oppressed teaches us that the 'state of emergency' in which we live is not the exception but the rule."[37] As Giorgio Agamben has shown in his recent study of the state of exception in the twentieth century, "The voluntary creation of a permanent state of emergency (though perhaps not declared in the technical sense) has become one of the essential practices of contemporary states, including so-called democratic ones."[38] The modern nation-state thrives on the sense of emergency and the need for exceptional measures to combat chaos. Chile under Pinochet lived seventeen years under one or another of the various "states of exception."

36. *Torture in Brazil: A Report by the Archdiocese of São Paulo*, ed. Joan Dassin (New York: Vintage, 1986), pp. 13-15.

37. Walter Benjamin, "Theses on the Philosophy of History," in *Illuminations,* ed. Hannah Arendt (New York: Schocken, 1968), p. 257.

38. Giorgio Agamben, *State of Exception* (Chicago: University of Chicago Press, 2005), p. 2. Agamben points out that it was the democratic tradition, not the absolutist one, that created the modern state of exception (p. 5).

In the current context in the United States, 9/11 and terrorism are constantly invoked to keep ever present the sense that we live in exceptional times. We are constantly told that "everything changed" on September 11, 2001. Before terrorism, however, it was communism that served as justification for exceptional measures. Agamben reaches farther back and shows how the state of exception has been used in the United States since the Civil War to absorb legislative powers into the executive.[39] Political theorist Carl Schmitt understood that the exception was the source of rule and rules and unapologetically made it the center of his definition of sovereignty. Schmitt had tried to rescue democracy in the Weimar Republic by strengthening the hand of the government to act. His position led him within a few short years to become something of the official jurist of Hitler's government, until falling out of favor with the Nazi Party in 1936.[40] Schmitt's brief flirtation with Nazism has not erased his influence, which in the United States has largely been channeled into neoconservative circles through Leo Strauss. In Schmitt's famous dictum, "Sovereign is he who decides on the exception." The mere proceduralism of liberal democracy was incapable of dealing with threats to state order. The sovereign cannot be subject to the law at all times but must be given the power to rise above the law and decide in exceptional circumstances.[41] Only thus can the state ensure order and stability.

The other definition for which Schmitt is famous is his definition of the political. According to Schmitt, "The specific political distinction to which political actions and motives can be reduced is that between friend and enemy."[42] This distinction is what makes an action political. "The political is the most intense and extreme antagonism, and every concrete antagonism becomes that much more political the closer it approaches the most extreme point, that of the friend-enemy grouping."[43] The problem with liberalism, according to Schmitt, is that in its illusory search for peace and comfort, it threatens to deprive us of our enemies, whom we desper-

39. Agamben, *State of Exception*, pp. 19-22.

40. Michael Hollerich, "Carl Schmitt," in *The Blackwell Companion to Political Theology*, ed. Peter Scott and William T. Cavanaugh (Oxford: Blackwell, 2004), pp. 108-9.

41. See Carl Schmitt, *Political Theology: Four Chapters on the Concept of Sovereignty* (Cambridge, Mass.: MIT Press, 1985), pp. 5-15.

42. Carl Schmitt, *The Concept of the Political* (New Brunswick, N.J.: Rutgers University Press, 1976), p. 26.

43. Schmitt, *Concept of the Political*, p. 29.

ately need. If the state is deprived of enemies, then the friend-enemy distinction will break out into religious, economic, and cultural arenas, and chaos will reign. To have common enemies is the true source of political unity.

The shadow of Schmitt looms large over the kind of exceptionalism represented by Alberto Gonzales and many others in the Bush administration. The friend-enemy distinction as the basis of political action can be seen clearly in George W. Bush's speech to a joint session of Congress on September 20, 2001: "Either you are with us, or you are with the terrorists." The exceptional nature of this situation has been used to promote a Schmittian view of sovereignty, most recently seen in the revelation that Bush secretly approved domestic spying by the National Security Agency without FISA court approval and without seeking a change in the existing law. "Sovereign is he who decides on the exception." At the same time, however, McCain's more benign version of American exceptionalism appears to have gained the upper hand, with President Bush reluctantly agreeing not to veto McCain's anti-torture amendment.

I wish I could take more encouragement from this small victory, but I am afraid that McCain's amendment — however well intentioned and potentially useful — will serve to reaffirm our amnesia and push the issue of torture back down to a subterranean level. When President Bush signed the bill outlawing the torture of detainees, he quietly reserved the right to bypass the law under his powers as commander in chief. As reported in the *Boston Globe,* "Bush issued a 'signing statement' — an official document in which a president lays out his interpretation of a new law — declaring that he will view the interrogation limits in the context of his broader powers to protect national security. This means Bush believes he can waive the restrictions, the White House and legal specialists said."[44] According to David Golove, a New York University law professor who specializes in executive power issues, "The signing statement is saying 'I will only comply with this law when I want to, and if something arises in the war on terrorism where I think it's important to torture or engage in cruel, inhuman, and degrading conduct, I have the authority to do so and nothing in this law is going to stop me.' They don't want to come out and say it directly because

44. Charlie Savage, "Bush Could Bypass New Torture Ban," *Boston Globe,* January 4, 2006.

it doesn't sound very nice, but it's unmistakable to anyone who has been following what's going on."[45]

There is a subtle interplay between visibility and invisibility here that in my book I refer to as the "striptease of power." The Chilean secret police depended on invisibility. They "disappeared" people in the middle of the night, and they tortured without leaving marks on the victim's body. At the same time, however, it was crucial that the operations of the secret police be widely known among the populace in order to achieve the desired effect of social control. The omnipotence of the state must be made present, but it is most powerful precisely when it is invisible, internalized in the anxieties of the people. The liturgy of torture realizes the state's terrible might, but it remains out of grasp yet palpable.

It was important for the regime, therefore, both to deny and simultaneously to affirm the existence of state terror. In an interview with journalist Patricia Politzer, Chilean Colonel Juan Deichler exemplified this double logic. After disputing the number of the permanently disappeared in Chile, Deichler said:

> Besides, I think that all these disappeared people were like rabid dogs, full of rage! And rabies must be eliminated, although by no means do I justify it. Neither in the Army, nor in any institution of National Defense are the disappearances justified. On the other hand, are they all disappeared? A neighbor of mine was crying about a disappeared person and two weeks later he arrived from Argentina. There are a lot of myths about this disappearance thing![46]

Colonel Deichler justifies the disappearances, then denies justifying them, then casts doubt on their existence altogether. Spokespersons for the Pinochet regime became adept at this type of discourse.

In the United States, this type of striptease is represented by President Bush's declaration in Panama that "we do not torture" while simultaneously seeking to dilute or kill McCain's amendment banning torture.[47] Torture functions as a taboo, widely known, but about which we cannot

---

45. Quoted in Savage, "Bush Could Bypass."

46. Interview in Patricia Politzer, *Miedo en Chile* (Santiago: CESOC, 1985), p. 67; my translation.

47. "Bush Declares 'We Do Not Torture,'" *Washington Post*, November 7, 2005.

speak. On the one hand, denying that we torture is crucial to maintaining the imagination of the United States as morally exceptional. On the other hand, retaining the prerogative to torture is essential for maintaining the imagination of the American nation-state as protector from the subhuman forces that threaten us. The drama of torture must never be played out on a fully public stage. At the same time, the widespread imagination of torture is important for fostering both the dire sense of emergency and exception in which we live and the sense that the state will do whatever is necessary to protect us from the threat it helped create.

Imagining Different Bodies

We should not cease to demand that the state renounce torture, but we must also be aware that expecting the state to be the champion of human rights may be like asking the fox to guard the henhouse. We must look to other types of social bodies to promote the dignity of the human person. My own work as a Christian theologian deals with the nature of the church as an alternative social body. Unfortunately, the Chilean church's resistance to state discipline was initially sapped by its own ecclesiology. In a well-intentioned attempt to extricate itself from coercive politics, the Catholic Church since the 1930s had accepted a distinction between "political" and "social" realms, vacating the former and trying to influence the latter through the articulation of general values to individual Christians. The church saw itself not so much as a body in its own right but as the "soul of society," effectively handing the bodies of Christians over to the state. When the state began to torture those bodies, the church was at first at a loss to respond, having already "disappeared" itself through its own ecclesiology.

Fortunately, a significant portion of the church was able to break out of this paradigm and, drawing on the theology and practice of the Eucharist, made the church a visible body in direct contradiction to the regime's strategy of disappearance. The church reappeared by denying the Eucharist to torturers, providing a space for grassroots groups to organize, and participating in street protests against the regime and its policy of torture. The Eucharist provided Christians with an imagination of another kind of body, the body of Christ, a community convinced it is the living body of the Son of God who was tortured to death by the state. As Paul tells the Corinthian church that they are the body of Christ, he reminds them that in this body the pain of one member is the pain of all (1 Cor. 12:26).

The Sebastian Acevedo Movement against Torture in Chile was a group of priests, nuns, and laypeople who took this imagination of the body of Christ to the streets. At a prearranged time, they would appear in front of torture centers and government buildings, block traffic, pass out leaflets, and perform ritual actions denouncing torture. They made visible in their own bodies what the regime tried to conceal. They were usually beaten and arrested. As one member wrote, "If to some extent we share the sufferings of the tortured, He who was tortured by Roman justice and nailed on the Cross accompanies us and we for our part accompany Him, because He identifies Himself with the tortured."[48] The movement assumed the communicability of pain in the body of Christ: "With symbolic gestures that expressed our desires, we were able to break the isolation of their incommunication, take their chained hands, embrace their broken bodies. We believe that there exist mysterious channels that can make the solidarity of friends reach those who languish in the deepest dungeons."[49] It is this solidarity of friends that the church must oppose to the imagination of enemies. The body of Christ transgresses national borders and embraces people of every nation. The first job of the church in the United States is to tell the truth: This is not an exceptional nation and we do not live in exceptional times, at least as the world describes it. Everything did not change on 9/11; for Christians, everything changed on 12/25. When the Word of God became incarnate in human history, when he was tortured to death by the powers of this world, and when he rose to give us new life — it was then that everything changed. Christ is the exception that becomes the rule of history. We are made capable of loving our enemies, of treating the other as a member of our own body, the body of Christ.

As a Christian theologian, my primary appeal is to the church to resist the imagination of the state, but this appeal is by no means limited to the church. We should cooperate across religious boundaries to foster alternative imaginations and alternative bodies. If we tell the truth, we will resist the politics of fear that makes torture thinkable. In concrete terms,

---

48. José Aldunate, "La Acción que Habla a las Conciencias," in *La No Violencia Activa: presencia y desafíos,* ed. José Aldunate, SJ, et al. (Santiago: ILADES, 1988), p. 5; my translation.

49. José Aldunate, quoted in Hernán Vidal, *El Movimiento Contra la Tortura "Sebastián Acevedo"* (Minneapolis: Institute for the Study of Ideologies and Literature, 1986), p. 74; my translation.

this means refusing to fight in unjust wars, refusing to use unjust means, and refusing to be silent when the nation-state institutionalizes "exceptional measures." We must, in short, create spaces to live inside of God's imagination.

CHAPTER 9

My Enemy, Myself: A Sermon

Fleming Rutledge

> *There is therefore now no condemnation for those who are in Christ Jesus.*
>
> Romans 8:1

> *You have heard that it was said, "You shall love your neighbor and hate your enemy." But I say to you, Love your enemies and pray for those who persecute you.*
>
> Matthew 5:43-44

My work takes me to churches all over America, to small churches and large churches of all denominations. They all seem to have one thing in common: They aren't praying for our enemies. Our troops, yes; our enemies, no. There is a fine prayer for enemies in the Episcopal Prayer Book, in which we shall join at the end of this sermon, but I have never heard it used except when I requested it myself.

Nor do I hear the churches discussing issues such as the use of state-sponsored torture. University towns like Princeton may be exceptions, but as a former member of a university church (at the University of Virginia), I can testify that such congregations have their own problems and tend to be smug about their liberal commitments. (You can let me know later where Trinity Church fits on that spectrum.) Speaking of the American churches generally, the issue of torture barely registers. The news magazines have been running cover stories on American-sponsored torture of suspected terrorists ever since the Abu Ghraib pictures first came out, but only a minuscule number of our citizens seem interested.[1] In fact, in my lifetime I do not remember any major public question being so studiously ignored as this one. We need to ask ourselves why this is so.

Last year in my home state of Virginia, a black man named Julius Earl Ruffin was released from prison after twenty-one years of incarceration for a crime he did not commit. In 1982, an all-white jury convicted him of assaulting a white woman solely on the basis of her doggedly insistent visual identification of him as her assailant. He was released after being exonerated through DNA testing. The white woman, whose name was Ann Meng, did a rare thing. She wrote to him expressing her profound remorse for misidentifying him. She sat next to him at a state government hearing designed to discuss reparations for him, and she testified on his behalf. She stated that she, like members of Mr. Ruffin's family, believed that the all-white jury identified more with her, the victim, than with the accused black man. And she said this to the government panel: "I feel a personal responsibility for Mr. Ruffin's incarceration. However, our system of criminal justice also must bear some responsibility. There was no one on this jury who saw themselves, or their son, or their brother, when they looked at Mr. Ruffin."[2]

That, it seems to me, is the heart of the matter. We do not care about torture in Iraq or Afghanistan because we do not see ourselves, or anyone in our families, as members of the same species as a prisoner being tortured. I read a newspaper column the other day by a politically conservative woman who said she could not get worked up about the fact that American citizens were being spied upon. The reason for her indifference, I thought, was that she had never had her own phone tapped, or a family member's phone tapped, and in her passionate loyalty to the present administration she could not imagine such a thing ever happening to her. She thinks of herself as invulnerable to such intrusions. Those of us of a certain age, however, can remember only too well the FBI surveillance of

---

1. Mark Danner has for many years been a burr under the saddle of the American government. He gets published, but he says that it seems no one is listening.
2. Tim McGlone, "State Urged to Pay for 21 Lost Years," *Norfolk Virginian-Pilot*, February 4, 2004.

Martin Luther King Jr. and of our own friends who had done nothing more sinister than protest against the Vietnam War.

To be able to see an accused human being as potentially our own son, or brother, or indeed as our own selves — that is the significance of the well-known saying, "There but for the grace of God go I." These words were first said by a sixteenth-century Englishman, John Bradford, who, when watching a group of prisoners being led off to the gallows, did not say, "They are getting what they deserve." Rather, he said, "There but for the grace of God goes John Bradford."[3] This simple saying has been preserved against the odds for more than four hundred years because it expresses the deepest, most fundamental truth about God and the human race. Have you noticed how often these days advertising speaks of what we deserve? Just two examples from my recent listening: "You deserve an Audi!" and "Come to Mt. Sinai Hospital for the health care you deserve." Where did this idea of "deserving" come from? Who decides who deserves what? We now know that after 9/11 there was a secret White House rewrite of military law. Vice President Cheney described it this way: "We think [this plan] guarantees that we'll have [available and ready] the kind of treatment of these individuals that *we believe they deserve.*"[4] I am not making a partisan political comment but giving a simple human gut reaction when I say that I would not want to find myself on the wrong side of this vice president. Yet he too is a human being like me, equally undeserving of the grace of God and equally sought after by God.

Dietrich Bonhoeffer wrote that torture was inflicting pain "while taking advantage of a relative superiority of strength."[5] The Christian, by definition, does not take advantage of superior strength.[6] Columnist Andy Crouch writes, "If Christians are sometimes called to acquire power [and

3. John Bradford (1510-1555); cited in *Bartlett's Familiar Quotations.*

4. Tim Golden, "After Terror: A Secret Rewriting of Military Law," *New York Times*, October 24, 2005; italics added.

5. Dietrich Bonhoeffer, *Ethics* (New York: Macmillan, 1965), p. 185. Bonhoeffer's point about taking advantage is conspicuously missing from the Justice Department's definition of torture, but it is crucial. (The department's infamous August 1, 2002, memo on interrogation was written largely by John Yoo of the Berkeley law faculty. To be considered torture, says the memo, techniques [what a word!] must produce suffering "equivalent to the pain accompanying serious physical injury such as organ failure, impairment of bodily function, or even death." This has been widely and repeatedly quoted.)

6. That is the whole point of C. S. Lewis using a lion, traditionally the most lordly and powerful animal, as a symbol of Christ in the Chronicles of Narnia.

we often are], we should probably begin by watching our Lord abandon it."[7] Children need to be taught from an early age that they should never bully another person, that is, take easy advantage of a "relative superiority of strength." The term used by the US military forces to denote Iraqi prisoners is PUC (pronounced "puck") meaning "person under control." The emphasis here is on the superior strength of the captor and the impotence of the captive.

We would not have to teach this if there were not a component in human nature that delights in the suffering of others. There have been numerous reports that abuse of Iraqi prisoners was the result of American troops "blowing off steam." This was said offhandedly, as though it was no big deal, as if it were well understood that causing pain or humiliation to another person was a handy stress reliever.

One of the soldiers who testified for a Human Rights Watch report last fall said, "In a way it was sport."[8] People typically will deny these tendencies in themselves, but they have not understood the dark undercurrents in the human psyche. In the Christian tradition these dark undercurrents are called by the name of sin. When Lent comes, as it soon will, we in the churches will go through the traditional motions of confessing our sins. It would be a good thing if we as a nation genuinely came together to identify and repent of our sins. Our greatest presidents, Washington and Lincoln, called for repentance on a national scale; it is hard to imagine any president doing so today.

In the recent book *Washington's Crossing*, which describes a certain event that took place somewhere around Princeton, the historian David Hackett Fischer describes how George Washington personally set the American policy toward "persons under control":

> After the battles in New York, thousands of American prisoners of war were treated with extreme cruelty by British captors. . . . Some [Americans] escaped, and their reports had the same impact as those of American prisoners of the Japanese in the second World War. . . . [But] an American policy on prisoners emerged after the battle of Trenton. George Washington ordered that Hessian captives would be treated as

7. Andy Crouch, "Always in Parables," *Christianity Today*, February 2004.
8. Human Rights Watch, "Torture in Iraq," *New York Review of Books*, November 3, 2005.

human beings with the same rights of humanity for which Americans were striving. The Hessians . . . were amazed to be treated with decency and even kindness. The same policy was extended to British prisoners after the battle of Princeton. Washington ordered one of his most trusted officers . . . to look after them: "You are to take charge of [211] privates of the British Army. . . . Treat them with humanity and let them have no reason to complain of our copying the brutal example of the British army in their treatment of our unfortunate brethren."

Hackett concludes, "Congress and the Continental army generally adopted [this] 'policy of humanity.' Their moral choices in the War of Independence enlarged the meaning of the American Revolution."[9] The argument of those who support torture as a means of extracting information is that since 9/11 we are dealing with a different type of enemy, an enemy that does not deserve to be treated as George Washington treated the Hessians. But this is not a new argument. This idea that the human race can be divided up into the deserving and the undeserving is a universal notion. Making distinctions on this basis is something we all do from birth, and the distinction between the righteous and the unrighteous is built into religion. That's why Paul's declaration in Romans 3 is so irreligious and radical: "For there is no distinction, since all have sinned and fall short of the glory of God; they are now justified by his grace as a gift, through the redemption that is in Christ Jesus" (vv. 22-24).

So now it is time to make the transition from American values to the universal Christian gospel. From the standpoint of Christ Jesus, any talk of "deserving" is treacherous territory. Everybody seems to love the hymn "Amazing Grace," but not everybody understands what it means. The very meaning of the word "grace" is "undeserved favor." If it is deserved, then it is not grace and it is certainly not amazing.

Amazing grace can be understood fully only from the standpoint of the Christian gospel. The teaching of Jesus about love for the enemy makes no sense at all if it is detached from his death and resurrection. If it were not for Good Friday and Easter, we would be justified in putting his teachings in a nice gilded box that we could bring out for admiration on ceremonial occasions and keep respectfully on a shelf the rest of the time. We

---

9. David Hackett Fischer, *Washington's Crossing* (New York: Oxford University Press, 2004), pp. 378-79.

cannot make Jesus into a nice religious teacher. Without the cross, we could not take his teaching seriously. The Christian faith rests on a unique, unrepeatable event that has fundamentally altered the way we understand reality. The cross shows us that in Jesus Christ we see God exchanging his divine life for the life of his enemies.

Who were these enemies? Trinity Church and guests, a few minutes ago I was a stranger to you and you to me. But now in the power of the gospel we are one. Listen to Romans 5:

> While we were still weak, at the right time Christ died for the ungodly. Indeed, rarely will anyone die for a righteous person. . . . But God proves his love for us in that while we still were sinners Christ died for us. . . . While we were [God's] enemies, we were reconciled to God through the death of his Son. (vv. 6-8, 10)

And in 1 Peter we read:

> For Christ also suffered for sins once for all, the righteous for the unrighteous, in order to bring you to God. He was put to death in the flesh, but made alive in the spirit. (3:18)

Do you see how this is inclusive of everyone? Peter and Paul show how we are all recipients of the undeserved grace of God. This is what makes us brothers and sisters beyond any distinction that we can dream up.

What would you want done with the body of your brother, or your father, or your sister? It is remarkable that we have this epistle lesson appointed for today: "Do you not know that your body is a temple of the Holy Spirit within you, which you have from God? . . . Therefore glorify God in your body" (1 Cor. 6:19-20). Paul is teaching the Corinthians about bodily life. The Corinthian congregation was very "spiritual." They thought that bodily life wasn't important to God; it was the "spirit" that counted. Paul's letter to them is a reprimand and a corrective. God is not to be glorified in vague, mystical, amorphous ways but in the actual, bodily life of Christian disciples.[10] The body is the person, a very Hebrew idea.

But there is more. Here is the complete text: "Or do you not know that

---

10. The Corinthians passage is specifically about sexual morality, but there can be no doubt that it applies to all bodily life.

your body is a temple of the Holy Spirit within you, which you have from God, and that you are not your own? For you were bought with a price; therefore glorify God in your body." You were bought with a price. What price is that? The price was the life of the Son of God, who exchanged his perfectly righteous life for the universally unrighteous lives of sinful human beings. When I look at another human being, even if he is my enemy — especially if he is my enemy — I am looking at a human being for whom Christ died and for whom he was raised from the dead. That is the only way in which the teaching of love for the enemy can be understood.

Anyone can do good things for their friends. All good soldiers will die for their comrades in arms. That has always been the rule of the battlefield. There is nothing specifically Christian about it. The way that we embody Christ is by refusing to do bodily harm to our enemies when they are disarmed and in our power.[11] That is the Christian gospel in action. To my brothers and sisters in the Spirit: May the same Spirit, the Spirit of our Lord Jesus Christ, give us the eyes to understand, through these passages from the word of God, that it is us, we ourselves, who have been the enemies of God. Before we can begin to conceive of love for our own enemies, we need to be able to think of ourselves this way: "There but for the grace of God go I." The one who stands judged and condemned is my brother; nay, he is I myself. "There is therefore now no condemnation for those who are in Christ Jesus" (Rom. 8:1).

Let us pray: O God, the Father of all, whose Son commanded us to love our enemies: Lead them and us from prejudice to truth; deliver them and us from hatred, cruelty, and revenge; and in your good time enable us all to stand reconciled before you; through Jesus Christ our Lord. Amen.

---

11. The phrase "disarmed and in our power" is important. I am not necessarily recommending a thoroughgoing pacifism. There may be times when an armed and threatening enemy must be stopped by physical means.

PART THREE

JEWS SPEAK OUT

Therefore was Adam created single,
to teach you that the destruction of any person's life
is tantamount to destroying a whole world
and the preservation of a single life
is tantamount to preserving a whole world.

Sanhedrin 4:5

CHAPTER 10

Torture and Torah: Defense of Dignity and Life in Jewish Law

Melissa Weintraub

Guantánamo, circa 2002: Men are in dog leashes, being forced to perform dog tricks and wear lacy lingerie on their heads. Female interrogators — dressed in skimpy mini-skirts — are straddling the laps of traditional Muslim men, rubbing their breasts against their backs, and wiping feigned menstrual blood on their faces. Some detainees are being subjected to dogs to scare them, others bombarded with painfully bright lights and loud violent music, left naked in isolation, hooded, spat on, urinated on, exposed to extreme cold to the point of induced hypothermia, and deprived of food and sleep.[1]

Torture joins slavery as the practice most unanimously condemned in international law as well as the domestic laws of most nations, including the United States. The Geneva Conventions, drafted by the nations of the world in response to the atrocities of World War II, enshrined an international consensus that certain moral horrors and savage inhumanities must be prohibited even in time of war, and designated torture as foremost among these baseline standards of conduct. The Convention Against Torture, a treaty to which the United States is a signatory, states that "no exceptional circumstances whatsoever, whether a state of war or a threat of

---

1. See for example, "Detainees Accuse Female Interrogators: Pentagon Inquiry Is Said to Confirm Muslims' Accounts of Sexual Tactics at Guantánamo," *Washington Post*, February 10, 2005, p. A01. For additional references, see Melissa Weintraub, "Kvod Ha-Briot: Human Dignity in Jewish Sources, Human Degradation in U.S. Military Detention," available online at http://rhr-na.org/torture/tortureresources.html, pp. 1-11.

war, internal political instability or any other public emergency, may be invoked as a justification of torture."

Nevertheless, from the pages of *Newsweek* to the leading journals of philosophy and public policy — from Hollywood to Capitol Hill — our post-9/11 nation has posited torture as a subject for moral deliberation and equivocation. May torture — or its milder cognates — ever be deemed permissible? Is torture an unseemly but necessary component of the state's right and responsibility to protect its citizens from terror, the message of the Fox Channel's *24* to its viewers each week?

In this essay I will present insights from the Jewish legal-ethical heritage as one compelling ground for moral reasoning in relation to this most important ethical question of our time. I will interrogate torture's rationales from the perspective of Jewish ethics in order to argue for an absolute proscription against torture.

Three prefatory remarks about Jewish ethics:

First: Jewish law, or halakhah, is classically the primary arena in which both general ethical principles and specific norms are articulated and regulated. For the purposes of this discussion, I will use the terms "Jewish ethics" and "Jewish law" interchangeably, bracketing the potential for collisions between them.[2]

Secondly, Jewish law is often contrasted with American and international secular law for its preoccupation with duties as opposed to rights. In what follows, I presuppose this distinction to be overstated, for Jewish law arguably takes cognizance of "rights" implicitly as derivatives of religious duties. That is, rather than designating a right to life, Jewish law enjoins a negative commandment against homicide and a positive responsibility to heal and safeguard life from harm, etc.[3]

Third, in what follows I will take the term "God" for granted, not be-

---

2. Much traditional Judaism considers "ethics" and "law" to be coterminous, and does not countenance the possibility of an independent ethical inquiry into the morality or immorality of any given law. See Aharon Lichtenstein, "Does Jewish Tradition Recognize an Ethic Independent of Halakha?" in *Modern Jewish Ethics,* ed. Martin Fox (Columbus: Ohio State University Press, 1975), p. 62, and David Weiss Halivni, "Can a Religious Law Be Immoral?" in *Perspectives on Jews and Judaism,* ed. Arthur Chiel (New York: Rabbinical Assembly, 1978), p. 167. For a critique of this position from the standpoints of Conservative and Reform Judaism, see Seymour Spiegel, "Ethics and the Halakha," *Conservative Judaism* 25 (1971): 33-40, and the essays in D. J. Silver, ed., *Judaism and Ethics* (New York: Ktav, 1970).

3. Haim Cohen, *Human Rights in Jewish Law* (New York: Ktav, 1984), pp. 18, 36.

cause I presume that this term is transparently meaningful, but because traditional Jewish ethics is theocentric through and through. Jewish ethics posits our responsibilities as deriving from our relationship with a Creator — to whom we are viewed as owing our lives, our conscience, and our limited freedom. Readers are invited, as I step into the Jewish hermeneutical horizon, to perform their own necessary translations.

My essay will pivot on two principles in Jewish law, twin commandments granted trumping priority relative to many other religious obligations, namely: 1) the imperative to honor the dignity of the human person, viewed as imbued with God's image; and 2) the kindred, and at times conflicting obligation to defend human life at great cost. The question of torture throws into relief both the tension and the inextricability of these two principles, for they mutually rest on a concept of human personhood as a sacred and inviolable trust from God.

Defining Torture

First, what is torture? How has it been variously defined? What practices constitute torture as opposed to other methods of interrogation?

Defining torture has itself become a vexed and politicized business in our country in the last five years. The Convention Against Torture, to which the United States is a signatory, defines torture as "any act by which severe pain or suffering, whether physical or mental, is intentionally inflicted on a person."

Torture is generally distinguished from other forms of cruelty or sadism in terms of its official context: torture entails purposeful acts of harm inflicted by agents of the state on those in their custody in order to coerce, intimidate, or punish. Torture by definition consists of an assault upon one who is, at least at the moment, defenseless. The utter asymmetry of power between torturer and tortured is one of the ways torture is distinguished from killing on the battlefield.[4]

We have all heard the current U.S. administration claim that "we do not torture." The administration has been able to make this claim in part by relying on a farcically narrowed definition of torture. An infamous 2002 memo, issued by the Department of Justice's Office of Legal Counsel

---

4. Lisa Hajjar, "Torture and the Future," *Middle East Report Online*, May 2004.

(OLC), redefined torture as "physical pain accompanying serious injury such as organ failure, impairment of bodily functions, or even death."[5] The purpose of this constrictive definition, the memo implied, was to drive a wedge between "torture" and what is termed in international law as CID — cruel, inhuman, and degrading treatment, also known euphemistically as "moderate physical pressure," "enhanced interrogation techniques," or "torture lite." The memo urged that "the criminal statute penalizes only the most egregious conduct . . . only the worst forms of cruel, inhuman, or degrading treatment or punishment." In other words, this innovative definition attempted to provide U.S. interrogators with wriggling room to brush up as closely as possible against the "torture" chalk line without being held liable for crossing it.

The category of torture in international precedent is not as elastic as the administration's narrowed definitions might lead one to think. In 1971, British interrogators in Northern Ireland subjected Irish Republican Army members and sympathizers to hooding and loud noise, and deprived them of sleep, food, and drink for several days. They bound them in "stress positions," forcing them to stand shackled against the wall for excruciating lengths of time. Long-term studies of these men revealed that beyond the temporary pain they endured, most of them experienced lifelong debilitating physical and mental effects, including loss of motor coordination, blackouts, hallucinations, violent headaches, severe insomnia, chronic depression and anxiety, suicidal tendencies, and heart attacks before the age of forty. Most of them were never again able to maintain functional personal or professional relationships.[6] In 1976, the British government accepted that these techniques constitute torture and decided to forego their use, in accordance with a minority opinion of the European Court of Human Rights.[7] In a case against Israel in 1997, the U.N. Committee against Torture

---

5. The full text of the Bybee memo is available online at http://www.washingtonpost.com/wp-srv/nation/documents/dojinterrogationmemo20020801.pdf. The O.L.C. issued a revised memo in December 2004 after the original memo became public. The revised memo departs from the first memo in several subtle respects, including an expanded definition of torture, but still emphasizes that for treatment to qualify as torture it must inflict "severe physical pain" of "duration" and "intensity" and not only pain that is "mild" or "transitory."

6. John Conroy, *Unspeakable Acts, Ordinary People: The Dynamics of Torture* (New York: Knopf, 2000), pp. 6, 45, 127.

7. In *Ireland v. the United Kingdom* (1976), the European Commission of Human Rights, by a unanimous decision, ruled that these techniques amounted to torture. The Irish

determined that a similar list of practices, particularly when used in combination over an extended length of time, produce pain and suffering extreme enough to be described as torture.[8] This U.N. decision helped prompt the Israeli Supreme Court to outlaw these techniques categorically in 1999.

In other words, international precedent recognizes as torture the very techniques adopted in U.S. detention in Iraq, Afghanistan, and Guantánamo since 2001. But it is important not to overstate the significance of these rulings. There is no precise moral or legal bright line between "torture" and "cruel, inhuman and degrading treatment." Article 4 of the Geneva Conventions bans slavery, torture, and cruel, inhuman, and degrading treatment, without distinction, as war crimes "shocking the conscience of humanity." Vladimir Bukovsky — a former Soviet prisoner of war subjected to similar methods by the KGB — has noted that "the attempt to make a distinction between torture and CID techniques is ludicrous" to anyone who has been on the receiving end of these techniques.[9]

From the perspective of Jewish law, what matters is not whether these techniques are labeled "torture" or "cruel, inhuman, and degrading treatment," but rather the evidence that these are well-researched efforts to shatter the personalities of those who endure them. In 1956, two psychiatric consultants to the American Department of Defense produced a study of the effects of these very techniques — then employed by the KGB — on the human personality, describing them as inducing hallucinations and delirium, catatonic apathy, loss of control over bodily functions, and befuddled suggestibility to the point that suspects were unable to determine truth from falsehood.[10] An official Army investigation of abuses at Guan-

---

government then appealed the decision to the European *Court* of Human Rights — not yet satisfied with the decision since no one had been held accountable for the use of torture, and no legal sanction had been issued to ensure these techniques would not be used in the future by other governments within the Court's jurisdiction. In a decision that stunned the Irish government and the international law community, the *Court* then overturned the *Commission's* ruling that the techniques amounted to torture, ruling that they instead were inhuman and degrading treatment, but not torture. The Court's reversal of the original decision was rendered after three days of hearings in which no witnesses were present. See Conroy, *Unspeakable Acts*, pp. 136-37 and 185-87.

8. CAT/C/SR.297/ADD.1, *Conclusions*, paragraphs 4-6. A summary of the U.N. decision is available online at http://www.unhchr.ch/tbs/doc.nsf/0/b51bae20771d616a80256513005275 ab?Opendocument.

9. Vladimir Bukovsky, "Torture's Long Shadow," *Washington Post*, Dec. 18, 2005, p. B1.

10. Lawrence E. Hinkle Jr. and Harold G. Wolff, "Communist Interrogation and Indoc-

tánamo in 2005 acknowledged that forced nudity and other aforementioned degrading techniques are "authorized approaches called 'ego down' or 'futility,' which are used to make the interrogation subject question his sense of personal worth."[11] They are, in short, purposive efforts at dehumanization — attempts to penetrate to the core of a suspect's personality in order to destroy his sense of self-respect. They are calculated attempts to turn the body and psyche against themselves, to force a body to become an accomplice in its own self-destruction and betrayal.

It is this extreme debasement and contempt for human dignity with which we must contend in considering the moral status of these techniques in Jewish ethics and law.

Kvod Ha-briot: The Trumping Priority of Human Dignity in Halakha

The most fundamental assumption of Jewish ethics is that there is something intrinsically and ineradicably sacred about the human person, the human body and spirit as such. This idea originates in the first chapter of the Book of Genesis, in the idea that the human being is created *btselem Elohim,* in the image of God.

On the basis of this assumption, Judaism formulates several injunctions. I want to stress two overriding, interrelated prohibitions that derive from this premise of sacred personhood. 1. A prohibition against murder in Genesis 9:6: "Whoever sheds the blood of a man, by man shall his blood be shed, for in the image of God he made man." As we will see in the next section, we are not only admonished to refrain from harming life, but commanded positively to do all we can to protect life from third-party harm.

2. A prohibition against violations of dignity. Classical Jewish literature refers to human dignity by the term *kvod ha-briot* — the dignity of "created beings" rather than the dignity of "human beings" — grounding the requirement to protect human dignity in the divine origins of the hu-

---

trination of Enemies of the State," *American Medical Association Archives of Neurology and Psychiatry,* 76:2, 1956, cited in Conroy, *Unspeakable Acts,* pp. 127-28.

11. "Report Discredits F.B.I. Claims of Abuse at Guantánamo Bay," *New York Times,* July 14, 2005.

man. On the basis of this concept of human beings as the earthly vestige of the divine, early rabbinic commentary presents humiliation as an outrage against God, and the refusal to debase others, even in retaliation, as the supreme principle of the Torah, the practical outcome of the commandment to love one's neighbor: "R. Akiva says, 'Love your fellow as yourself.' This is the greatest principle in the Torah. You must not say, 'because I have been humiliated, let my fellow also be humiliated. . . . For, as Rabbi Tanhuma pointed out, if you act thus, realize who it is that you have really humiliated.' He made him in the likeness of God" (Genesis Rabbah 24:7).

The ontological fact of our creation in God's image enjoins us to moral behavior — commands us to work actively to honor the lives and dignity of other human beings, likewise bestowed with intrinsic sanctity.

Human dignity is arguably the foundational and aspirational ideal of Jewish law. The rabbis grant human dignity the power to displace other religious commandments: *kvod ha-briot docheh lo taaseh*. The injunction to avoid humiliating or contemptuous behavior takes legal precedence over all other rabbinic verdicts.[12] The rabbis present this override not as an extra-legal moral standard, but as a formal principle built into the inner workings of the law itself. From the rabbinic perspective, this is an astonishing idea. Most legal systems are hesitant to admit of opportunities for their rulings to be abrogated. In Jewish law, rabbinic rulings are conceived of as originating in divine will, not in human authority. Yet the rabbis designate human dignity as the litmus test for their sacred law, a seeming recognition that were the law to participate in dishonoring the human person, it would betray its own *raison d'être*. What are some of the practical implications of this lofty principle?

1. We are not to debase the human body. For many authorities, the idea that the human body is the corporeal representation of divinity gives rise to legal prohibitions against tattooing and piercing, let alone outright abuse and degradation of the body. The law prohibits dishonoring even

---

12. See Babylonian Talmud Brachot 19b, Shabbat 81a-b, and Megillah 3b. The parallel text in the Jerusalem Talmud *(Yerushalmi)* presents the opinion of R. Zeira that even Torah commandments are temporarily overridden where they conflict with human dignity (JT Kilayim 9:1). The *Yerushalmi* seems to consent to R. Zeira's opinion, citing it in another context to demonstrate that a Torah obligation may indeed be set aside for the sake of human dignity (JT Nazir 7:1; JT Ber. 3:1). For an overview of this concept in Jewish law, see Nahum Rakover, "The Protection of Human Dignity," *Jerusalem, City of Law and Justice*, ed. by Ravoker, Library of Jewish Law, pp. 210-11.

the dead body of a criminal convicted of a capital crime. As the twelfth-century biblical commentator Rashi comments on this prohibition: "Because man is made in the image of his Creator, to humiliate his body is to demean the Heavenly King."[13]

2. We are not to shame others through demeaning speech, threats, or insults. Doing so is conceived of as a form of violence akin to murder. The Talmud states: "He who publicly shames his fellow is as though he shed blood," and describes the act of shaming as "whitening the face" — stamping out another's spirit, turning another into a living corpse. Shaming, teaches the Talmud, constitutes an irreparable wrong more serious than any monetary wrong because it permanently injures another's personhood rather than his replaceable property.[14] Rabbinic sources display extraordinary sensitivity to shame-induced pain through a number of other extensive measures as well; one may not remind a person of something shameful in his family's past; one may not reprove someone in public; one must make every attempt to remove visible material differences in clothing and even wedding gifts to preclude humiliation to the poor or disenfranchised.[15]

Whose humanity is worthy of such honor? May one forfeit the right to dignified treatment? The sources teach us that the obligation to treat others with dignity and avoid shaming is not conditional on what sort of person we imagine stands before us. We are to honor the dignity of the criminal offender, even if he himself has disavowed it.[16] The Talmud voices anxiety over the inevitable humiliation involved in arrest, before a person, presumed innocent, has been convicted through due process of law.[17] The texts present the offender's dignity, even post-conviction, as standing independent of his personal attributes and actions, intrinsic to his humanity.

The Israeli Supreme Court extends these halakhic concepts to contemporary, concrete cases involving the rights and dignity of prisoners. Citing the principle of *kvod ha-briot* (human dignity) as developed in the halakha, the Israeli High Court has determined in several landmark deci-

---

13. Deut. 21:23, Rashi ad. loc.

14. Babylonian Talmud Baba Metzia 58b-59a.

15. Mishnah Taanit 4:8 and Babylonian Talmud Moed Katan 27b-28a. Meiri, Bet Habehirah, Moed Katan 27a.

16. Babylonian Talmud Baba Kama 79b (see Rashi ad. loc.), Menahot 99b, and BT Baba Metzia 58b

17. Jerusalem Talmud Sanhedrin 7:10. Cf. Maimonides, Mishneh Torah, Hilkhot Sanhedrin 24:10.

sions that prisoners must be provided with all of their basic human needs, physical, religious, and cultural, and treated as civilized people:[18]

> Imprisonment requires, by its nature, denial of freedom, but this denial does not justify, by its nature, violation of human dignity. Imprisonment that protects the human dignity of the prisoner is possible. The prison's walls do not have to separate between the prisoner and humanity . . . A prison is forbidden to become a concentration camp, and the prison cell is forbidden to become a cage. With all the problems inherent in this, a cultured society must ensure the minimum humane standards of imprisonment.[19]

> A free and civilized society is distinguished from a barbaric and oppressive society by the degree to which it treats a human being as a human being. . . . Just as the [Talmudic] rabbis were bold enough to waive all prohibitions instituted by them where necessary to preserve human dignity, [our law] should be cautious in sacrificing human dignity on the altar of any other requirement whatsoever.[20]

Citing the overriding importance of human dignity, the Israeli Supreme Court in 1999 categorically outlawed torture and cruel, inhuman, and degrading treatment — including the specific methods prevalent in U.S. military detention since 2001. The court rejected the logic implicit in the Bush administration's invented category of the "enemy combatant" that the "ter-

18. "It is firmly entrenched in our law that the fundamental rights of man 'survive' also behind prison walls, and are granted to the prisoner (and the detainee) also in his prison cell." See PPA 4463/94, *Golan v. Prison Service*, PD 50(4) 136, at 152-153. Cf. the comments of vice-president of the Supreme Court, Haim Cohen: "It is the right of a person in Israel who is sentenced to imprisonment (or who is lawfully detained) to be incarcerated in conditions that allow him to live a cultured life." HCJ 221/80, *Darwish v. Prison Service*, PD 50(4) 136, at 538. In *Darwish v. Prison Service*, the majority of the Court ruled that the right to a bed is derogated in the face of security considerations; H. Cohn gave a dissenting opinion that a bed is a bare minimum cultural need for *every* person, created in God's image. See HCJ 221/80, *Darwish v. Prisons Service*, PD 35 (1) 536.

19. Justice A. Barak, HCJ 540/84-546, *Yosef et al. v. Director of the Central Prison in Judea and Samaria*, PD 40 (1) 567 at 572-573.

20. Justice Haim Cohen, *Katlan et al. v. The Prison Service et al.* (1980), 34(3) PD 294 at 305-307. Cited and translated in Nahum Rakover, *Modern Applications of Jewish Law*, Library of Jewish Law, 1992, pp. 199-202.

rorist" forfeits the protections granted all other human beings on account of their being human. The court, rather, determined that its agents must "preserve the human image" and dignity of even those detainees known to be directly involvement in terror activities including suicide bombings.[21]

But Does Torture Save Lives? The Jewish Counterargument

As a Rabbi and activist against torture, I would love to bang my gavel now and authoritatively declare, "Case closed."

But torture cannot be repudiated absolutely on grounds of human dignity without reckoning with the other and still weightier moral and legal override of Jewish tradition. For alongside the injunction to safeguard human dignity on the basis of sacred human personhood, we are enjoined to an at times competing positive obligation to defend human life at almost any cost. Surely, goes the Jewish counterargument, lost lives would hurt more than the bending of our other principles? Even were the law to take into account the dignity of the interrogated as absolute, might we not also be compelled to suspend this noble ideal (not to forsake it, but to deflect it) in favor of the greater moral imperative of protecting innocent life?[22]

Consider the proverbial example, trotted out consistently to challenge an absolutist prohibition against torture. Known as the "ticking bomb" case, it presents some version of the following hypothetical: a captured fanatic has set a hidden nuclear device in the heart of a major metropolis, set to go off within hours. The authorities are certain that the prisoner in their hands is the perpetrator whose knowledge could avert the catastrophe and spare thousands of innocents, even a whole nation, and the nonviolent devices of their most expert interrogators have not yielded enough information to locate and deactivate the bomb.

Should we really, ask the thinkers who present this scenario, damn thousands rather than suspend our moral commitments? "It seems fanatical," says Harvard law professor Charles Fried, "to maintain the absoluteness of the judgment to do right even if the heavens will in fact fall." Fried, who is

---

21. HCJ 5100/94, *Public Committee Against Torture in Israel v. The State of Israel.* Full text of the decision is available online at http://www.jewishvirtuallibrary.org/jsource/Politics/GSStext.html.

22. See Michael Broyde, "Jewish Law and Torture," *Jewish Week,* July 7, 2006.

generally critical of sacrificing rights on the altar of cost/benefit analysis, nonetheless leaves the door open for this "catastrophe exception."[23]

The ticking bomb scenario is often invoked by defenders of the "lesser evil" argument. The "lesser evil" argument does not represent a shallow or coarse utilitarianism. It offers no pretense that it is right to sacrifice the lives of the few for the so-called greater good. It instead appreciates Jack Bauer and the C.I.A. he represents for their willingness to dirty themselves morally so that the rest of us might remain clean. For though torture is bad, would it not be even worse to sacrifice the lives of innocent civilians by tying the hands of intelligence officers who might otherwise thwart "ticking bombs" and massive loss of life? I will interrogate the assumptions of the "lesser evils" argument and the hypothetical "ticking bomb" case in what follows. But first, let me lay out a general framework for the imperative to defend life in Jewish law.

A Framework from Jewish Law

Rodef: *The Trumping Priority of Sacred Life*

The sanctity of human life is perhaps Judaism's most preoccupying value. Life — the tradition teaches — is *kinyan ha-kadosh barukh hu,* the property of God rather than of human beings, a principle whose practical implications include not only a prohibition against murder, but a prohibition against suicide and a refusal to allow murder to go unpunished.[24]

Jewish law recognizes not only a right to self-defense, but a positive duty to protect endangered life, elevating the "Good Samaritan" principle to the status of a legal requirement: "If one pursues his fellow in order to kill him . . . all Israelites are commanded to save the pursued, even at the cost of the pursuer's *(rodef)* life."[25] One who witnesses another in mortal

---

23. Charles Fried, *Right and Wrong* (Cambridge, Mass.: Harvard University Press, 1979), p. 10.

24. Maimonides, Mishneh Torah, Hilkhot Rotzeah 1:4.

25. Maimonides, Mishneh Torah, Hilkhot Rotzeah 1:6. As Chaim Povarsky elaborates, the principle of self-defense and defense-of-others *(rodef)* are related in later *halakhic* sources. For an extensive discussion of the relation between these two principles, see Povarsky's "The Law of the Pursuer and the Assassination of Prime Minister Rabin," *Jewish Law Association Studies IX,* ed. E. A. Goodman (Binghamton, N.Y.: Global Academic Publishing, 1997).

danger is obligated to attempt to save the would-be victim from harm as well as the perpetrator from committing a sin.[26] The law commands that we hinder perpetrators with force, even lethal force, where no other means for preventing a grave and imminent crime are available.

The justification for self-defense implicitly relies on a "lesser evils" argument. Because life is sacred, created in God's image, violence is absolutely wrong. But where life is threatened and violence could protect it, defensive force is less wrong than standing idly by as innocent life comes to harm. Given the overwhelming sanctity of life, however, the Rabbis recognize the enormous danger of providing a legal override to the prohibition against force, and so place stringent limitations on the application of self-defense.[27]

A Principle of Minimum Possible Harm

Force must be the minimal necessary to thwart a grave harm. The Talmud teaches that if Person A could have averted Person B's attack by maiming

---

26. See Mishnah Sanhedrin 8:7; Babylonian Talmud Sanhedrin 73ff.; Shulhan Arukh, Hoshen Mishpat 425:1-2. Rashi and Tosafot, ad. loc. Sanhedrin 73a.

27. Some contemporary Jewish legal scholars argue that the *rodef* (self-defense and defense-of-others) literature, with its stringent preconditions, applies only to society-based situations and not to wartime conditions. Generally these arguments are made from silence: references to the *rodef* principle do not frequent discussions of war — and commentators do not object when traditional texts describe war contexts that clearly violate *rodef* standards — so therefore the *rodef* preconditions must not apply to war. This essay will apply these standards to the case of torture on four grounds: (1) several classical and contemporary traditional Jewish legal decisors *do* explicitly apply these principles to battlefield contexts (eg. Sifte Hachahim 32:8; Immanuel Jakobovits, *Tradition: Journal of Orthodox Jewish Thought* 4:2, p. 202; Shimon Weiser, "Purity of Arms: An Exchange of Letters," *Niv Hamidrashiyah* 11 [1974]: 211-12). (2) Given the historical realities of the Jewish people during previous eras of Jewish history, there is a general paucity of *halakhic* treatment of war ethics generally, and no separate area of law governing *ius in bello* ("battlefield ethics") in *halakhah*. The most obvious place to turn, in developing Judaism's positions on "battlefield ethics," is to general principles of self-defense, which closely resemble the ethical constraints of other *ius in bello* traditions. There is no reason to argue that these standards are *too* stringent when they are legitimately applied by other ethical systems and are the closest the Jewish system has to "rules of engagement." (3) The *rodef* principle is particularly germane to any discussion of torture, for the interrogation room lies closer to the courtroom than the heat of the battlefield. Torture is often justified with criminal defenses — like the "necessity" defense — that resemble the *rodef* defense.

Person's B limb, rather than by killing him, Person A is liable for Person B's death. In other words, shoot at the feet before the chest.[28]

The Absolute, Equal Value of Innocent Human Lives

Jewish law insists on the equal value of human lives. The Mishnah, the earliest code of Jewish law, states unequivocally: "One life may not be given priority over another."[29] The Talmud extends this principle to its extreme conclusion, posing a hypothetical in which a man is given an impossible choice: slay another innocent person or surrender his own life. The Talmud enjoins him to do the latter, asking rhetorically: "What makes you think that your blood is redder? Perhaps his blood is redder."[30] And later commentaries gloss: "Who says your life is more beloved by God than his? Perhaps his life is more beloved."[31] These basic principles are applied by analogy to all other cases of kill or be killed — cases in which one can find no way to avoid imperiling oneself without committing violence against another. The tradition insists that one must die before bringing harm to another innocent person.

According to a striking first-century text that became the basis for reams of later legislation, the law instructs that we are prohibited from surrendering a single innocent life even to protect an entire community from destruction.[32] Each individual life, in other words, is an infinite end in and of itself, so sacred that it cannot be subjected to the moral calculus of utilitarian cost/benefit considerations. The practical implication: We may use force only against an attacker, who temporarily forfeits his right to life in the moment of the attack. We are not permitted reckless or negligent harm to befall innocent third parties in the name of our personal or collective self-defense.

Force must be a spontaneous reaction to a situation of present danger, not a premeditated act of pre-emption or revenge. One may not kill or in-

---

28. See Babylonian Talmud, Sanhedrin 74a and Shulhan Arukh, Hoshen Mishpat 421:13.

29. M. Ohalot 7:6, Rambam, Hilkhot Rotzeah 1:9 and Hilkhot Yesodei Ha-Torah 5:5, 5:7.

30. Babylonian Talmud 74a and Pesahim 25b.

31. Rashi, ad. loc. Pesahim 25b.

32. See for example, Tosefta, Terumot 7:20, Jerusalem Talmud Terumot 8:4, Maimonides, Mishneh Torah, Hilkhot Yesodai Ha-Torah 5:5, Rav Avraham Kook, Mishpat Kohen 143.

jure a harm-doer to avenge or punish a finished crime, or to prevent a future threat. Punishment is reserved for the system of justice — with its careful inquiry into the facts, its procedural safeguards, and its presumption of innocence. One may cause harm in self-defense only in a moment of unavoidable urgency, when life is in immediate danger.[33]

A Certainty, or Reasonableness Standard

One must be reasonably certain that a threat is real, and force necessary to repel it.[34] As in criminal law, this is an extremely difficult standard to apply. As one American domestic case puts it: "Detached reflection cannot be demanded in the presence of an uplifted knife."[35] Nonetheless, the standard requires some minimal degree of objective, reasonable threat and likelihood that force will help avert it.

The American Military Context

The remainder of this piece will draw these compelling standards into dialogue with the question of torture in an American military context.

The Minimum Possible Harm Standard

What would "minimal possible harm" look like in an interrogation room? Are there alternative means to protect public safety and innocent lives?

Two points: First, torture doesn't seem to work very well. The research demonstrates that torture provides largely unreliable information, if not absolute fabrication, driven by both the victim's psychological instability while experiencing excruciating pain and his belief that he will be able to bring his torment to an end with a story — any story.[36] As the straight-shooting John McCain likes to say, "Torture is just stupid." (This from a

---

33. See for example, Rambam, Mishneh Torah, Hilkhot Gneiva 9:7-10, Resp. Maharam bar Barukh cited in Mordekhai, Baba Kamma 196, and Rashi, ad. loc., Ex. 22:1.

34. See for example, Maimonides, Mishneh Torah, Hilkhot Rotzeah 1:7, Hilkhot Gneiva 9:10, 9:12, Rivash Responsa 238. See also Mekhilta Nezikin 13, 101 and Rashi and Ralbag ad loc. 22:2.

35. *State v. Bryant*, 671 A.2d 1058 (N.J. Sup. Ct. App. Div. 1996).

36. Conroy, *Unspeakable Acts*, p. 113, p. 170.

man who once confessed to the North Vietnamese the entire lineup of the Green Bay Packers rather than the members of his flight squadron.) As John Langbein, who has meticulously researched the rise and fall of the use of torture in the European criminal justice system, asserts: "History's most important lesson is that it has not been possible to make coercion compatible with truth."[37]

Second, there are demonstrated, alternative ways of getting the information we need to protect lives. Research demonstrates that rapport-building — winning over informants through the earning of their confidence — is the most effective method of interrogation, followed by nonviolent ruses that catch suspects by surprise.[38] Cyril Cunningham, who served in the Ministry of Defense of the U.K., once quipped, "The best interrogator I ever met . . . had the demeanor of an unctuous parson."[39] FBI documents claim that in Guantánamo, "every time the FBI established a rapport with a detainee, the military would step in and the detainee would stop being cooperative."[40] In the aftermath of the 1999 Israeli Supreme Court decision, a new generation of interrogators has developed a host of alternative interrogation techniques. Danny Rothschild, formerly a high official in the Israeli security service, claims: "The results are the same. Which shows you could have done without brutal interrogation."[41] Physical coercion is neither the least harmful nor the most effective means of obtaining the information we need to protect ourselves. Much false information tends to be disclosed in the face of agonizing pain, and research demonstrates that prisoners tend to cooperate more readily when their trust has been earned.

Given that there is little demonstrated proof that torture "works," and that alternative, effective means are available to gather intelligence necessary to protect American lives, torture would not be permissible according to the "minimum possible harm" standard.

---

37. John H. Langbein, "The Legal History of Torture," in *Torture: A Collection*, ed. by Sanford Levinson (New York: Oxford University Press, 2004), p. 101.

38. Jane Mayer, "Whatever It Takes," *The New Yorker*, Feb. 19, 2007.

39. Quoted in Conroy, *Unspeakable Acts*, p. 44.

40. Quoted in Anne Applebaum's editorial, "The Torture Myth," *Washington Post*, January 12, 2005, p. A21, available online at http://www.washingtonpost.com/wp-dyn/articles/A2302-2005Jan11.html.

41. Quoted in Joseph Lelyveld, "Interrogating Ourselves," *New York Times Magazine*, June 12, 2005.

The Equality of Innocent Lives

Jewish law, as discussed above, rejects the cost-benefit logic of sacrificing a few innocents for the sake of a net saving of life.

Most of those who defend torture rely on the assumption that the person being tortured is not a mere suspect; he is a confirmed perpetrator, a terrorist, the worst of the worst. In real life, however, interrogators rarely know that they have the "right" person before them, particularly when detainees have been gathered in broad round-ups and granted few due process protections, including the habeas corpus to challenge the legality of their detentions or the right to see the evidence against them.

Again, two empirical points: one contemporary, one historical. One of the many consequentialist arguments against torture — again from the historian's corner — is that torture has metastatic tendencies. Like a disease, it is infectious; invariably, it spreads.[42] Between 1987 and 1999, Israel justified "moderate physical pressure" under "ticking bomb" conditions. Later data revealed that 85 percent of the Palestinians who passed through the Israeli military detention system during these years were subjected to these techniques, regardless of the charges against them, or lack thereof.[43]

Perhaps this tendency for "torture creep" would not be so morally troubling if not for the evidence that under emergency military conditions, a lot of innocent people get vacuumed into the system. In our own military context, the statistics are so damning that it is difficult to absorb them without denial. As of 2003, the International Committee of the Red Cross estimated that between 70 and 90 percent of those held in Abu Ghraib were there "by mistake"; later official Army inquiries dropped that

---

42. See for example, Michael Ignatieff, *The Lesser Evil: Political Ethics in an Age of Terror* (Princeton: Princeton University Press, 2004), p. 136.

43. Btselem — the Israeli Center for Human Rights in the Occupied Territories — published a report in 1998 detailing the methods used by the GSS prior to 1999 as well as stories of prisoners who underwent interrogation. The Btselem report argues, however, that most cases in which "ticking bomb" justifications were invoked before the Supreme Court were later found to be unsubstantiated. The report follows several stories of detainees who were interrogated with a "ticking bomb" justification and never indicted for any criminal offense (pp. 31-32). If those being tortured were all "ticking bombs," why, asked the report, did interrogators take weekends off? "The lethal bomb ticks away during the week, ceases, miraculously, on the weekend, and begins to tick again when the interrogators return from their day of rest." The full text of the report is available online at http://www.btselem.org/English/Publications/Summaries/199802_Routine_Torture.asp.

estimate to two-thirds. At Guantánamo, official reports estimated that 40 percent of detainees never belonged there.[44] Eighty-five percent of those captured at Bagram in Afghanistan were released without any charges or evidence of terror links.[45] There were reports of routine physical and psychological ill-treatment and abuse at each of these facilities.

If we imagine as true for even one moment that our lives belong to God, that all human lives are equally beloved to God, that one infinite soul may outweigh a whole community, and that it is simply not up to us to decide, how could we permit a policy that consistently results in the destruction of so many lives?

The Principle of Imminent Danger

The well-documented use of "torture lite" in American detention facilities has not been restricted to cases in which interrogators were fighting a clock against an imminent attack. U.S. military personnel have used physically coercive techniques not to deactivate looming bombs, nor even only to foil future attacks, but also to obtain information about who was involved in previous attacks, to learn who is generally hostile to American policies, to punish, intimidate, and pacify detainees, and to send a message to detainees' families and communities back home.

Jewish law requires that violence be used in self-defense only as an expression of unavoidable urgency, when life is in immediate peril. Such a standard would allow the killing of a suicide bomber strapped with explosives, or return of enemy fire in battle. It would not permit deliberate, routine, premeditated violence in the cool, calculated conditions of the interrogation room in which a subject is at one's mercy and poses no immediate threat to life.

But what about a true "ticking time bomb" case? you might ask. Might not all of these criteria — "imminent danger," "minimum possible harm," and "no third party innocents" — be satisfied in the limited circumstance of the "ticking time bomb," in which a suspect in custody knows the location of a hidden explosive device that threatens life on a grand scale and has resisted nonviolent means of interrogation? It is time to test the abso-

---

44. Lelyveld, "Interrogating Ourselves."

45. Tim Golden, "Army Faltered in Investigating Detainee Abuse," *New York Times,* May 22, 2005.

lute prohibition of torture in Jewish law — the edifice I have been slowly building from all sides — against this worst-case scenario.

The problem with the "ticking bomb" case is that it seems never to have occurred in the real world. It is an implausible hypothetical that relies on several dubious preconditions: You know an attack is due to occur imminently. You know the person in front of you is the right person, harbors the information that could avert an attack, and will reveal reliable information once subjected to pain.

These circumstances are unlikely even within the realm of the thought experiment in which they, indeed, seem exclusively to reside. The "real-life" uncertainty about these variables tends rather to slide habitually towards normalization. For how certain does one have to be that the party before you knows something? Can one torture on mere suspicion? Why not torture hundreds, if not thousands, in a context like Iraq, in which everyone is a potential enemy, in which everyone may know something, and there are always bombs primed to explode, if not in an hour, then tomorrow, or next week?

On the empirical, historical level, defense of torture under "ticking bomb" conditions has invariably opened the door to the routinization of torture; this has been the case in Algeria during the French occupation, in Israel and the occupied territories, and now in Iraq and Afghanistan. Once advanced preparation and legal authorization for "the ticking bomb" exception had occurred, torture became entrenched as an administrative practice and customary procedure for interrogation and governance, not in isolated circumstances in which harsh treatment heroically fended off catastrophe, but rather as an ongoing and somewhat arbitrary regime of cruel and dehumanizing treatment.

The "ticking bomb" scenario is an artificial philosopher's case that cannot withstand its exposure to real world conditions. As New York University law professor Aziz Huq has said about this case, "Laws must comport to the world in which we live, not the world with which the Fox channel presents us. It is morally fraudulent to make law on the basis of infidelity to reality."[46] It is not only fraudulent, but actually quite dangerous to use this case to govern our moral and legal reflection about torture in the real world.

46. Public Lecture, "When Does Prosecution Become Persecution? Torture: Is it Ever Moral?" Jan. 25, 2007.

There is one remaining criterion for the use of force in Jewish law, and for those readers who are not sold on moralizing absolutes, but care primarily about pragmatic consequences, this one is for you.

The Reasonableness, or Certainty, Standard

I have stated that in Jewish law one must be reasonably certain that a threat is real and that force will contribute to averting it. This sort of standard, as any criminal lawyer will tell you, is difficult to adjudicate. It is deeply subjective in a barroom brawl, let alone in a world like the one in which we live — a world in which shadowy "threats" are pervasive and ongoing on the one hand, haphazard and unpredictable on the other. In our struggle to protect the public from terror, how do we ascertain: a) the degree of actual versus perceived threat, and b) what force will contribute to ameliorating these threats, rather than to exacerbating them? These may seem like tactical questions — but as Jewish law recognizes, it is impossible to disentangle moral questions from the practical, empirical, and even political "real-world" situations in which they arise.

Consider the following. In 1995, a man named Yigal Amir assassinated the Prime Minister of Israel on grounds of the defense-of-life principles I have laid out. He argued that Yitzhak Rabin, in pursuing a path of territorial accommodation, was endangering the survival not only of the State of Israel, but of the entire Jewish people.

We may rightfully shake our heads in disbelief or disgust. But in Israel, many halakhic decisors didn't quite know what to do with Amir's reasoning, for many agreed that Oslo did present a danger to the Jewish people. In the end, one ground for the rejection of Amir's reasoning was uncertainty.[47] After all, at least half of the Israeli voting public believed that terminating the peace process would be at least as dangerous as its continuation.

In closing, I want to name four reasons why torturing detainees is at least as dangerous to the American people as refraining from doing so.

First, even if torture helps win a battle, it typically helps lose the larger war.[48] In the aftermath of Abu Ghraib, bipartisan military and political commentators joined in recognizing that America had just granted Osama bin Laden his most effective propaganda campaign and recruitment tool

47. See for example Povarsky, "The Law of the Pursuer," p. 180.
48. Ignatieff, *The Lesser Evil*, pp. 19-20.

yet.[49] Even if torturing detainees were to help garner "actionable intelligence" on terror networks (setting aside for the moment torture's questionable efficacy) — what good is a military tactic that helps break a terror cell while alienating allies and moderates and engendering hatred and resentment in an entire population?[50] Thomas Friedman has been particularly eloquent on this point: "I am convinced that more Americans are dying and will die if we keep the Gitmo prison open than if we shut it down. . . . Why care? It's not because I am queasy about the war on terrorism. It is because I want to win the war on terrorism. . . . This is not just deeply immoral, it is strategically dangerous. . . . I would rather have a few more bad guys roaming the world than a whole new generation."[51]

Second, we will not ultimately help the American people to live in greater security by fanning existing hostilities and bolstering the idea that America is an "evil occupier" intent on brutalizing and dehumanizing the Muslims over whom it seeks to rule. Perhaps nothing has done more to erode America's global political legitimacy and credibility than the torture scandals of the last five years as well the total impunity of those public officials who should have been held accountable for them.[52]

Third, torture endangers our own soldiers, weakening longstanding international protections against the mistreatment of POWs and eviscerating our ability to oppose similar practices when used against American citizens.[53]

---

49. See Phillip Carter, "The Road to Abu Ghraib," *Washington Monthly*, November 2004. Available online at www.washingtonmonthly.com/features/2004/0411.carter.html. Also Bob Herbert, "It Just Gets Worse," *New York Times*, July 11, 2005.

50. Ignatieff, *The Lesser Evil*, p. 82; and Michael Walzer, *Arguing About War* (New Haven: Yale University Press, 2005) p. 9.

51. "Just Shut it Down," *New York Times*, May 27, 2005.

52. See Samantha Powers, "Fixing Foreign Policy," *Harvard Magazine*, July-August 2006.

53. Former Secretary of State Colin Powell's criticism of the Bybee memo — which argued for the elimination of Geneva protections in Guantánamo and Afghanistan — is available online at http://msnbc.msn.com/id/4999363/site/newsweek. Powell's claims: "[The Bybee memo] will reverse over a century of U.S. policy and practice in supporting the Geneva Conventions and undermine the protections of the law of war for our troops, both in this specific context and in general." See also the critical memo of William H. Taft IV, legal advisor to the State Department, available online at http://www.fas.org/sgp/othergov/taft.pdf. For an expanded version of this argument, cf. Carter, "The Road to Abu Ghraib."

And finally, and in conclusion, torture threatens to destroy the idea of America — everything we stand for — the only real counteragent to terror.

Is this our America? Men in dog leashes, being forced to perform dog tricks, and wear bras and lingerie on their heads? Female interrogators — dressed in lacy thongs — straddling the laps of traditional Muslim men, and wiping feigned menstrual blood on their faces? What has become of America?

One does not need to be a Jew, or even a religious person, to believe that there is something inviolably sacred about the human person. Every moral and religious system of which I am aware advances some notion of basic human dignity and condemns such total violations of the human body and spirit.

The sanctity of human personhood lies at the core and foundation of our nation's history, enshrined in our constitution through the prohibitions against cruel treatment and self-incrimination. The repudiation of the rack and the screw — along with due process protections and the separation of powers — were seen by our constitutional forefathers as the foundation for the modern rule of law, an enlightened repudiation of persecution and tyranny, essential for conditions of human dignity, liberty, security, and well-being to thrive. The Supreme Court has long denounced physical and psychological cruelty on the part of governmental agents as "revolting," "shocking," and "alien" to the most sacred values on which America was founded.[54] Let us heed the historian's warning: when democracies are brought to their knees by terrorism, it is not in military defeat, but in eroding their own ideals through overreactions — think of Argentina, Colombia, Peru, or our own America during the "Red Scare." Terrorism tends to menace democratic states most by weakening their own constitutional and ethical commitments.[55]

---

54. See for example, *Culombe v. Connecticut,* 367 U.S. at 581 (1961) for a summary of "[a] cluster of convictions, each expressive in a different manifestation of the basic notion that the terrible engine of the criminal law is not to be used to overreach individuals who stand helpless against it. Among these are the notions that men are not to be imprisoned at the unfettered will of their prosecutors, nor subjected to physical brutality by the officials charged with the investigation of crime. This principle, branded into the consciousness of our civilization by the memory of the secret inquisitions, sometimes practiced with torture, which were borrowed briefly from the continent during the era of the Star Chamber, was well known to those who established the American governments."

55. Ignatieff, *The Lesser Evil,* p. 61.

To paraphrase law scholar Lisa Hajjar, If America sacrifices the one right that is considered most sacrosanct and inalienable by U.S. and international law — the one right the civilized world agrees all human beings should have simply by virtue of being human — it is not only the "terrorists" who will lose. It is the humans.[56]

56. Hajjar, "Torture and the Future."

CHAPTER 11

Developing a Jewish Theology Regarding Torture

Edward Feld

The Torah — the first book of Jewish instruction — mandates the Sabbath as, among other things, an act of remembrance: remembrance of creation and remembrance of the Exodus. Deuteronomy 5:12-14 reads:

> Observe the Sabbath day and keep it holy, as the Lord your God has commanded you. Six days you shall labor and do all your work, but the seventh day is a Sabbath of the Lord your God. You shall not do any work — you, your son or your daughter, your male or female servant, your ox or your ass, or any of your cattle, or the stranger in your settlements so that your male and female servant may rest as you do. Remember that you were a slave in the land of Egypt and the Lord your God freed you from there with a mighty hand and an outstretched arm; therefore the Lord your God has commanded you to observe the Sabbath day.[1]

Remember your own history of oppression, so that you learn not to oppress others.

In this telling of the fourth commandment, the reason for the Sabbath is so that the least of you may have some rest. The reason why all work must stop is that if it did not, you might be able to arrange for your own

---

1. All biblical quotations are taken from *JPS Hebrew-English Tanakh*, 2d ed. (Philadelphia: The Jewish Publication Society, 2003).

rest — you would take off from work whenever you needed to — but the least among you, the servant, might be given the work that you are not doing. The Sabbath, then, is instituted to protect the poor and powerless, who might otherwise never be given rest. This is the condition of slavery that you once experienced: oppressive, unceasing labor. What you should have learned from that experience is how easily abused the powerless are. In the Torah, it is consistently the memory of the slavery in Egypt and the Exodus from Egypt that serve as the warrant for the care of the poor and the stranger.

Interestingly, the story of the Exodus in fact begins with the following verses:

> A new king arose over the land of Egypt who did not know Joseph. And he said to his people, "Look, the Israelite people are much too numerous for us. Let us deal shrewdly with them, so that they may not increase; otherwise in the event of war they may join our enemies in fighting against us and rise up from the ground." (Exod 1:8-10)

So the slavery of the Jewish people begins with: first, defining a people as "other"; second, seeing them as potential enemies; and finally, enslaving this "other" and defining it as self-protection.

Note the prescience of these verses. Over and over, Jews would be persecuted on the same grounds: Suspicion of their otherness allowed people to define Jews as outside the pale, and then as enemies of the state, so that in the end, having been declassified from the protections of citizenship, Jews were persecuted, enslaved, and not infrequently tortured. Grisly records exist of torture by the Inquisition; of pogroms perpetrated by Russians, Ukrainians, and Poles; and of twentieth-century horrors committed by Germans and their allies. These persecutions all had the same quality: First, the larger culture defined a group of people as other, then they were seen as enemies, and finally all was permitted in the war against them. The Nazis did not begin with the slaughter of Jews but with the cultural creation of otherness and enmity. The Jew had to be defined as outside the human family before the slaughter could begin, before all could be permitted. And we should never forget that the Inquisition and Nazism had at least this in common: Both of them thought that they were engaging in heroic work to bring a better future.

In speaking about torture in our synagogue in Amherst over the High

Holy Days, I once read a portion of a transcript from a torture session of the Spanish Inquisition. This female victim of the Inquisition keeps on repeating again and again — she is in obvious pain as the inquisitor keeps on ordering one turn of the screw and then another — "Tell me what you want me to say. I will say anything you want, señor." A woman in our congregation later protested against my sermon because she said that it had upset her fourteen-year-old son. It is human nature to want to suppress that which is painful. But if we are part of a culture inflicting suffering, then we are commanded to remember — to remember our own painful stories and to keep in mind the knowledge of the suffering of others.

The other remembrance the Sabbath asks us to engage in is the remembrance of creation: The version of the Decalogue in Exodus explains that the reason for the observance of the Sabbath is that it re-creates the pattern of creation. We are to live with the knowledge that all of life is a gift and that each human being is created in the image of God. That first great compendium of rabbinic teaching, the Mishnah, teaches as follows:

> Why was Adam created singly: to teach you that if anyone destroys one soul, scripture considers it as if a whole world was destroyed, and if anyone save a person's life then scripture considers it as if a whole world was maintained. Also, for the sake of peace between peoples, that no person could say my ancestry is greater than yours and so that no one should say that there is more than one creator. How great is the Holy One, for a person creates many coins from the same mold and they are all similar to each other, but the sovereign of the universe, the Holy One forms each human in the mold of that first person but no human being is like another. Therefore every human being must say: the world was created for me.[2]

Interestingly, the context of this dictum in the Mishnah is the warning that the court is to give to witnesses in a capital case to take care with their words, because a life is at stake. What is being argued for here is the sacredness of the life of the suspected criminal. This person who is on trial is in the image of God. It was for this person that the world was created. In Jewish readings of the text of Genesis, that sense of the sacredness of each human being is not simply confined to some inner being — the soul of a per-

---

2. Mishnah Sanhédrin 4:5.

son — but the very body of the person. And so it is not surprising to read the following command regarding the criminal: "If a person is guilty of a capital offense and is put to death, and you impale the person on a stake, you must not let the corpse remain on the stake overnight, but must bury the corpse the same day. For an impaled body is an affront to God: You shall not defile the land the Lord your God is giving you to possess" (Deut. 21:22-23).

Note again that we are talking here of the body of a criminal. Yet in the biblical account the body of this person is no less sacred than that of any other person. Indeed, Jewish burial practice is derived from this law, and burial for everyone is done as quickly as possible. In other words, the treatment of the criminal becomes the norm of how we treat everyone. Just as the Sabbath is instituted for the protection of the slave, so now the treatment of the body of the criminal becomes the norm for all. How we treat the least of society is the standard for how everyone ought to be treated.

Interestingly, the midrash adds the following footnote to the biblical verses we have just read: "This injunction of the Bible is meant to prevent the kind of behavior the government adopts nowadays."[3] The midrash is specifically commenting on the Roman practice of a torturous death in which bodies were displayed on posts for days. The rabbis applied the biblical exhortation in opposing and criticizing the governmental practice of their day.

What the rabbis of the midrash and the Mishnah formulated were behaviors that would honor human beings in both body and spirit. They defined this as a principle of Jewish law: *kavod habriot*, the need to honor all living beings.

What torture seeks to do is the opposite of the application of this principle. Rather than honoring the prisoner as a fellow human being, the prisoner is to be broken, and the means to do this is the infliction of pain and degradation. Many cases of torture, such as those practiced at Abu Ghraib, are simply committed to humiliate the captive — physically, mentally, sexually, and religiously. Some of what occurred and continues to occur is simply the expression of raw revenge and hatred. Some of it manifests the worst kinds of ethnic and religious bigotry. Muslims or Arabs or Asians are seen as other, as not having the same commitments to life and human dignity that we do; therefore, they need to be treated differently than we

3. Sifre Deuteronomy, ad loc.

would treat Westerners. Whatever the motive, what is intended is the reduction of the other, the captive, the one in my possession, to powerlessness so that he or she and I both know that I am superior.

Torture in connection with interrogation may be more cold-blooded, but it has some of the same features. What we seek to do by torturing prisoners is to take away their will, their choice. We wish to rule totally over them so that they will tell us all we want. We want to take over their will, deprive them of choice. We want them to betray themselves, to betray what they most believe in, to betray what they hold sacred, to betray their own sense of honor. We want to shame them. We disorient them by sleep deprivation or by application of heat or cold. We make them beg for food. We use physical pain to make them "go out of their mind." We want to deprive them of their fundamental self-respect, their autonomy, their rationality, their will. We want to take away from them those fundamental aspects by which we define our humanity. Not infrequently, to have been subject to torture is to be harmed for life, because the very meaning of life has been so fundamentally challenged.

There is another way of relating to one's enemies. I was present at a swearing-in ceremony for Israeli soldiers that took place on an army base after basic training. The chaplain who spoke at the service said to these soldiers: "Do not ever refer to the people whom you fight by slang epithets. Do not even refer to them as Arabs, because you are not fighting all Arabs. The people whom you fight are presently your opponents, but you must always believe that one day they may be your friends." It was an extraordinary statement by an army chaplain. It was extraordinary for soldiers to hear this as they swore to do their duty for their country.

The contemporary Jewish philosopher Emmanuel Lévinas, who was himself imprisoned by the Germans who occupied France, characteristically remarked, "To be able to see in the face of the other, in the face of those who would try to kill me, in the face of the criminal, the face of God, this is the hardest challenge of the religious enterprise."[4] Lévinas insisted that he had a moral responsibility even toward the Nazi captain who commanded his work camp.

The Jew who observes the Sabbath is taught that there are limits that have to be placed on what he or she wants to do. Indeed, the Jewish com-

---

4. Emmanuel Lévinas, *Difficult Freedom: Essays on Judaism* (Baltimore: Johns Hopkins University Press, 1990), p. 10.

mitment to law is fundamentally based on an understanding of the need for
limits. Lévinas argues that all of Jewish religious law is a way of channeling
our raw emotions and directing us toward an appreciation of otherness.

The theological understandings and the historical remembrances that
I have outlined here animated the Israeli Supreme Court to outlaw the use
of torture in its 1999 decision. Previously an Israeli commission had allowed the use of torture under some extreme circumstances — the ticking
bomb, for example. But the Supreme Court found that once exceptions
were made, security services used this loophole to apply the exemption
more broadly so that torture became widely used in interrogation processes. So the Supreme Court of Israel found it necessary to make its findings absolute and said as much in its decision:

> This is the destiny of democracy — it does not see all means as accept-
> able, and the ways of its enemies are not always open before it. A democ-
> racy must sometimes fight with one hand tied behind its back. Even so,
> a democracy has the upper hand. The rule of law and the liberty of an
> individual constitute important components in its understanding of se-
> curity. At the end of the day, they strengthen its spirit and this strength
> allows it to overcome its difficulties. We are not isolated in an ivory
> tower. We live the life of this country. We are aware of the harsh reality
> of terrorism in which we are, at times, immersed. The possibility that
> this decision will hamper the ability to properly deal with terrorists and
> terrorism disturbs us. . . . In deciding the law, we must act according to
> our purest conscience. (Israeli Supreme Court, Judgment on the Inter-
> rogation Methods Applied by the GSS, par. 39, 40)

Even in a time of war, even faced with terrorism, with an enemy that
targets civilians and does not act within the bounds of morality as we
know it, we are still enjoined not to give up our own moral center. Israel
has been under constant attack, yet its Supreme Court has issued one of
the most sweeping condemnations of torture — including what some have
called "light" torture, such as sleep deprivation.

Rabbi Nahman, one of the great Hasidic masters, who lived at the end
of the eighteenth century and the beginning of the nineteenth, tells a story
of a kingdom where the crops had gone bad and the food everyone ate was
poisonous and making them insane. The king turned to his counselor and
asked, "What can we do?" The counselor advised that everyone mark their

forehead with a sign so that as each person peered into their neighbor's face they would remember what they were feeling was the result of their insanity, and they would recall what it was like to be sane.

What is the religious task of the hour? It is to look into our neighbor's face and recognize how easily it is for us to be overcome by enmity and rage. Our task is the task we have always had: Amid the craziness of our world, amid the insanity of history, we are to teach the world that if you want to find God, look into the face of the other. Make sure you see the face of God even in the person you suspect of being your enemy, even in the face of the criminal.

Shabbat Shalom — may our invocation of the Sabbath send us on the ways of peace.

CHAPTER 12

These Things I Remember as I Pour Out My Heart: A Sermon for Kol Nidre 5766

Ellen Lippmann

A painful rabbinic story: When they led Rabbi Akiva to the executioner, it was time for reciting the Shema. With iron combs they scraped away his skin as he recited Shema Yisrael, freely accepting the yoke of God's sovereignty. "Even now?" his disciples asked. He said to them, "All my life I have been troubled by the verse: 'Love the Eternal your God . . . with all your soul,' which means even if God takes your life. I often wondered when I would be able to fulfill that obligation. And now that I have the opportunity, should I not do so?!" He left the world while uttering *Ekhad* — God is one.[1]

Eleh ezkerah v'nafshi alai esh'p-kha: These things I remember as I pour out my heart. After the Yom Kippur Avodah service tomorrow we will read *Eleh Ezkerah* — "These Things I Remember," a poem about ten martyrs who died under Roman persecution for teaching Torah. It entered the Ashkenazic liturgy in the Middle Ages, a "cry of anguish and bewilderment at the savagery of Jewish fate during the Crusades."[2]

We Jews know about torture, by the Romans, the Crusaders, the Spanish Inquisitors, the Nazis. All these we remember and pour out our hearts.

So if we know and remember what it is to be a victim of torture, why am I talking about torture tonight? I am talking about it because as a member of the Executive Committee of Rabbis for Human Rights —

1. Talmud Berakhot 61b.
2. Jonathan Magonet, *Hadeish Yameinu,* p. 621.

North America (RHR), I have been in on the Rabbis Campaign Against Torture from the beginning, and have had a chance to hear from experts, learn from rabbinic sources, and advocate with those in Washington who are finally beginning to work against it.

But mostly, I am talking about it because I wept when I realized how far our country has fallen. This was in June, when I heard Josh Rubinstein, regional director of Amnesty International in the northeast U.S., say, "We have always worked with centers for treatment of torture victims from countries around the world, but never in thirty years of my work in this field have we had to look at victims of torture committed by our own country."

I startled myself by weeping, but after his talk I broke down. I wept for my country, and how far we have come from the ideals I learned to love as a child. I wept for shame. When I told this to friends, some said, "How naïve can you get? The United States has been involved in torture and abuse the world over for years!"

I know that. And yet . . .

We have crossed a line here, damaging further our reputation abroad and our safety there and here, and pouring out a little more of our hearts with each incident, each humiliation, each conviction of a Pfc. Lynndie England while higher level officials remain at large.

Kolot member Elizabeth Holtzman, writing in *The Nation* in July, said that "President Bush likes to blame a few 'bad apples' for the serious mistreatment of Iraqi prisoners. But the problem is not limited to a few bad apples at the bottom of the barrel." She strongly advocated holding senior officials accountable and urged Congressional action: a special prosecutor, legislation, hearings, press conferences, and more.

It is gratifying that the Senate, led by Senator John McCain (who knows of torture firsthand), has finally voted — decisively — to bring military prison camps under the rule of law, banning the use of cruel, inhuman, or degrading treatment (which was already illegal).

Two weeks ago a delegation of rabbis met with Senator McCain and presented him with our Rabbinic Letter against Torture, a document signed by close to 600 rabbis. He told them how much he appreciated our efforts and how important public opinion is to the success of his initiative. The rabbis made a commitment to him to do all we can to support his efforts and other similar initiatives aimed at ending torture. Before we at RHR began this Campaign Against Torture, I was — maybe like you — someone who either read about sexually-charged torture with creepy fascination or turned the page as fast as I could. In either case, I certainly didn't feel I was reading or thinking about human beings being tortured. Yet torture, like terror, is about human abuse of other humans, and I think we ought to pay more attention. Hayder Sabbar Abd reported that seven men were all placed in hoods . . . and the beating began. "'They beat our heads on the walls and the doors.' . . . He said his jaw had been broken . . . he received fifty blows in two hours. . . . 'When we refused to take off our clothes, they beat us and tore our clothes off with a blade.'" He saw himself in the photos from Abu Ghraib, naked, his hand on his genitals, a female soldier pointing and smiling with a cigarette in her mouth.[3]

It is painful to face these truths, yet it is a painful honor, as my friend Rabbi Margaret Holub has said. It is an honor to be part of a group that has gotten 600 rabbis and untold numbers of other Jews to sign on to letters against torture, that has been able to meet with the key legislators, that is getting out a Jewish voice that has been largely silent about torture.

And it is an honor to realize that one place we can look to for support is Israel and a landmark 1999 decision by the Israeli Supreme Court. I, and many of you, have been critical of much of Israel's behavior in the last many years, and we are often fearful as Jews because of how Israel's behavior is perceived by the rest of the world. In the case of torture, we can now — since 1999 — hold Israel up as an example. Would that the U.S. government would adopt a ruling as clear and important as that of the Israeli Supreme Court! We should be proclaiming it from the rooftops!

The background: In 1988, the Landau Commission there authorized the use of "moderate physical pressure" in what they called "ticking bomb" situations, in which a suspect is thought to know of an immediate threat. Soon, though, most or all Palestinian detainees were treated as potential "ticking bombs." In 1999, the Supreme Court in Israel, recognizing that most Palestinians were being tortured in some way, ruled that torture and other cruel, degrading, and inhumane means of interrogation are illegal. The ruling states, in part, that "although a democracy must fight with one hand tied behind its back, it nonetheless has the upper hand. The rule of law and the liberty of an individual constitute important components in its understanding of security. At the end of the day, they strengthen its spirit and this strength allows it to overcome its difficulties."

I asked Ken Roth, executive director of Human Rights Watch, what the

---

3. *Washington Post*, January 2002.

effect on the ground had been after the decision. He replied that it had made a huge difference: that the use of torture by Israel since 1999 has been nothing like it had been before the ruling; not that there is no torture, but that it is enormously reduced.

These things I remember and my heart grows strong.

So what is the matter, the heart of the matter? Why haven't Americans, Jews or not, responded in full voice to the outrageous abuses and torture by our government? Is it just that it is all so far away, and we can barely manage to get through our days as it is? Or is it that we are ambivalent? The people being tortured are almost all Muslim prisoners, and as Jews and New Yorkers we have been given reason to fear Muslim terror.

Yet our fear is precisely why we must take extra precaution, remember the words of Israeli Chief Justice Barak, and maintain the democratic ideals that should keep this country and us Jews safer. Torture does not succeed in getting accurate information, and outrage against U.S. torture practices will only add fuel to terrorists' fire. Just as we are to know the heart of the stranger, so too we know what it is to see our tortured leaders made martyrs. Shall we watch as the United States becomes like ancient Rome, creating martyrs from "religious fanatics"? Shall we become like the Crusaders, or the Spanish Inquisitors?

> The inquisitors ordered Maria Lopez, a Jewish prisoner of the Spanish Inquisition, to be taken to the torture chamber and to be undressed and placed on the rack of torment and to be tied with some hemp ropes. She was . . . admonished by the . . . inquisitors to tell the truth: who were those persons whom she had seen commit those heretical crimes of which she is accused? . . . The order was made to pour water with a pitcher and to put something additional upon her face on top of the silk headdress that she had on her face. It was ordered for the ropes to be tightened with a tourniquet and it was tightened with two tourniquets. . . .[4]

A researcher named John Conroy found that studies of bystanders suggest that dehumanization tends to accompany feelings of powerlessness to help. Torture heralds the breakdown of empathy, in other words; we fail to see the one tortured as a human being. That is certainly true for

---

4. Renee Levine Melammed, *Heretics or Daughters of Israel: The Crypto-Jewish Women of Castile* (New York: Oxford University Press, 2001), pp. 136-37.

the torturer, who long ago stopped seeing the victim as human. Yet Conroy suggests that it is true for us, as well. We too see "torture victim" when we ought to see human being.

Seeing "torture victim" allows us to stop seeing, to turn away, to turn the page, to turn to the needs of everyday life. Yet on this day, when our task is to turn, to ask God to turn us, we cannot turn away. Part of our *teshuva,* our turn, on this Yom Kippur, must be to turn toward hope. Signing on to the Jewish Campaign Against Torture letter is a small step that will take a few minutes, as I said earlier. Yet the many small steps added together, even from just this one gathered community, will add weight to the understanding of human dignity, of Jewish memory, of empathy and compassion. Write to Senators McCain and Levin and others who are going to try to keep this issue alive even in the face of a presidential veto — or write to the president, write to the press.

But is there something we can do that comes first, something to remind us of humanity, of *k'vod ha-briot,* the dignity of a human being who was created in the image of God? What can we do to ensure that every time we see someone being degraded in a military prison camp, we see "human being"? What must we do to make that turn, that slight shift of mind that changes everything? The Hasidic teacher Zeev Wolf of Zhitomer taught that *teshuva* happens in an instant, and happens all the time. Let's us try to make those instant shifts every time we read the paper, every time we see a disturbing photograph, every time we hear about the kind of gruesome torture that makes us want to flinch and turn away instead. Let that shift to seeing "human being" be our *teshuva* on this Yom Kippur.

Akiva, flayed to the bone, understood the words of the Shema as he never had before. It gave him hope even in death, hope that he was fulfilling the desire of his God. Can we on this Yom Kippur find the hope to answer the call to love God with all our hearts, with all our souls, with all our strength, without having to be tortured? Can we find hope in the letters we sign, the calls we make, the shifts that will form our *teshuva?* The Senate is finally awake and public opinion may be following. There is room to hope for the results of our actions. Can we then muster enough memory and heart to respond to God's words, Akiva's words, with our actions? If God on this day is called by the name He told Moses — *El Rahum vHanun* — then we must rise to meet that challenge and ourselves be compassionate and loving, with all our hearts, all our souls, all our strength.

These things I remember as I pour out my heart.

CHAPTER 13

What We Pray For: Principles of Faith

Rabbis for Human Rights

We, members of Israeli Rabbis for Human Rights, affirm in our daily prayers and blessings that:

G-d and Human Beings

G-d is sovereign over the universe. All humankind is created in G-d's image and is an active partner with G-d in perfecting the world. (Shabbat 10a, 119b)

Abraham

When G-d chose our father Abraham, G-d promised,

> All the families of the earth shall bless themselves by you. (Gen. 12:2)

and that he would instruct his children and posterity to keep the way of the Lord by doing what is just and right (Gen. 18:19). As descendants of Abraham, we must fulfill his legacy of

> compassion, generosity, and sensitivity. (Yevamot 79b)

In accordance with our Torah tradition, the world will declare in admiration,

What great nation has laws and rules as just as all this Teaching that I set before you this day? (Deut. 4:8)

Torah

The essence of Torah, as summarized by Hillel:

What is hateful to you, do not do to others,

reflects the historic experience and ethical consciousness of the Jewish people. Both this historic experience and ethical consciousness must sensitize us to defend the right of all who dwell among us.

When a stranger resides with you in your land, you shall not wrong him. The stranger who resides with you shall be to you as one of your citizens: you shall love him as yourself, for you were strangers in the land of Egypt: I am the Lord your G-d. (Lev. 19:33-34)

Kiddush HaShem

Exemplary conduct of Israel is a sanctification of G-d's name (*Kiddush HaShem*): shameful conduct is a defamation of G-d's name (*Chilul HaShem*).

Preserving Life

G-d's name is sanctified through the respect we show for the human worth and dignity of all G-d's creatures.

Sanctity of Human Life

Our Mishnah teaches:

Therefore was Adam created single, to teach you that the destruction of any person's life is tantamount to destroying a whole world and the preservation of a single life is tantamount to preserving a whole world. (Sanhedrin 4:5)

And again in the words of Rabbi Akiva:

Beloved is Man who was created in (G-d's) image. (Pirkei Avot 3:18)

Our ideal state being when

We shall beat our swords into plowshares . . . (Isa. 2)

and with our concern for human dignity and the preservation of life, be they Jews or Arabs, we are deeply disturbed by and seek to remove excesses and abuses such as:

Expropriation of land;
Uprooting of trees;
Demolition of homes;
Torture through the use of "moderate physical or psychological pressure";
Coercion and torture to extract confession or to incriminate others;
Bullying and humiliating, which is demoralizing both to perpetrator and victim: and we wish to save our children from the temptation to these vices.
The exercise of double standards by, or the granting of relative immunity to those who wield political or military power and authority, in the pursuit of criminal proceedings in general, through delay, evasion, and protection;
Shooting to kill when life is not in immediate danger;
Collective punishment of "children for the sins of their parents" and "parents for the sins of their children";
Imprisonment without trial in administrative detention;
Removing the rights of residence through confiscation of identity cards;
Sale of weapons to aggressive regimes;
Undercover killings.

As Rabbis for Human Rights in Israel, we are committed to the principles stated in Israel's Declaration of Independence:

to foster the development of the country for the benefit of all the inhabitants, based on freedom, justice and peace as envisaged by the prophets of Israel: to ensure complete equality of social and political rights to all its inhabitants, irrespective of religion, race, and sex: to guarantee freedom of religion, conscience, language, education, and culture; to guard the holy places of all religions: and to be faithful to the principles of the Charter of the U.N.

We pray to bring nearer the day for the fulfillment of the prophecies

The remnant of Israel will not act iniquitously, nor speak falsely; neither shall there by found in their mouths the tongue of deceit. (Zeph. 3:13)

When nation will not lift up sword against nation, and no longer train for war. (Isa. 2)

Who is mighty? One who transforms one's enemy into one's friend. (Avot D'Rabbi Natan 23)

PART FOUR

MUSLIMS SPEAK OUT

Whoever kills a person [wrongfully], . . .
it is as though he had killed all humankind.
And whoever saves a life,
it is as though he had saved
all humankind.

Qur'an 5:32

CHAPTER 14

Stopping Oppression: An Islamic Obligation

Ingrid Mattson

> *A person should help his brother, whether he is an oppressor or is being oppressed. If he is the oppressor, he should prevent him from continuing his oppression, for that is helping him. If he is being oppressed, he should be helped to stop the oppression against him.*[1]

The terrorist attacks of September 11, 2001, have raised important questions about the role of Muslim leaders in shaping a responsible discourse of resistance to oppression and injustice. In this article, I will examine some of the issues that have been raised in this regard and will consider the question, what kind of leadership do Muslims need in the face of oppression? In particular, I will consider the role of American Muslims in the context of world events following the terrorist attacks of September 11. I will acknowledge that since Muslim leadership must be responsive to events, this question cannot be answered completely in isolation of specific circumstances. The appropriate response will necessarily depend on the nature of the threat. At the same time, I will stress that any truly appropriate response must be firmly rooted in faith. A faith-based response is one that recognizes the omniscience of God, and the limits of human un-

---

1. *Sahih Muslim: being traditions of the sayings and doings of the Prophet Muhammad as narrated by his companions and compiled under the title al-Jamiʿ-us-Sahih,* trans. and ed. ʾAbdul Hamid Siddiqi, 4 vols. (Beirut: Dar al-Arabia, n.d.), vol. 4, p. 1367.

derstanding. Faith urgently demands that we recognize the omnipotence of God, and the limits of human authority. Finally, faith demands that we acknowledge the absolute accountability of each individual before God, and that communal solidarity should never impede honest self-criticism, nor should it lead to injustice against other groups.

Within hours of the September 11 attacks, Muslim leaders worldwide, including the Chief Mufti of Saudi Arabia and the leaders of all major Islamic organizations in the United States, issued strong statements denouncing the attacks as sinful and illegal. In the weeks and months following the attacks, Muslim scholars and leaders wrote articles analyzing the Islamic legal basis for classifying these acts as terrorism or brigandry. War (jihad) is permitted in Islamic law, they explained, but only a legitimate head of state can conduct a war. They further argued that there are strict rules in Islamic law governing the conduct of warfare, for example, civilians cannot be targeted and property cannot be wantonly destroyed.[2] This was an entirely appropriate and correct response.

At the same time, many Muslim leaders have not felt comfortable with the American military response to the acts of terrorism, apprehensive that it will lead to further interventions in Muslim lands that will only increase the suffering of ordinary people. In addition, Muslims perceive that Israeli aggression against Palestinians continues without American sanction; indeed, enormous financial and military support for Israel has continued. It seems that any Palestinian resistance to Israeli occupation is termed "terrorism" and is responded to with overwhelming force. The result is the Palestinians themselves are increasingly showing less restraint in the force they employ to defend their families and lands.

How should American Muslims respond to this expansion of American military force, to this increase in Israeli action, and to the further radicalization of Muslim resistance in Palestine and elsewhere? In the heightened tension that has ensued since the terrorist attacks, many have argued that it has become more important than ever for American Muslims to act as ambassadors for America to the Muslim world, and as ambassadors for Islam to the American public. This is a natural role for American Muslims,

---

2. The articles, op-eds, press releases, and statements are so numerous that the best way to access them is through links collected on the Muslims Against Terrorism website: http://www.matusa.org. A brief overview of the statements made by major Muslim leaders was published in a full-page ad in the *New York Times* and other major American newspapers on October 17, 2001.

but it will have efficacy only if they are perceived as sincere advocates for, and honest critics of each community to which they belong.

To a great extent, the terrorist attack of September 11 exacerbated a double bind American Muslims have been feeling for some time now. It has seemed, so often in the past, that we have had to apologize for reprehensible actions committed by Muslims in the name of Islam. We would tell other Americans, "People who do these things — oppression of women, persecution of religious minorities, terrorism — have distorted the 'true' Islam." And so often we have had to tell other Muslims throughout the world that America is not as bad as it appears. We tell them, "These policies — support for oppressive governments, enforcement of sanctions against Iraq, lack of support for Palestinians — contradict the 'true' values of America." The line between apologetics and the desire to foster mutual understanding has not always been clear.

What is needed now from American Muslims, therefore, is to seriously heed the words of the Prophet Muhammad that if we really want to help our "brothers," not only must we support them against those who would harm them, but also we must stop them from committing oppression against others. The critical situation we find ourselves living in today is the result, to a great extent, of allowing injustice and oppression to continue unchecked. Muslims, for example, did not criticize the Taliban strongly enough for their oppression of many groups of people in Afghanistan, thinking that they should "support" the struggling rulers in a chaotic situation. The American government has not criticized sufficiently the brutality of the Israeli government, believing that it needs to be "supportive" of the Jewish state. The result is that oppression, left unchecked, can increase to immense proportions, until the oppressed are smothered with hopelessness and rage.

The first duty of Muslims in America, therefore, is to help shape American policies so they are in harmony with the essential values of this country. In the realm of foreign policy, this "idealistic" view has been out of fashion for some time. Indeed, the American Constitution, like foundational religious texts, can be read in many different ways. The true values of America are those which we decide to embrace as our own. There is no guarantee, therefore, that Americans will rise to the challenge of defining themselves as an ethical nation; nevertheless, given the success of domestic struggles for human dignity and rights in the twentieth century, we can be hopeful.

At the same time, on the pragmatic level, there are strong arguments for the benefits of upholding international law and fostering human rights in foreign relations. As Robert Crane, president of the Washington-based Islamic Institute for Strategic Studies, has argued, it is truly in the best interest of the United States to act according to a consistent moral standard in international relations.[3] The United States has learned a hard lesson that international cooperation is essential to fighting terrorism. Other nations will be more willing to cooperate with us on this issue if we compromise on issues important to them, even if we can achieve short-term gains pushing our own agenda. The best strategy for achieving national security needs to be reconsidered in an age of transnational terrorism and narcotic networks, and proliferating nuclear, chemical, and biological weapons.

If Muslim Americans are to participate in such a critique of American policy, however, they will only be effective if they do it, according to the Prophet's words, in a "brotherly" fashion. This implies a high degree of loyalty and affection. This does not mean, however, that citizenship and religious community are identical commitments, nor that they demand the same kind of loyalty. People of faith have a certain kind of solidarity with others of their faith community that transcends the basic rights and duties of citizenship. But most faith groups, including Islam, obligate believers to honor their covenants and contracts, including those that entail obtaining permission to enter a country as a visitor or becoming a citizen. Islam further obligates the believer to provide for his neighbors and make them feel secure, without regard to their religious status or identity. The Prophet Muhammad said, "None of you believes who eats while his neighbor goes to bed hungry," and he said, "None of you believes whose neighbor does not feel secure from (your) harm." It is therefore a religious obligation for Muslims in America to promote what is in the best interest of the American people, in terms of their security and basic needs. Muslim Americans cannot be a special interest group concerned only with the rights of Muslims in America and abroad.

At the same time, Muslims in America urgently need to address injustice when it is committed in the name of Islam. The most difficult part of fulfilling this responsibility is to achieve recognition, by other Muslims, that one is speaking about Islam with some authority. After all, Islam is not self-explanatory; it is a religious tradition that needs to be interpreted and

---

3. Robert Crane, "A Wake-up call for America and Muslims World-Wide," *Islam21* (September 2001). Available online at http://www.islam21.net/pages/keyissues/key7-2.htm.

claimed. As a practicing Muslim, I believe that there is a core of fundamental beliefs and practices that distinguish authentic Islam from deviations. I also believe that apart from this essential core, the task of interpreting the application of Islamic norms to human society is an enormously complicated task, which inevitably leads to a broad range of opinion and practice. I agree with "Sunni" Muslims, the majority of the Muslim community worldwide, that after the death of the Prophet Muhammad, no one has the right to claim infallibility in the interpretation of sacred law. At the same time, this does not mean that all opinions are equal, nor that everyone has the ability to interpret law. Without the intense study of Islamic texts and traditions under qualified scholars and without the presence of a stable Muslim community through which one can witness the wisdom of the living tradition, the chances of an ordinary believer arriving at a correct judgment about most legal issues are slim. This is one of the reasons why revolutionary leaders who arise in periods of great instability often are accused of having superficial knowledge of sacred texts, and little knowledge of the actual application of law, despite being apparently sincere in their desire to relieve people of oppression.

It is also the case that it is often exceedingly difficult to sustain a self-critical attitude within revolutionary movements. When external threats are immense, dysfunction within a community is usually given little attention. This difficulty is apparent in any nation that faces a challenge to its security. Even many Americans have little patience for complaints about violations of immigrants' rights, racial profiling, or transgressions of internationally recognized rights of war captives in the wake of September 11. The international Muslim community, feeling under siege for centuries since the beginning of European colonial rule, has similarly had great difficulty sustaining a self-critical attitude. Bold, charismatic revolutionary leaders have won the hearts of the people because they have given some hope for success against oppression. The inability of such leaders to address internal dysfunction has seemed less important for many people.

A number of scholars have pointed out that the revolutionary discourse of many modern Muslim leaders has most in common with the ideologies of resistance employed by Third World national liberation and self-determination movements. Khaled Abou El Fadl writes that

> modern nationalistic thought exercised a greater influence on the resistance ideologies of Muslim and Arab national liberation movements

than anything in the Islamic tradition. The Islamic tradition was reconstructed to fit Third World nationalistic ideologies of anti-colonialism and anti-imperialism rather than the other way around.[4]

Before colonialism, authority was acquired by religious leaders in a much more subtle process, and religious leaders who advocated extreme hostility or aggression against the state were usually marginalized. After all, most Muslims did not want to be led into revolution, they simply wanted their lives to be better. In general, the most successful religious leaders were those who, in addition to serving the spiritual needs of the community, were able to moderate how state power was exercised on ordinary people, and in some sense, acted as intermediaries between the people and state. However, at those times when forces hostile to the practice of Islam attacked or occupied Muslim lands, for example, during the Mongol invasions, (Christian) Crusades, European colonialism, and the Soviet invasion of Afghanistan, meaningful mediation was often impossible. At such times, the people needed revolutionary leaders; leaders who were not able to stand against occupying forces were marginalized, and their opinions were considered lacking in authority. Many historically Muslim lands have undergone unending turmoil since the beginning of European colonialism. Continued occupation and imperialism by foreign powers has allowed revolutionary discourse to take firm root in much of the Muslim world. Oppressive circumstances have disabled many Muslims, making them blind to the effectiveness of peaceful avenues of change, and deaf to the arguments of generations of Muslim scholars that revolt and lawlessness usually cause more harm to society than even government corruption. At the same time, when corruption is severe, when people are suffering continually under an oppressive government, a scholar who remains silent will lose all authority with the majority of people.

This is the reason why it is so difficult to find authentic, authoritative Muslim voices advocating peaceful resistance to oppression. Religious leaders who speak out in a peaceful way against injustice will remain marginalized if their speech has no effect. The majority of Muslims simply will not recognize such people as religious leaders. At the same time, in many parts of the world, even those who speak out against corruption in a

---

4. Khaled Abou El Fadl, "Islam and the Theology of Power," *Middle East Report* 221 (Winter 2001).

peaceful manner are jailed, tortured and killed.[5] Anwar Ibrahim, former Minister of Finance of Malaysia, for example, is widely believed to have been the victim of a state conspiracy in 1998 to prevent him from publicizing proof of widespread government corruption linked to the President of Malaysia. After the September 11 attacks, he published an article in which he linked the growth of extremism to such repression by the state, arguing that bin Laden and his protégés are the children of desperation; they come from countries where political struggle through peaceful means is futile. In many Muslim countries, political dissent is simply illegal. Yet, year-by-year, the size of the educated class and the number of young professionals continue to increase. These people need space to express their political and social concerns. But state control is total, leaving no room for civil society to grow.[6]

In such circumstances, very few people — only those who are willing to risk losing everything: their property, their families, their security, and their lives — will continue to speak out. Such individuals rarely limit their attempts to change state behavior through speech, because they have seen it to be ineffective. Indeed, in such circumstances, "extremism" might seem to be the only rational choice, because extreme actions are the only actions that seem to have an effect.

In this context, Muslim Americans need to deeply consider what kind of leadership they can and should exercise in the Muslim world. First of all, it is clear that we need to be lovingly self-critical of our own flaws, and of the errors committed by fellow Muslims, even those in difficult circumstances. We cannot allow unsubstantiated suspicions, vague accusations of conspiracies, and exaggerated protests of attempts to ensure security to be used as excuses for violating the rights of women, non-Muslims, and others. According to the words of the Prophet Muhammad, we are truly helping our fellow Muslims when we insist that they cease their injustice and oppression of others. During the Prophet's own life, despite persistent external attacks on the Muslim community, the Prophet did not shy from addressing injustice committed by individual Muslims. Indeed, by helping his companions leave their old culturally-acquired practices of brutality,

---

5. His story is told in *Renaissance Man: Dato Seri Anwar Ibrahim, Former Deputy Prime Minister of Malaysia*, UASR Regional Report Series 3 (Springfield, Va.: UASR Publishing Group Inc., 2001).

6. *Time*, Asian edition, October 15, 2001.

he helped them develop a communal solidarity that was the key to the security of the state.

At the same time, by focusing on the absolute primacy of an individual's relationship with God, the Prophet gave the early Muslims a measure of success that was not dependent on political achievement. Soumayya, the first martyr in Islam, a slave-woman who was killed by her polytheistic owner, was "successful" because she recognized only God as her true master. The Prophet Muhammad was unable to stop Soumayya from being oppressed and killed, because he had not yet been successful in establishing a state ruled by law; indeed, his own security was tenuous. All he could say to Soumayya and her husband Yassir as they were being killed was, "Patience, family of Yassir, for verily Paradise is yours."

Certainly Muslim Americans must, in the first place, pray for their oppressed brothers and sisters, and assure them that God will reward them if they suffer innocently. But what if such people react to their oppression with their own brutality? We need to examine the argument that oppressed people must use only nonviolent means of resistance, or confine military action to what is permitted by the law of war, even when such limited methods appear to be totally ineffective in stopping oppression. Is it possible that usual standards of morality in warfare and conflict must be ignored when it appears that great suffering cannot be stopped if resistance and retaliation is limited by these norms? This argument has been made many times in periods of crisis, leading the United States, for example, to drop atomic bombs on Japan, knowingly killing thousands of innocent civilians in the most horrible fashion.

Some Muslim leaders, using the same logic, have argued that standard Islamic limits on the means employed in warfare must be set aside if the brutal oppression of ordinary Muslims is to be stopped. They argue that in the Palestinian case, for example, some leaders have argued that peaceful means have not led to a lessening of Israeli oppression. During fifty years of diplomacy at the United Nations, they cite the numerous resolutions that have been passed in support of Palestinian statehood and in condemnation of Israeli oppression, but which the U.N. has been unable, or unwilling, to enforce. Millions of Palestinians continue to live in squalid refugee camps, and in daily humiliation and insecurity under Israeli rule. Faced with this reality, they suggest the Palestinians have no choice but to use any means to destabilize Israeli society, to force the Israelis to back off out of a desire to protect their own interests and true security for their citizens.

I believe this argument is flawed because it confuses the need to understand what might compel a desperate person to commit indiscriminate acts of violence and the need to provide strategies, which can be justified by faith, that might relieve such a person from suffering. Before we consider such strategies, however, we must seriously consider the deep suffering experienced by those who suffer persistent abuse and humiliation. We should not be surprised that extremely oppressive circumstances might lead an individual to disregard any moral code. To illustrate this point, we might want to consider this statement, make by a man who fled from American slavery to safety in Canada in the early nineteenth century:

> The abuse a man receives at the South is enough to drive every thing good from the mind. I sometimes felt such a spirit of vengeance, that I seriously meditated setting the house on fire at night, and killing all as they came out. I overcame the evil, and never got at it — but a little more punishment would have done it. I had been so bruised and wounded and beset, that I was out of patience. I had been separated from all my relatives, from every friend I had in the world, whipped and ironed till I was tired of it. On that night when I was threatened with the paddle again, I was fully determined to kill, even if I were to be hanged and, if it pleased God, sent to hell: I could bear no more.[7]

Reading such a statement from an Islamic perspective, it occurs to me that certainly one could say that such an act of violence, as well as other acts of terrorism, might lead a person to hell. It is also possible that God will forgive even such grave sins. But what if another individual, appalled, for example, at the treatment of this slave, unable to compel the abusive master to free him, encouraged him to commit this act of violence? What would be the weight of sin on such a person? At the same time, would it not be wrong for such a person to simply condemn as a grave sinner the desperate slave who has lashed out not only at his oppressor, but has inflicted violence on all those around his oppressor?

If we return once more to the example of the Prophet Muhammad for guidance, we see that he used a variety of techniques to relieve the suffer-

---

7. Benjamin Drew, *The Refugee, or the Narratives of Fugitive Slaves in Canada related by Themselves with An Account of the History and Condition of the Colored Population of Upper Canada* (Toronto: Prospero, 2000), p. 220.

ing of the unjustly oppressed, depending on his ability to help them. For the early martyrs, all he could do was pray for them and reassure them. Once he was recognized as a prophet by the people of Medina, he was able to do much more. Still, it has been argued convincingly by a number of scholars that political power was relatively decentralized during the time of the Prophet, and he often could use only moral persuasion and shaming to stop certain individuals from committing oppression.[8] Thus, Abu Masud al-Ansari, one of the early Muslims from Medina, related,

> I used to beat a young slave of mine until once I heard a voice behind me saying, "Know, Abu Masud, that God is more powerful over you than you are over him." I turned and lo and behold it was the Messenger of God. So I said, "He is free, Messenger of God, for the face of God." The Prophet said to me, "If you had not done so, hell-fire would have covered you."[9]

In other reports about the Prophet, we see him directly ordering a person to free a slave he has struck in anger.[10] In these cases, perhaps, the Prophet had the political authority to enforce such an order.

What we learn from the Prophet's example is that Muslims are required to help the oppressed within the limits of authority they possess. Thus, Muslims in America must demonstrate their empathy with their oppressed brethren through prayer and encouragement. They must use their legal rights to free speech to publicize the oppressors and shame them. They must work for a just political order, and in particular, encourage their government to make universal human rights a priority in foreign policy.

Americans, Muslims and non-Muslims, are not neutral outsiders to the conflicts in Muslim lands that have come to threaten our security. The United States government has a long history of negative interventions in the Middle East. Muslim Americans, too, have supported resistance movements with words and, in some cases, with money. What is of primary importance is that we ensure that our "help" does not in fact increase oppression and injustice.

8. W. Montgomery Watt, *Muhammad at Medina* (New York: Oxford University Press, 1956), pp. 228-38.

9. *Sahih Muslim*, vol. 3, pp. 883-84.

10. *Sahih Muslim*, vol. 3, p. 883.

During the Soviet occupation of Afghanistan, the United States gave support to a resistance movement that desperately needed to succeed. Nevertheless, not enough care was paid to the way this support could increase internal oppression among the Afghan people. In my own small way, I learned this lesson too. In 1988, I was working in an Afghan refugee camp in northern Pakistan. Part of my job was to register women for monthly widows' benefits. One day, a woman who had received her payment the day before walked into our office with a black eye. She told us that her brother-in-law had tried to take her money, and, when she refused, beat her. When we investigated further, we discovered that in some areas, corrupt tribal leaders were seizing all the widows' benefits and using the money to increase their power to oppress others. What this taught me is that one can do a little good to relieve the suffering of others, or one can do a great deal of harm.

We pray that Americans, Muslims and non-Muslims, will have the wisdom to know what is good, and the courage to stand up to oppression, whatever form it takes.

CHAPTER 15

Of Torture and Abuse

Taha Jabir Alalwani

Dignity is a distinguishing characteristic of the human being, bestowed upon him by God. The dignity of a human being is the essence of his humanity. Dr. Alalwani here answers questions submitted to him about violations against human dignity, particularly about torture and abuse, from a specifically Islamic perspective.

Q. How does Islam view torture?

A. Allah the Almighty has honored human beings and made them vicegerents on earth, so that they are responsible for conveying his revelation. Allah has put all of us through a test in life to see which of us is best in action. The dignity of a human being is the essence of his humanity; it is like a brain to the body. If the dignity of human being is humiliated, his humanity is de facto debased. Therefore, if we find a human being, a regime, or a party torturing someone, especially if that person is a prisoner or a captive, it means that the torturer's "animal qualities" have dominated his human characteristics. That is why he has oppressed his human brother, who could have been in his shoes in order to torture him — and it might happen one day.

Torture has been practiced by people since old times, during the struggle between the truth and falsehood, since Adam (peace be upon him). As we know, Islam commenced with Adam and ended with Muhammad (peace and blessings be upon him). All prophets of Allah, including Abraham (Ibrahim), Noah (Nuh), Isaac (Is-haq), Moses (Musa), Jesus ('Isa), and Muhammad (peace and blessings be upon them all), preached the same message — Islam. This resembles a program of study wherein each "prophet" gave a course and all courses have been re-edited and published in one book revealed to Muhammad (peace and blessings be upon him).

We know that the two sons of Adam (peace and blessings be upon him) disputed with each other, as one of them was righteous while the other was deviant. When each of them offered a sacrifice to Allah, it was accepted from the righteous, while it was not accepted from the other. The deviant brother threatened his brother with death, and then executed him, while the righteous brother said, "Surely I wish that you should bear the sin committed against me and your own sin, and so you would be of the inhabitants of the Fire, and this is the recompense of the unjust" (Al-Ma'idah 5:29).

Torture has been used by those who want to enslave human beings.

Therefore, torture is a battle between truth and falsehood, Islam and disbelief. It has been used by those who want to enslave human beings to make them bow down to them; and when the latter refuse to surrender, the former resort to acts of humiliation and torture in order to debase their victims' human dignity.

Islam considers all human beings to be part of one family. If those torturers had realized that they are torturing their human brothers and sisters, they would never have thought of committing such a heinous act.

Islam came when oppression and tyranny were rampant among people. Yet Islam elevated the status of human beings and established justice on earth, which is the most important value after belief in Allah.

So all these acts, committed from the time of Adam until the present time, are signs of the ignorance and injustice from which people are suffering. Torturing captives and prisoners is a sign of the lack of moral values, justice, and human dignity.

Q. Is it justified in Islam to torture a prisoner or an accused person for the purpose of getting information?

A. This act is totally contradictory to justice; it is unacceptable, by all means. To force an accused person or a prisoner to admit to something is not permitted in Islam, nor is it acceptable from a human point of view. Such an act is only accepted by people of no faith, by oppressors and tyrants who want to convert people into slaves. All faiths condemn this act.

The history of Islam shows that the Prophet (peace and blessings be upon him) used to tell the criminals who came to him voluntarily, admitting their crimes, to repent and seek forgiveness from Allah.

Torturing prisoners and accused persons at the time of investigation in an attempt to make the accused testify against himself is a flagrant violation of human dignity. Therefore, it is the duty of the judge to refuse all information obtained under duress and force.

Q. What is Islam's position on international human rights? Can the Islamic perspective contribute to working against torturing and prisoner abuse that is widespread in many Muslim countries, including your country of origin, Iraq?

A. Islam is a holy and sacred religion that cannot be viewed through the wrong practices of some of its followers.

I think that all Muslims today are required to work in the field of human rights and to promote any effort in this regard. Muslims have lost many of their human rights and much of their dignity, especially in many Arab and Muslim countries. Therefore, we need to work together to restore some of these denied rights.

We should work with all human rights organizations, even those that don't proceed from a religious point of view. The Prophet (peace and blessings be upon him) used to say: "I witnessed a peace treaty conducted in the house of 'Abdullah Ibn Jud'an such that even if I were invited to a similar alliance or treaty in Islam, I would have welcomed the idea." So we need to promote any organization that works in the field of human rights.

Q. How do we interpret violations carried out by Muslim leaders if we say that the Islamic perspective of human rights is superior to the Western one?

A. Islam is a religion and a mission, and people implement it in different degrees. While some people apply Islam in an excellent manner, others misrepresent Islam. In no case should we blame Islam for the mistakes of its followers. Islam is a holy and sacred religion that cannot be viewed through the wrong practices of some of its followers.

Q. Does Islam allow Muslims to behead civilians and prisoners of war?

A. As a matter of principle, Islam forbids targeting civilians and those who don't contribute to the war. A Muslim fighter can only target those who attack him and wage war against his country.

As for civilians or those who oppose the war, it is unacceptable to kill them under any circumstances. That is why the Prophet (peace and blessings be upon him), and Muslim caliphs after him, used to advise the leaders of the Muslim army in all battles not to kill monks, civilians, or whoever surrenders and decides to leave off the battle. This is because fighting, in the perspective of Islam, is like a surgery sought only as the last resort. Allah commanded us to establish peace unhesitatingly: "O you who believe! Enter into peace wholeheartedly" (Al-Baqarah 2:208). Therefore, fighting is an exceptional case; if it happens, it has to be limited to the warring parties.

Killing captives is unjustifiable in the perspective of Islam, except in case of retaliation or responding to the same tactic the enemy is using. If there is a war between Muslims and non-Muslims and the non-Muslim army kills Muslim captives systematically — only in this case it is allowed that captives be killed in return, in conformity with Allah's saying, "Whoever then acts aggressively against you, inflict injury on him according to the injury he has inflicted on you, and be careful (of your duty) to Allah and know that Allah is with those who guard (against evil)" (Al-Baqarah 2:194).

Q. What is your analysis of the American and international response to the abuse of Iraqi prisoners as shown by many news agencies?

A. People have a common human mind and a common heritage that was established by many factors, at the top of which is religion. That produced certain common values among people, which enabled them to distinguish good from bad, to promote what is good and condemn what is bad. There can be no doubt that those who abused the Iraqi detainees, and ordered this to happen, or approved of it, have already lost all these basic values.

If the Americans or the world condemned these attacks, it is because of those common values we mentioned, and not because of racial superiority; otherwise they would have never allowed such atrocities to happen or even occupied the country in the first place.

The Qur'an sanctions the removal of dictatorship and tyranny and the

177

restoration of rights, dignity, and freedom to the oppressed. However, it is unreasonable to claim that you came to protect the rights of the oppressed and remove dictatorship and establish justice in the land while you practice a similar form of oppression, whatever the reasons or motives behind it might be. Therefore, this condemnation of prisoner abuse is attributed to those common human values among people and not because of a racial superiority.

Q. What is the best thing for me as a Muslim to do about the photographs from Abu Ghraib?

A. The best thing you can do now is to build awareness among the people worldwide. It is important to tell the entire world that this act is unacceptable, awful, and outrageous. All human beings must stand together in rejection of this kind of torture, and work more closely to stop any similar action in any corner of the earth.

I think the pictures help people to understand what really happened, and how urgently they are required to take immediate action. Such pictures disturb the people more than anything else would do.

Q. In view of the recent events in Iraq, why is it un-Islamic to kill the captives while the Americans are doing much worse?

A. A few months ago we at the Graduate School of Islamic and Social Sciences in Virginia organized a conference that was attended by many scholars: Jews, Christians, and Muslims, some of whom were experts in religious wars throughout history. In this conference, there was unanimity concerning the fact that all wars waged nowadays, especially those between the "superpowers" and other countries, whatever the reason behind this war — are all illegitimate and unacceptable, except those launched in self-defense. This is because for a war to be legitimate there are lots of conditions that must be met, and these are missing in the wars of today. Also, the politicians and rulers who lead their country to wars are often motivated by a "hidden agenda," which is not declared. Moreover, the weapons used in these wars do not discriminate between combatants and civilians, children or the aged, and so on.

Conversely, Islam has taught us that no one can be targeted in the war except those who set out with the intention to fight. To kill children, women, and old people that do not fight, even to the point of destroying infrastructure, cutting down trees, or demolishing houses — all these acts are condemned by all religions.

Q. As there is no free press in Islamic countries, how do we know what's happening in their jails? What would you call the murder of a Canadian journalist in an Iranian jail? Not torture?

A. No, I affirm that this act is unacceptable regardless of to whom it is attributed. Whether done by Muslims or non-Muslims, in a Muslim country or in a non-Muslim one, any act that infringes on human dignity is unacceptable, and we must do whatever we can to stop it.

Q. If Islam condemns torturing civilians and prisoners, then why do the human rights organizations focus on the Arab and Muslim countries in tracking or recording the violation records of human rights?

A. Torture techniques have been practiced by many countries, including the U.S. and Great Britain, but the problem is that people always fear to criticize the strong countries, but once a weak country violates any of the human rights they are always attacked. I am not here to defend the Arab countries, but I must say that the U.S. has now become an expert in "promoting" tyrants, oppressors, and unjust rulers, who add to the suffering of the *Ummah,* the Muslim community, and the loss of Arab and Muslim dignity.

Q. The world witnessed a flagrant violation of human rights at the time of the Iranian Revolution in regards to Sunnis in Iran, and also by the Americans in Iraq. How do we interpret these violations if we say that the Islamic perspective of human rights is far superior to the Western one?

A. I didn't like to identify any particular country. Islam is a religion and a mission, and people implement it in different degrees. While some people apply Islam in an excellent manner, others misrepresent Islam. In no case should we blame Islam for the mistakes of its followers. As I have said, Islam is a holy and sacred religion that cannot be viewed through the wrong practice of some of its followers.

Q. What do you think is the best action that we have to do as Muslims against these events in Iraq?

A. I think the best thing is to raise awareness among the American people, to show them the lies that were told to them: WMD, nuclear weapons, linkage to al-Qaeda, and so forth. All these lies have to be explained and shown to them, because the American people have been misled. Next to this, we need to take an active and more effective role, by demanding accountability for any persons guilty of prisoner abuse. We should protest and write to all government departments: the state department, our local police station, etc.

CHAPTER 16

A Call for Dialogue: A Sermon

Yahya Hendi

If one were to believe the morning news and the pictures of the recent events in the Middle East, one would have to conclude that we are at the dawn of a clash of religions and civilizations.

The three Middle Eastern and monotheistic religions have been used to advocate hate, when they can be used to advocate love and coexistence. We can make a historic decision to succeed in our dialogue efforts — if not internationally, at least here in our beautiful country.

Judaism, Christianity, and Islam each claim the same historical legacy within the prophetic tradition, although each may interpret specific historical and prophetic events differently. While each of the three religions has dogma unique to itself, the core is essentially similar.

In Judaism, the word "shalom" is derived from the word *shalem,* which means "complete," or "perfection"; therefore, peace in Judaism means perfection and completion. This perfection involves three levels of relationships: between man and himself, between man and his fellow man, and between the nation of Israel and all other nations.

In Christianity, one would consider how Jesus manifested unconditional love for all people. He gave himself to save sinners. He called his disciples to love their enemies, to rely only on faith. Above all, Jesus called on one to judge oneself before judging others and to criticize oneself before criticizing others.

The very word "Islam," from the Arabic *silm,* includes peace, according to a tradition of the Prophet Muhammad. Peace is one of the prerequisites of Islam. Islam states that a Muslim is one from whose tongue and hand all people are safe. One of the attributes of God described in the Qur'an is As-salaam, that is, peace and security. When war breaks out, the Qur'an teaches that peace and reconciliation are the best of all actions.

One would have to conclude that peace, reconciliation, and dialogue are an expression of faith. Peace-building and reconciliation are values we all have to commit ourselves to and encourage, because reality demands them and because our religious traditions require them.

It is true that ignorance, religious extremism, terrorism, and fears generated from past encounters have widened the gap between us and created a sense of mistrust and rejection. The Arab-Israeli conflict and its consequences, the tragic attacks of September 11, 2001, the implications of the War in Iraq, and irresponsible statements by politicians and religious leaders have led us to the path of bitterness and alienation.

There is another path we can model, the path of love, reconciliation, and dialogue, which streams from our religious commitment to a God of love.

Yet, the fruits of religious convictions and our love of God are not achieved in a vacuum. They are achieved and found in the context of human relationships. Indeed, we cannot understand love except as we see it striving on behalf of all its enemies.

All of us, Americans in general and committed Jews, Christians, and Muslims in particular, must find within our own traditions sound reasons to value other faiths without compromising our own. We should not tolerate voices of divisiveness. We must use 9/11 to explore the best in each of us. So let us all choose to be united with all of our differences for the best of this nation and all of humanity.

The major burden, however, falls on all religious communities. Our communities, guided by wise leadership, need to overcome longstanding prejudices and resentments. Each tradition has sacred teachings that can be enlisted to build bridges of respect and reconciliation. Wise religious leadership consists of identifying those teachings and educating all peoples in that spirit.

Let today's events inspire us to find a common forum with a common action for the common good of all. Let dialogue become a part of our culture.

CHAPTER 17

Fatwa Against Religious Extremism

Fiqh Council of North America

December 7, 2007

The Fiqh Council of North America wishes to reaffirm Islam's condemnation of terrorism and religious extremism.

Islam strictly condemns religious extremism and the use of violence against innocent lives. There is no justification in Islam for extremism or terrorism. Targeting civilians' life and property through suicide bombings or any other method of attack is *haram* — prohibited in Islam — and those who commit these barbaric acts are criminals, not "martyrs."

The Qur'an, Islam's revealed text, states: "Whoever kills a person, unless it be for murder or for spreading mischief in the land, it is as though he had killed all mankind. And whoever saves a person, it is as though he had saved all mankind" (Qur'an 5:32).

Prophet Muhammad said there is no excuse for committing unjust acts: "Do not be people without minds of your own, saying that if others treat you well you will treat them well, and that if they do wrong you will do wrong to them. Instead, accustom yourselves to do good if people do good and not to do wrong [even] if they do evil" (Al-Tirmidhi).

God mandates moderation in faith and in all aspects of life when He states in the Qur'an: "We made you to be a community of the middle way, so that [with the example of your lives] you might bear witness to the truth before all mankind" (Qur'an 2:143).

In another verse, God explains our duties as human beings when he says: "Let there arise from among you a band of people who invite to righteousness, and enjoin good and forbid evil" (Qur'an 3:104).

Islam teaches us to act in a caring manner to all of God's creation. The Prophet Muhammad, who is described in the Qur'an as "a mercy to the worlds," said: "All creation is the family of God, and the person most beloved by God [is the one] who is kind and caring toward His family."

In the light of the teachings of the Qur'an and Sunnah we clearly and strongly state:

1. All acts of terrorism targeting the civilians are *haram* (forbidden) in Islam.
2. It is *haram* for a Muslim to cooperate or associate with any individual or group that is involved in any act of terrorism or violence.
3. It is the duty of Muslims to cooperate with the law enforcement authorities to protect the lives of all civilians.

We issue this fatwa following the guidance of our scripture the Qur'an and the teachings of our Prophet Muhammad — peace be upon him. We urge all people to resolve all conflicts in just and peaceful manners. We have deep concern for the suffering and pain of millions of Muslims in different parts of the world. We deplore those who cause death and destruction to them. However, we urge Muslims to not lose their moral grounds. God's help is with those who follow the right path.

We pray for the defeat of extremism, terrorism and injustice. We pray for the safety and security of our country the United States and its people. We pray for the safety and security of all inhabitants of this globe. We pray that interfaith harmony and cooperation prevail both in the United States and everywhere in the world.

CHAPTER 18

Universal Islamic Declaration
of Human Rights (1981)

Islamic Council of London

This is a declaration for mankind, a guidance and instruction to those who fear God. (Qur'an Al-Imran 3:138)

Foreword

Islam gave to mankind an ideal code of human rights fourteen centuries ago. These rights aim at conferring honor and dignity on mankind and eliminating exploitation, oppression, and injustice.

Human rights in Islam are firmly rooted in the belief that God, and God alone, is the Law Giver and the Source of all human rights. Due to their divine origin, no ruler, government, assembly, or authority can curtail or violate in any way the human rights conferred by God, nor can these rights be surrendered.

Human rights in Islam are an integral part of the overall Islamic order and it is obligatory on all Muslim governments and organs of society to implement them in letter and in spirit within the framework of that order.

It is unfortunate that human rights are being trampled upon with impunity in many countries of the world, including some Muslim countries. Such violations are a matter of serious concern and are arousing the consciences of more and more people throughout the world.

We sincerely hope that this Declaration of Human Rights will give a powerful impetus to the Muslim peoples to stand firm and defend resolutely and courageously the rights conferred on them by God.

This Declaration of Human Rights is the second fundamental document proclaimed by the Islamic Council to mark the beginning of the fifteenth century of the Islamic era, the first being the Universal Islamic Declaration announced at the International Conference on the Prophet Muhammad (peace and blessings be upon him) and his Message, held in London from 12 to 15 April, 1980.

The Universal Islamic Declaration of Human Rights is based on the Qur'an and the Sunnah and has been compiled by eminent Muslim scholars, jurists, and representatives of Islamic movements and thought. May God reward them all for their efforts and guide us along the right path.

> O men! Behold, We have created you all out of a male and a female, and have made you into nations and tribes, so that you might come to know one another. Verily, the noblest of you in the sight of God is the one who is most deeply conscious of Him. Behold, God is all-knowing, all aware. (Qur'an, Al-Hujurat 49:13)

Preamble

WHEREAS the age-old human aspiration for a just world order wherein people could live, develop, and prosper in an environment free from fear, oppression, exploitation, and deprivation remains largely unfulfilled;

WHEREAS the Divine Mercy unto mankind reflected in its having been endowed with superabundant economic sustenance is being wasted, or unfairly or unjustly withheld from the inhabitants of the earth;

WHEREAS Allah (God) has given mankind through His revelations in the Holy Qur'an and the Sunnah of His Blessed Prophet Muhammad an abiding legal and moral framework within which to establish and regulate human institutions and relationships;

WHEREAS the human rights decreed by the Divine Law aim at conferring dignity and honor on mankind and are designed to eliminate oppression and injustice;

WHEREAS by virtue of their divine source and sanction these rights can neither be curtailed, abrogated, or disregarded by authorities, assemblies, or other institutions, nor can they be surrendered or alienated;

Therefore we, as Muslims, who believe

a) in God, the Beneficent and Merciful, the Creator, the Sustainer, the Sovereign, the sole Guide of mankind and the Source of all Law;

b) in the Vicegerency *(Khilafah)* of man who has been created to fulfill the will of God on earth;

c) in the wisdom of divine guidance brought by the prophets, whose mission found its culmination in the final divine message that was conveyed by the Prophet Muhammad (peace be upon him) to all mankind;

d) that rationality by itself without the light of revelation from God can neither be a sure guide in the affairs of mankind nor provide spiritual nourishment to the human soul, and, knowing that the teachings of Islam represent the quintessence of divine guidance in its final and perfect form, feel duty-bound to remind man of the high status and dignity bestowed on him by God;

e) in inviting all mankind to the message of Islam;

f) that by the terms of our primeval covenant with God our duties and obligations have priority over our rights, and that each one of us is under a bounden duty to spread the teachings of Islam by word, deed, and indeed in all gentle ways, and to make them effective not only in our individual lives but also in the society around us;

g) in our obligation to establish an Islamic order

i) wherein all human beings shall be equal and none shall enjoy a privilege or suffer a disadvantage or discrimination by reason of race, color, sex, origin or language;

ii) wherein all human beings are born free;

iii) wherein slavery and forced labor are abhorred;

iv) wherein conditions shall be established such that the institution of family shall be preserved, protected and honored as the basis of all social life;

v) wherein the rulers and the ruled alike are subject to, and equal before, the Law;

vi) wherein obedience shall be rendered only to those commands that are in consonance with the Law;

vii) wherein all worldly power shall be considered as a sacred trust, to be exercised within the limits prescribed by the Law and in a manner approved by it, and with due regard for the priorities fixed by it;

viii) wherein all economic resources shall be treated as divine blessings bestowed upon mankind, to be enjoyed by all in accordance with the rules and the values set out in the Qur'an and the Sunnah;

ix) wherein all public affairs shall be determined and conducted, and the authority to administer them shall be exercised after mutual consultation *(Shura)* between the believers qualified to contribute to a decision which would accord well with the Law and the public good;

x) wherein everyone shall undertake obligations proportionate to his capacity and shall be held responsible pro rata for his deeds;

xi) wherein everyone shall, in case of an infringement of his rights, be assured of appropriate remedial measures in accordance with the Law;

xii) wherein no one shall be deprived of the rights assured to him by the Law except by its authority and to the extent permitted by it;

xiii) wherein every individual shall have the right to bring legal action against anyone who commits a crime against society as a whole or against any of its members;

xiv) wherein every effort shall be made to

(a) secure unto mankind deliverance from every type of exploitation, injustice and oppression,

(b) ensure to everyone security, dignity and liberty in terms set out and by methods approved and within the limits set by the Law;

Do hereby, as servants of Allah and as members of the Universal Brotherhood of Islam, at the beginning of the Fifteenth Century of the Islamic Era, affirm our commitment to uphold the following inviolable and inalienable human rights that we consider are enjoined by Islam.

I. Right to Life

    a) Human life is sacred and inviolable and every effort shall be made to protect it. In particular no one shall be exposed to injury or death, except under the authority of the Law.

    b) Just as in life, so also after death, the sanctity of a person's body shall be inviolable. It is the obligation of believers to see that a deceased person's body is handled with due solemnity.

II. Right to Freedom

    a) Man is born free. No inroads shall be made on his right to liberty except under the authority and in due process of the Law.

    b) Every individual and every people has the inalienable right to freedom in all its forms — physical, cultural, economic, and political — and shall be entitled to struggle by all available means against any infringement or abrogation of this right; and every oppressed individual or people has a legitimate claim to the support of other individuals and/or peoples in such a struggle.

III. Right to Equality and Prohibition Against Impermissible Discrimination

    a) All persons are equal before the Law and are entitled to equal opportunities and protection of the Law.

    b) All persons shall be entitled to equal wage for equal work.

    c) No person shall be denied the opportunity to work or be discriminated against in any manner or exposed to greater physical risk by reason of religious belief, color, race, origin, sex, or language.

IV. Right to Justice

    a) Every person has the right to be treated in accordance with the Law, and only in accordance with the Law.

    b) Every person has not only the right but also the obligation to protest against injustice; to recourse to remedies provided by the Law in respect of any unwarranted personal injury or loss; to self-defense against any charges that are preferred against him and to obtain fair adjudication before an independent judicial tribunal in any dispute with public authorities or any other person.

c) It is the right and duty of every person to defend the rights of any other person and the community in general (*Hisbah*).

d) No person shall be discriminated against while seeking to defend private and public rights.

e) It is the right and duty of every Muslim to refuse to obey any command which is contrary to the Law, no matter by whom it may be issued.

V. Right to Fair Trial

a) No person shall be adjudged guilty of an offense and made liable to punishment except after proof of his guilt before an independent judicial tribunal.

b) No person shall be adjudged guilty except after a fair trial and after reasonable opportunity for defense has been provided to him.

c) Punishment shall be awarded in accordance with the Law, in proportion to the seriousness of the offense and with due consideration of the circumstances under which it was committed.

d) No act shall be considered a crime unless it is stipulated as such in the clear wording of the Law.

e) Every individual is responsible for his actions. Responsibility for a crime cannot be vicariously extended to other members of his family or group, who are not otherwise directly or indirectly involved in the commission of the crime in question.

VI. Right to Protection Against Abuse of Power

Every person has the right to protection against harassment by official agencies. He is not liable to account for himself except for making a defense to the charges made against him or where he is found in a situation wherein a question regarding suspicion of his involvement in a crime could be reasonably raised.

VII. Right to Protection Against Torture

No person shall be subjected to torture in mind or body, or degraded, or threatened with injury either to himself or to anyone related to or held dear by him, or forcibly made to confess to the commission of a crime, or forced to consent to an act which is injurious to his interests.

VIII. Right to Protection of Honor and Reputation

Every person has the right to protect his honor and reputation against calumnies, groundless charges, or deliberate attempts at defamation and blackmail.

IX. Right to Asylum

a) Every persecuted or oppressed person has the right to seek refuge and asylum. This right is guaranteed to every human being irrespective of race, religion, color, and sex.

b) Al Masjid Al Haram (the sacred house of Allah) in Mecca is a sanctuary for all Muslims.

X. Rights of Minorities

a) The Qur'anic principle "There is no compulsion in religion" shall govern the religious rights of non-Muslim minorities.

b) In a Muslim country religious minorities shall have the choice to be governed in respect of their civil and personal matters by Islamic Law, or by their own laws.

XI. Right and Obligation to Participate in the Conduct and Management of Public Affairs

  a) Subject to the Law, every individual in the community *(Ummah)* is entitled to assume public office.
  b) Process of free consultation *(Shura)* is the basis of the administrative relationship between the government and the people. People also have the right to choose and remove their rulers in accordance with this principle.

XII. Right to Freedom of Belief, Thought, and Speech

  a) Every person has the right to express his thoughts and beliefs so long as he remains within the limits prescribed by the Law. No one, however, is entitled to disseminate falsehood or to circulate reports which may outrage public decency, or to indulge in slander, innuendo, or to cast defamatory aspersions on other persons.
  b) Pursuit of knowledge and search after truth is not only a right but a duty of every Muslim.
  c) It is the right and duty of every Muslim to protest and strive (within the limits set out by the Law) against oppression even if it involves challenging the highest authority in the state.
  d) There shall be no bar on the dissemination of information provided it does not endanger the security of the society or the state and is confined within the limits imposed by the Law.
  e) No one shall hold in contempt or ridicule the religious beliefs of others or incite public hostility against them; respect for the religious feelings of others is obligatory on all Muslims.

XIII. Right to Freedom of Religion

Every person has the right to freedom of conscience and worship in accordance with his religious beliefs.

XIV. Right to Free Association

a) Every person is entitled to participate individually and collectively in the religious, social, cultural, and political life of his community and to establish institutions and agencies meant to enjoin what is right (*ma'roof*) and to prevent what is wrong *(munkar)*.

b) Every person is entitled to strive for the establishment of institutions whereunder an enjoyment of these rights would be made possible. Collectively, the community is obliged to establish conditions so as to allow its members full development of their personalities.

XV. The Economic Order and the Rights Evolving Therefrom

a) In their economic pursuits, all persons are entitled to the full benefits of nature and all its resources. These are blessings bestowed by God for the benefit of mankind as a whole.

b) All human beings are entitled to earn their living according to the Law.

c) Every person is entitled to own property individually or in association with others. State ownership of certain economic resources in the public interest is legitimate.

d) The poor have the right to a prescribed share in the wealth of the rich, as fixed by *Zakah*, levied and collected in accordance with the Law.

e) All means of production shall be utilized in the interest of the community *(Ummah)* as a whole, and may not be neglected or misused.

f) In order to promote the development of a balanced economy and to protect society from exploitation, Islamic Law forbids monopolies, unreasonably restrictive trade practices, usury, the use of coercion in the making of contracts and the publication of misleading advertisements.

g) All economic activities are permitted provided they are not detrimental to the interests of the community *(Ummah)* and do not violate Islamic Laws and values.

XVI. Right to Protection of Property

No property may be expropriated except in the public interest and on payment of fair and adequate compensation.

XVII. Status and Dignity of Workers

Islam honors work and the worker and enjoins Muslims not only to treat the worker justly but also generously. He is not only to be paid his earned wages promptly, but is also entitled to adequate rest and leisure.

XVIII. Right to Social Security

Every person has the right to food, shelter, clothing, education, and medical care consistent with the resources of the community. This obligation of the community extends in particular to all individuals who cannot take care of themselves due to some temporary or permanent disability.

XIX. Right to Found a Family and Related Matters

a) Every person is entitled to marry, to found a family, and to bring up children in conformity with his religion, traditions, and culture. Every spouse is entitled to such rights and privileges and carries such obligations as are stipulated by the Law.

b) Each of the partners in a marriage is entitled to respect and consideration from the other.

c) Every husband is obligated to maintain his wife and children according to his means.

d) Every child has the right to be maintained and properly brought up by its parents, it being forbidden that children are made to work at an early age or that any burden is put on them which would arrest or harm their natural development.

e) If parents are for some reason unable to discharge their obligations towards a child it becomes the responsibility of the community to fulfill these obligations at public expense.

f) Every person is entitled to material support, as well as care and protection, from his family during his childhood, old age, or incapacity. Parents are entitled to material support as well as care and protection from their children.

g) Motherhood is entitled to special respect, care, and assistance on the part of the family and the public organs of the community *(Ummah)*.

h) Within the family, men and women are to share in their obligations and responsibilities according to their sex, their natural endowments, talents, and inclinations, bearing in mind their common responsibilities toward their progeny and their relatives.

i) No person may be married against his or her will, or lose or suffer diminution of legal personality on account of marriage.

XX. Rights of Married Women

Every married woman is entitled to:

a) live in the house in which her husband lives;

b) receive the means necessary for maintaining a standard of living which is not inferior to that of her spouse, and, in the event of divorce, receive during the statutory period of waiting *(iddah)* means of maintenance commensurate with her husband's resources, for herself as well as for the children she nurses or keeps, irrespective of her own financial status, earnings, or property that she may hold in her own rights;

c) seek and obtain dissolution of marriage *(Khul'a)* in accordance with the terms of the Law. This right is in addition to her right to seek divorce through the courts.

d) inherit from her husband, her parents, her children, and other relatives according to the Law;

e) strict confidentiality from her spouse, or ex-spouse if divorced, with regard to any information that he may have obtained about her, the disclosure of which could prove detrimental to her interests. A similar responsibility rests upon her in respect of her spouse or ex-spouse.

XXI. Right to Education

    a) Every person is entitled to receive education in accordance with his natural capabilities.

    b) Every person is entitled to a free choice of profession and career and to the opportunity for the full development of his natural endowments.

XXII. Right of Privacy

Every person is entitled to the protection of his privacy.

XXIII. Right to Freedom of Movement and Residence

    a) In view of the fact that the World of Islam is veritably *Ummah Islamia,* every Muslim shall have the right to freely move in and out of any Muslim country.

    b) No one shall be forced to leave the country of his residence, or be arbitrarily deported therefrom without recourse to due process of Law.

Explanatory Notes

1. In the above formulation of human rights, unless the context provides otherwise:

    a) the term "person" refers to both the male and female sexes.

    b) the term "Law" denotes the *Shari'ah,* i.e., the totality of ordinances derived from the Qur'an and the Sunnah and any other Laws that are deduced from these two sources by methods considered valid in Islamic jurisprudence.

2. Each one of the human rights enunciated in this declaration carries a corresponding duty.

3. In the exercise and enjoyment of the rights referred to above every person shall be subject only to such limitations as are enjoined by the Law for the purpose of securing the due recognition of, and respect for, the rights and the freedom of others and of meeting the just requirements of morality, public order and the general welfare of the community *(Ummah)*.

The Arabic text of this Declaration is the original.

Glossary of Arabic Terms

Hisbah   Public vigilance, an institution of the Islamic State enjoined to observe and facilitate the fulfillment of right norms of public behavior. It consists in public vigilance as well as an opportunity to private individuals to seek redress through it.

'Iddah   The waiting period of a widowed or divorced woman during which she is not to remarry.

Khalifah   The vicegerency of man on earth, or succession to the Prophet, transliterated into English as the caliphate.

Khul'a   Divorce a woman obtains at her own request.

Ma'roof   Good act.

Munkar   Reprehensible deed.

Shari'ah   Islamic Law.

Sunnah   The example or way of life of the Prophet (peace be upon him), embracing what he said, did, or agreed to.

Ummah Islamia   World Muslim community.

Zakah   The "purifying" tax on wealth, one of the five pillars of Islam obligatory on Muslims.

References

Note: The Roman numerals refer to the topics in the text. The Arabic numerals refer to the Chapter and the Verse of the Qur'an, i.e., 5:32 means Chapter 5, Verse 32.

I.

1. Qur'an Al-Maidah 5:32
2. Hadith narrated by Muslim, Abu Daud, Tirmidhi, Nasai
3. Hadith narrated by Bukhari

II.

4. Hadith narrated by Bukhari, Muslim
5. Sayings of Caliph Umar
6. Qur'an As-Shura 42:41
7. Qur'an Al-Hajj 22:41

III.

8. From the Prophet's address
9. Hadith narrated by Bukhari, Muslim, Abu Daud, Tirmidhi, Nasai
10. From the address of Caliph Abu Bakr
11. From the Prophet's farewell address
12. Qur'an Al-Ahqaf 46:19
13. Hadith narrated by Ahmad
14. Qur'an Al-Mulk 67:15
15. Qur'an Al-Zalzalah 99:7-8

IV.

16. Qur'an An-Nisa 4:59
17. Qur'an Al-Maidah 5:49
18. Qur'an An-Nisa 4:148
19. Hadith narrated by Bukhari, Muslim, Tirmidhi
20. Hadith narrated by Bukhari, Muslim
21. Hadith narrated by Muslim, Abu Daud, Tirmdhi, Nasai
22. Hadith narrated by Bukhari, Muslim, Abu Daud, Tirmidhi, Nasai
23. Hadith narrated by Abu Daud, Tirmidhi
24. Hadith narrated by Bukhari, Muslim, Abu Daud, Tirmidhi, Nasai
25. Hadith narrated by Bukhari

V.

26. Hadith narrated by Bukhari, Muslim
27. Qur'an Al-Isra 17:15
28. Qur'an Al-Ahzab 33:5
29. Qur'an Al-Hujurat 49:6

30. Qur'an An-Najm 53:28
31. Qur'an Al Baqarah 2:229
32. Hadith narrated by Al Baihaki, Hakim
33. Qur'an Al-Isra 17:15
34. Qur'an At-Tur 52:21
35. Qur'an Yusuf 12:79

VI.

36. Qur'an Al Ahzab 33:58

VII.

37. Hadith narrated by Bukhari, Muslim, Abu Daud, Tirmidhi, Nasai
38. Hadith narrated by Ibn Majah

VIII.

39. From the Prophet's farewell address
40. Qur'an Al-Hujurat 49:12
41. Qur'an Al-Hujurat 49:11

IX.

42. Qur'an At-Tawba 9:6
43. Qur'an Al-Imran 3:97
44. Qur'an Al-Baqarah 2:125
45. Qur'an Al-Hajj 22:25

X.

46. Qur'an Al Baqarah 2:256
47. Qur'an Al-Maidah 5:42
48. Qur'an Al-Maidah 5:43
49. Qur'an Al-Maidah 5:47

XI.

50. Qur'an As-Shura 42:38
51. Hadith narrated by Ahmad
52. From the address of Caliph Abu Bakr

XII.

53. Qur'an Al-Ahzab 33:60-61
54. Qur'an Saba 34:46

55. Hadith narrated by Tirmidhi, Nasai
56. Qur'an An-Nisa 4:83
57. Qur'an Al-Anam 6:108

XIII.
58. Qur'an Al Kafirun 109:6

XIV.
59. Qur'an Yusuf 12:108
60. Qur'an Al-Imran 3:104
61. Qur'an Al-Maidah 5:2
62. Hadith narrated by Abu Daud, Tirmidhi, Nasai, Ibn Majah

XV.
63. Qur'an Al-Maidah 5:120
64. Qur'an Al-Jathiyah 45:13
65. Qur'an Ash-Shuara 26:183
66. Qur'an Al-Isra 17:20
67. Qur'an Hud 11:6
68. Qur'an Al-Mulk 67:15
69. Qur'an An-Najm 53:48
70. Qur'an Al-Hashr 59:9
71. Qur'an Al-Maarij 70:24-25
72. Sayings of Caliph Abu Bakr
73. Hadith narrated by Bukhari, Muslim
74. Hadith narrated by Muslim
75. Hadith narrated by Muslim, Abu Daud, Tirmidhi, Nasai
76. Hadith narrated by Bukhari, Muslim, Abu Daud, Tirmidhi, Nasai
77. Qur'an Al-Mutaffifin 83:1-3
78. Hadith narrated by Muslim
79. Qur'an Al-Baqarah 2:275
80. Hadith narrated by Bukhari, Muslim, Abu Daud, Tirmidhi, Nasai

XVI.
81. Qur'an Al Baqarah 2:188
82. Hadith narrated by Bukhari
83. Hadith narrated by Muslim
84. Hadith narrated by Muslim, Tirmidhi

XVII.

85. Qur'an At-Tawbah 9:105
86. Hadith narrated by Abu Yala 3/4 Majma Al Zawaid
87. Hadith narrated by Ibn Majah
88. Qur'an Al-Ahqaf 46:19
89. Qur'an At-Tawbah 9:105
90. Hadith narrated by Tabarani 3/4 Majma Al Zawaid
91. Hadith narrated by Bukhari

XVIII.

92. Qur'an Al-Ahzab 33:6

XIX.

93. Qur'an An-Nisa 4:1
94. Qur'an Al-Baqarah 2:228
95. Hadith narrated by Bukhari, Muslim, Abu Daud, Tirmidhi, Nasai
96. Qur'an Ar-Rum 30:21
97. Qur'an At-Talaq 65:7
98. Qur'an Al-Isra 17:24
99. Hadith narrated by Bukhari, Muslim, Abu Daud, Tirmidhi
100. Hadith narrated by Abu Daud
101. Hadith narrated by Bukhari, Muslim
102. Hadith narrated by Abu Daud, Tirmidhi
103. Hadith narrated by Ahmad, Abu Daud

XX.

104. Qur'an At-Talaq 65:6
105. Qur'an An-Nisa 4:34
106. Qur'an At-Talaq 65:6
107. Qur'an At-Talaq 65:6
108. Qur'an Al-Baqarah 2:229
109. Qur'an An-Nisa 4:12
110. Qur'an Al-Baqarah 2:237

XXI.

111. Qur'an Al-Isra 17:23-24
112. Hadith narrated by Ibn Majah
113. Qur'an Al-Imran 3:187

114. From the Prophet's farewell address
115. Hadith narrated by Bukhari, Muslim
116. Hadith narrated by Bukhari, Muslim, Abu Daud, Tirmidhi

XXII.
117. Hadith narrated by Muslim
118. Qur'an Al-Hujurat 49:12
119. Hadith narrated by Abu Daud, Tirmidhi

XXIII.
120. Qur'an Al-Mulk 67:15
121. Qur'an Al-Anam 6:11
122. Qur'an An-Nisa 4:97
123. Qur'an Al-Baqarah 2:217
124. Qur'an Al-Hashr 59:9

PART FIVE

TOWARD A SOLUTION

*Never underestimate the power of a small group
of dedicated people to change the world.
Indeed, it's the only thing that ever has.*

Margaret Mead

CHAPTER 19

Islam and Human Rights Today

Ann Elizabeth Mayer

Islam and Human Rights — Changing Subjects and Evolving Perspectives

Hoping to convert my advancing years into an asset, I offer a perspective on the mutability of the Islam and human rights nexus that exploits the long period during which I have explored the topic. For over two decades I have observed the relationship of Islam and human rights evolving, this coinciding with a period during which both Islam and human rights were themselves accommodating new strains and adjusting to fresh challenges. In the following, I offer assessments of the dynamics that affect this relationship and discuss some actual situations that have prompted adjustments or that will likely promote future evolution.

In addition to the Islam and human rights nexus evolving, over the last decades scholarly attitudes towards examinations of this relationship have also undergone a sea change. These days the pairing "Islam and human rights" and the comparisons that such pairing inspires seem to strike people as normal. In contrast, two decades ago I found that any mention that I was working on that relationship tended to be greeted with scowling objections to such an incongruous pairing or accusations that I had lapsed into "Western hegemonic discourse."

A human rights framework, so the conventional wisdom had it, could not and should not be applied when the subject was Islam. Behind such objections lay some stereotyping. In the main, Islam was viewed as a self-contained entity that was impervious to external influences, having its own unique system of authority dating back to seventh-century Arabia, with sources elaborated according to a distinctive internal logic. International human rights law was viewed as being located a world away, being tied to a United Nations system that was inaugurated in San Francisco in 1945. This system was seen as being closely tied to the Western heritage and dominated by Western nations. The scholarship that would later remind the world of the constructive contributions that Muslims had made to the creation of international human rights law had yet to appear.[1]

I grew interested in learning more about how Muslims thought about human rights during research trips in 1984 and 1985 to Sudan, where a brutal and arbitrary Islamization program was underway. I was exposed to the phenomenon of Muslims engaging in intense wrangling over how their religious heritage related to human rights.

As my Sudanese experience taught me, many Muslims who were committed to their faith were ready to use human rights as the appropriate criteria for critiquing governmental Islamization measures. They differentiated what they regarded as the authentic teachings of Islam from newly enacted Islamic laws sponsored by undemocratic regimes that wielded Islam as a tool of politics and as part of their quest for legitimation. Muslims supportive of human rights confronted other Muslims who were ready to applaud any efforts to implement Islamic law — including those made by dictatorial regimes — regardless of the suffering or inequities that applying such laws in seriously flawed legal systems might entail. The latter denounced as apostates Muslims who critiqued Islamization measures using what were supposedly Western human rights standards.

After my return to the United States, I tried to explain to skeptics that there was good reason for investigating a topic regarding which Muslims were deeply divided. I argued that the reasons for these disagreements merited study, urging that we needed to identify how stances on human rights correlated with the proponents' own interests and their positions on the contemporary political spectrum — mostly to encounter incredulous and even hostile reactions. Among other things, most of my interlocutors in the West insisted that Islam was inherently opposed to the values ex-

---

1. See the significant study published in 2004, Susan E. Waltz, "Universal Human Rights: The Contribution of Muslim States," *Human Rights Quarterly* 799 (November 2004): 26.

pressed in human rights. They were confident that human rights embodied quintessentially Western ideas that could not be exported to or successfully implanted in the landscape of the Muslim Middle East and North Africa, the parts of the Muslim world on which I conduct research. "You obviously need to learn about cultural relativism" was a common, scornful rejoinder when I mentioned my research.

I am very conscious of a dramatic expansion of the study of Islam and human rights, because when I started writing on this topic in the mid 1980s, useful source material was scant. In that era, I was delighted when assiduous research succeeded in locating the occasional pertinent document or a rare cogent analysis. In contrast, in 2005 when I worked on updating the fourth edition of my book *Islam and Human Rights: Tradition and Politics,*[2] a major problem was trying to sort through the staggering volume of relevant material to select the small percentage that my page limits would allow me to include. A topic that had been an orphan only two decades previous had become a preoccupation — not only among people living in Muslim societies, but also among the academics churning out the burgeoning scholarly literature in Europe and North America. A belated consciousness of Islam and human rights as encompassing a relationship eminently deserving of examination has led to the spawning of innumerable articles, books, websites, conferences, institutes, university courses, official pronouncements, and other activities, all testifying to how widely its importance has become recognized.

Problematic Stereotyping of the United States and Islam

At the same time that the field has progressed, I have noticed how often discussions of the Islam and human rights nexus remain affected by the misconception that human rights are grounded in values endorsed by the United States. Some confusion may be accounted for by the regularity with which the U.S. government publicly touts its commitment to human rights and lambastes other nations for what it claims are their shortcomings. However, the international human rights system is certainly not a creature of the United States. Instead, investigation reveals a longstanding U.S. es-

2. Ann Elizabeth Mayer, *Islam and Human Rights: Tradition and Politics,* 4th ed. (Boulder: University of Colorado Press, 2007).

trangement from international human rights law, both in terms of the U.S. refusal to be bound by international conventions and in terms of U.S. practice, which increasingly evinces a proclivity to flout international human rights law even where fundamental principles like the ban on torture are involved.[3]

Disregarding this reality, people frequently cling to the image of a natural polarization in which the West, led by the United States, espouses human rights, creating conflicts with Muslim societies, which reject human rights. The hypostatized Islamic hostility to human rights is often portrayed in ways that reflect the cultural stereotyping perpetrated by Samuel P. Huntington in his notorious article on the clash of civilizations.[4] Although this article has been roundly criticized, many in the West embrace Huntington's depiction of a monolithic Islamic culture being besieged by demands that it conform to an antipathetic Western cultural model that affronts Muslims' values.

On the other side, Huntington's Muslim counterparts have made analogous arguments, appealing to an Islamic cultural particularism that, it is claimed, makes Muslims reject "Western" international human rights models and excuses Muslim countries' noncompliance with human rights. For example, in a recent book Mashood Baderin espouses this thesis, demanding that allowances be made for Muslim countries' noncompliance with international human rights law on the basis that international law is infected with "a strict and exclusive Western perspective."[5]

The impression that Islam is inherently incompatible with human rights has been encouraged by the reservations that many Muslim coun-

---

3. Regarding recent developments confirming the U.S. failure to respect international human rights law, see the statement of Kenneth Roth, executive director of Human Rights Watch, who in the introduction to the Human Rights Watch's "World Report 2007" asserted that in the previous five years the United States had forfeited its credibility in the human rights domain and called for the European Union to take up the task of human rights advocacy. See Human Rights Watch, "World Report 2007," available online at http://www.hrw.org/wr2k7/essays/introduction/index.htm. For general background on the U.S. resistance to international law and to international human rights law see Harold Hongju Koh, "On American Exceptionalism," *Stanford Law Review* 1479 (2003): 55; Louis Henkin, "U.S. Ratification of Human Rights Conventions: The Ghost of Senator Bricker," *American Journal of International Law* 341 (1995): 89.

4. Samuel Huntington, "The Clash of Civilizations?" *Foreign Affairs* 22 (1993): 42.

5. See Mashood A. Baderin, *International Human Rights and Islamic Law* (Oxford: Oxford University Press, 2003), p. 27.

tries have continued to enter when they ratify human rights conventions. These reservations invoke supposedly unchangeable Islamic rules that are said to bar accepting any human rights that contravene them.[6]

Recourse to Islamic culture, conceived of as a bulwark against noxious "Western" freedoms, can provide a convenient rationale for governments' reluctance to comply with international human rights law. The idea that Islam should be classified as a religion that rejects the values of the U.N. human rights system has been fostered by some governments as well as some individual Muslims. But, this is only one part of a more complex picture.

In the 1980s, when I started critiquing such efforts to concoct Islamic alternatives to international human rights, I was often heatedly denounced for what was characterized as my cultural insensitivity; I was accused of using external criteria to pass judgment on a phenomenon that was presumed to be legitimate in Islamic terms. Now I can point to initiatives that come from the region that reject the legitimacy of invoking a supposed Islamic particularism to justify stripping Muslims of human rights. One example is the Beirut Declaration on the Regional Protection of Human Rights, which was produced in June 2003. This declaration issued from a conference organized by the Cairo Institute for Human Rights Studies with the participation of regional and international NGOs and various legal, academic, and media experts. More representative of Muslim opinion than are principles imposed by Iran's theocrats or the Saudi royal family, the declaration unequivocally denounces the kind of tactics utilized in documents like the Cairo Declaration. Principle 3 stipulates:

> Civilization or religious particularities should not be used as a pretext to cast doubt and to question the universality of human rights. The "particularities" that deserve celebration are those which make a citizen have a sense of dignity, equality, and enrich his/her culture and life, and promote his/her participation in their [*sic*] own country's public affairs. Assuring the tolerant principles of Islam and religions in general should not be put in a false contradiction to human rights principles. The conference [rejects the authority] of aged interpretations of Islam that distort Islam and insult Muslims and lead to violations of human rights, particularly when excluding women and not allowing freedom of thought, belief, creative art, literature and scientific research.[6]

6. Beirut Declaration on the Regional Protection of Human Rights Towards an Effec-

That is, the declaration called for drawing a clear distinction between Islam and what amounts to the political use of a supposed Islamic cultural particularism to justify discrimination and oppression.

Pressures for Rethinking Islam and International Human Rights Law

Those positing an essential incompatibility of Islam and human rights consistently tend to reify Islam, treating its doctrines as set in concrete. In reality, human understandings of the complex and enormously rich Islamic heritage are varied, fluid, and responsive to political developments. Opponents of change tend to overlook or deliberately disregard the lively contention that is going on within Muslim communities regarding controversial contemporary issues like human rights, with some Muslims at the conservative end of the spectrum denouncing human rights as part of a nefarious Western plot to undermine Islam and to corrupt Muslim societies and other Muslims at the opposite end of the spectrum comfortably embracing human rights as reaffirming the values that they cherish in their own heritage and affording remedies for the ills besetting their societies.

The versions of Islamic doctrine that reject human rights constitute only one part of a larger pattern of resistance to fresh modes of thinking about Islam that are already threatening to undermine old verities and entrenched hierarchies. Any signs of evolution distress reactionary ideologues and Muslims committed to the rules set forth in medieval jurisprudence. Debates over Islamic doctrines pertaining to human rights are thus linked to a broader contemporary phenomenon, in which many Muslims are reconceiving their religion and are daring to critique ossified jurisprudential methodologies and narrow mindsets. Muslims of varied backgrounds, who include philosophers, jurists, political scientists, sociologists, and human rights activists, are speaking up to demand a role in articulating Islamic precepts. Learned jurists have in effect forfeited the monopoly of authority that they exercised in the old days, when they alone explicated Islamic requirements.

---

tive Regional Protection of Human Rights, "Which Arab Charter on Human Rights?" available online at http://www.cihrs.org/prog_Activity_en.aspx?prog_id=8&prog_name=Other%20Activities.

It is in this context that the battle over Muslim women's quest for equality goes on, touching on one of the most sensitive areas in the debates about Islam and human rights. A relatively small movement until the 1990s, Islamic feminism has gained momentum, doing much to advance the idea that human rights complement the original vision of Islam, a vision that was subsequently corrupted and distorted by biased male interpreters.

Not only do Islamic feminists criticize what they see as patriarchal biases infecting traditional interpretations of the Islamic sources pertaining to women, but by issuing their bold proposals for rethinking the Islamic heritage, they have created shockwaves that have destabilized sclerotic modes of analysis more generally, opening doors to fresh approaches to the Islamic sources. Both men and women have made significant contributions to Islamic feminism, but contributions by women stand out as having special revolutionary potential. Aided by expanded access to the Internet, exegeses informed by gender consciousness are being widely disseminated, facilitating the exploration of Islam's potential to be conceived of as a religion supportive of women's equality.

At the same time that fresh intellectual currents are reshaping Muslims' understandings of their religion, we see that human rights concepts are evolving, as a comparison of the skeletal 1948 Universal Declaration of Human Rights with the vast panoply of subsequently developed instruments reveals. Including matters as wide-ranging as child labor; the International Criminal Court; water rights; economic, social, and cultural rights; the responsibilities of transnational corporations; and cultural diversity, these instruments cover problems that people in Muslim societies must care about and where they will see the benefits of overarching international standards.

Regardless of whether one is Muslim or non-Muslim, one can appreciate that the human rights policies and initiatives that the world requires to cope with urgent problems of this magnitude must reflect a sound global vision, one that does not admit of separate strategies with particularistic biases. That is, the dire predicament of humankind is making it essential to buttress the universality of human rights and to rebut arguments in favor of opting out — whether on a national, regional, or cultural basis, irrespective of whether excuses for opting out are being put forward by the United States or by governments of Muslim countries. Critical global problems that militate in favor of expanding the purview of international law may prompt many to rethink their former support for an Islamic particularism that erects a "cultural" wall between Muslims and international human rights law.

Muslims' assessments of the merits of opting out of international human rights law may also be affected by the way that the United States has been pursuing what it calls the "War on Terror." The U.S. government often acts in this war as if its expansively-defined national security needs justify overriding international law in general and international human rights law in particular. Due to the way that Washington officialdom links Islam with terrorism, all Muslims are exposed to being treated as sub-humans and presumed terrorists.

Conversely, Muslims can appreciate the vigor with which serious advocates of international human rights law have denounced the way that Muslims have been targeted and victimized. It should make an impression that the world's most important human rights NGO, Amnesty International, is now headed by Irene Khan, a Muslim woman from Bangladesh. Khan has infuriated the Bush Administration and its apologists with her outspoken condemnations of the U.S. violations of international human rights law perpetrated in the course of the War on Terror and has courted vituperative attacks from those quarters for daring to call the Guantánamo Bay detention camp "the gulag of our time."

An insightful article by the late Joan Fitzpatrick assesses the potential of the U.S. War on Terror to undermine human rights — often with particularly harsh consequences for Muslims, who find themselves especially vulnerable to abuse. Her article proposes that developments in the wake of the attacks on September 11, 2001, portend changes in international norms, including the increased legitimacy of preemptive defensive action, which would comprise actions of the kind exemplified by the U.S. attack on Iraq, an attack that was claimed to be a defensive response to a threat posed by Iraq's possession of weapons of mass destruction.

In her article Fitzpatrick also foresees counterterrorism producing new rules that could displace human rights law and international criminal law; the weakening of standards regarding arbitrary detention and the right to fair trials; and the undermining of bans on discrimination in connection with the targeting of non-citizens, Muslims, and Arabs as likely subversives or terrorists. In institutional terms, she views the pursuit of the War on Terror as being likely to add more fuel to the U.S. campaign against the International Criminal Court, as promoting the growing tendency to assert a U.S. exceptionalism, and as sharply reducing official U.S. criticisms of rights violations perpetrated by governments of Muslim countries in exchange for their cooperation in fighting terrorism.[7]

Those wedded to the notion that Islam bars compliance with "Western" international human rights law will need to think hard about the implications of insisting on Islamic exceptionalism at a juncture when the United States is essentially trying to rewrite international human rights law, creating new standards that aim to strip Muslims of many of its fundamental protections on the basis of this same sort of exceptionalism.[8] Muslims should question the benefits of adopting a stance that effectively makes them allies of a U.S. project that dismisses Muslims' claims to possess human rights on a par with other human beings. This situation might move some Muslims to mobilize in support of international human rights law — before it is irretrievably compromised.

Thus, the way people think about Islam and human rights continues to evolve at a juncture when around the world we observe many of the props of our familiar status quo eroding, raising the question for both religious thinkers and international lawyers about what constitute the appropriate principles for coping with our rapidly changing environment. This means that the nexus between the two cannot be expected to attain a stable equilibrium but will have to be renegotiated as understandings of Islam and human rights continue their metamorphosis. Many of these negotiations will take place at the level of governments of states that operate under the auspices of the U.N. system. They also will also take place within Muslim communities around the globe, as well as in the arena of scholarship.

Perceptions of U.S. Policies and Their Implications

Leaving Iran aside and surveying Muslim societies more generally, one realizes that changed circumstances could make the familiar preoccupation with the tensions between Islam and human rights in the area of civil and political rights eventually seem passé. Many factors are encouraging a

7. Joan Fitzpatrick, "Speaking Law to Power: The War Against Terrorism and Human Rights," *European Journal of International Law* 241 (2003): 28.

8. A stimulating assessment of how post-September 11 dynamics affect perspectives on human rights controversies is afforded in Shadi Mokhtari, "Human Rights in the Post-September 11th Era: Between Hegemony and Emancipation," *Muslim World Journal of Human Rights* 1, no. 1 (2006): 3.

reorientation towards what humankind needs to survive. The fact that U.S. policy on issues of economic and social rights is so at variance with the international human rights principles in this area may actually help disabuse people of the notion that human rights are tied to U.S. values.

Among the issues that are likely to preoccupy the world over the next years is the global water crisis — involving problems like grievous water shortages and gross disparities in access to safe drinking water.[9] Increasingly, the idea is catching on that the human right to water — a right that no one bothered to enumerate back in 1948 — might be one of the most crucial human rights, as well as being a right that must be addressed on a global basis for the world to find a viable solution to the water crisis. Showing how human rights law constantly evolves, a proposed new convention dealing with the human right to water is currently under discussion. Since most Muslim countries suffer from acute water deficits, which are predicted to worsen over the next decades, a new preoccupation with water as a human right may diminish interest in arguments regarding a supposed Islamic religious or cultural particularism that stands in the way of human rights.

Meanwhile, the United States has been promoting the notion that water resources should be privatized, treating water not as a human right but like any other commodity in the marketplace that can be controlled and marketed by transnational corporations. At the same time, the United States is insisting that human rights law does not apply to corporations.[10] Muslim countries may soon unite with a broader coalition of countries from the Global South that want to fight against projects to privatize water.[11] Instead of Muslim countries being placed on the defensive with regard to human rights, it may be the United States that will be pilloried for

9. A multi-agency United Nations report examines the world water crisis, surveying its causes and proposed solutions. See World Water Assessment Programme, UNESCO, "The U.N. World Water Development Report: Water for People, Water for Life" (2003), available online at http://www.unesco.org/water/wwap/wwdr/table_contents.shtml.

10. See "Statement by the U.S. Delegation to the 61st U.N. Commission on Human Rights," April 20, 2005, especially Item 17: Transnational Corporations, available online at http://geneva.usmission.gov/humanrights/2005/0420Item17TNC.htm.

11. Regarding the drive to privatize water and the resistance to this see Maude Barlow and Tony Clarke, *Blue Gold: The Fight to Stop the Corporate Theft of the World's Water* (New York: The New Press, 2002). On how water privatization clashes with human rights, see Jennifer Naegele, "What Is Wrong with Full-Fledged Water Privatization?" *Journal of Law & Social Challenges* 99 (2004): 6.

defying an emerging global consensus on the need to treat water as human right.

Water issues could help Muslims to realize new affinities for human rights, but other factors could aggravate Muslims' suspicions of human rights, such as the Bush Administration's interventions in the Middle East. These mean that U.S. human rights rhetoric keeps being associated with attempts to sugarcoat neo-imperialist projects that many Muslims claim have the goal of weakening Islam in order to dismantle resistance to U.S. domination. In this connection, the heavy-handed U.S. efforts to reduce the role of Islamic law in the post-invasion Iraqi constitution are likely to provoke a backlash.

After the 2003 invasion, U.S. officials, especially those in the United States Commission on International Religious Freedom (USCIRF), publicly pressed the urgency of enshrining provisions for religious freedom and protections for religious minorities — with the emphasis on Iraq's Christian minority — first in Iraq's 2004 Transitional Administrative Law and then in the 2005 constitution. In this connection, U.S. advisors campaigned to minimize if not eliminate provisions that could be used to uphold Islamic law, doing so with striking insensitivity to Iraqi attitudes.

When it was hectoring the Iraqis to adhere to U.S. instructions for how to draft the new constitution, the USCIRF invoked international human rights law, but in fact it only showed concern for a few rights that dovetailed with distinctive U.S. priorities, the few rights that the United States typically has in mind when it admonishes Middle Eastern countries to respect "human rights." Muslims' concern for their right to self-determination does not figure in this customized U.S. menu of human rights, in which securing freedom of religion is paramount.[12]

In public admonishments by the USCIRF, Iraqis were instructed that they needed to incorporate precisely the wording favored by U.S. authorities.[13] Despite the intense lobbying, Iraqis resisted, and Islam retains a larger role in the 2005 constitution than U.S. officialdom wanted to see. Even after the final constitution was issued, the USCIRF, dissatisfied with

12. See Ann Elizabeth Mayer, "Clashing Human Rights Priorities: How the United States and Muslim Countries Selectively Use Provisions of International Human Rights Law," *Satya Nilayam: Chennai Journal of Intercultural Philosophy* 44 (2006): 9, also available on my website at http://lgst.wharton.upenn.edu/mayera/Documents/satyanilayam06.pdf.

13. The record of the USCIRF's extensive interventions in post-invasion Iraq can be found on the USCIRF website, http://www.uscirf.gov.

the compromises that accommodated Iraqis' determination to show respect for Islam and Islamic law, continued to pressure the Iraqi government to make the amendments that the USCIRF claimed were necessary to tighten guarantees for religious freedom and the rights of religious minorities.[14]

What was at stake was not freedom of religion in the abstract but ensuring that Iraqi law protected religious freedom in a manner that served U.S. goals. These goals correlated with the ambitions of the Religious Right, which had seen its political potency mushroom since Bush replaced Clinton and for whose members converting Iraqi Muslims was a top priority. It was not difficult for Iraqis to ascertain the motives behind the calls for religious freedom. As one reads in the account by Ali Allawi, the former Iraqi Minister of Defense and Finance, Iraqis understood that the U.S. drive to secularize the Iraqi constitution and to provide guarantees for religious freedom was spearheaded by Christian activists.[15] Iraqis realized that would-be Christian missionaries were pushing for Iraq to adopt constitutional provisions that would forward their planned campaign to Christianize Iraq, a campaign that could be impeded by restrictive Iraqi constitutional provisions, such as ones that affirmed Iraq's identity as a Muslim country or that accommodated traditional Islamic rules barring apostasy. The aggressive U.S. deployment of human rights rhetoric as part of an endeavor designed to whittle down the role of Islam provided ammunition to Muslims who charge that human rights constitute a threat to Islam.

Viewed from a Middle Eastern vantage point, U.S. professions of solicitude for Muslims' human rights seem to reflect capricious politics and indefensible double standards. In the U.S. War on Terror, evidence of flagrant U.S. disregard for Muslims' human rights has provoked dismay and anger, which exposés of the vile abuse of prisoners in Abu Ghraib and the barbaric conditions at the Guantánamo detention camp can only intensify. In the background, resentment over the continued U.S. indifference to the denial of Palestinians' right to self-determination still festers, and U.S. backing for Israeli measures that have aggravated Palestinians' suffering intensifies Muslims' disgust at U.S. professions of support for democracy,

---

14. See, e.g., "Iraq: Human Rights in Jeopardy," in *The 2006 Annual Report of the USCIRF,* May 2006, pp. 9-17, available online at http://www.uscirf.gov/countries/publications/currentreport/2006annualRpt.pdf.

15. Ali Allawi, *The Occupation of Iraq* (New Haven: Yale University Press, 2007), p. 226.

which are seen as hypocritical if not mendacious. The way that human rights are opportunistically exploited to serve U.S. political objectives but otherwise disregarded can aggravate disenchantment with human rights on the part of those who fail to differentiate the consistent and universal principles of human rights from the vagaries of U.S. politics.

A related factor making Muslims associate appeals to human rights with nefarious U.S. policies is the humanitarian catastrophe that spread in the wake of the U.S. invasion and occupation of Iraq. It is hard to overestimate the negative impact that reports of Iraqis' acute misery since the 2003 U.S. takeover are having on Muslims' attitudes. Of course, U.S. leaders had set the stage for particularly bitter alienation by promising the world that Iraqis would enjoy vibrant democracy and prosperity once Saddam Hussein was overthrown — only to leave Iraqi society staggering under the impact of destructive military initiatives, rampant criminality, escalating sectarian violence, a collapsing infrastructure, shortages of essential commodities, and other ills that prompted millions of Iraqis who possessed the means to seek refuge in other countries.

Rather than imagining that the United States has been altruistically engaged in bestowing "the foreigner's gift," they are likely to make negative assessments. Harsh critiques of the U.S. misadventure in Iraq may provide ammunition for those in Muslim societies who argue that human rights are an instrument of Western hegemonic designs.

However, with the decline in secular ideologies like Arab socialism and the ascendancy of Islamism, hostile reactions to the U.S. deployment of human rights as part of its interventions in the Middle East may take on an Islamist coloration. Muslims who are outraged by the sufferings that their coreligionists have endured at the hands of U.S. forces in Iraq, Guantánamo, and elsewhere may be increasingly drawn to combinations of Islamism and nationalism that serve to mobilize resistance to U.S. diplomatic pressures and military and economic predations. This, in turn, could play into the hands of regimes and political movements that instrumentalize Islam as part of schemes to mobilize popular support and that also resort to retrograde readings of Islam to crush human rights.

Angry reactions to what are seen as U.S. manipulations of human rights to advance hegemonic designs could not only potentially discredit human rights but could also spill over into attacks on indigenous human rights NGOs and their critiques of repressive Islamist policies. That is, in lieu of fostering progress towards integrating human rights in the fabric of

Muslim societies and a harmonization of Islam and human rights, U.S. policies, ones that are ostensibly aiming to enhance Muslims' rights, may have reverberations that portend serious setbacks.

Conclusion

At the same time that people in Muslim societies and in Western milieus have been arguing about the relationship of Islam and human rights, both Islam and human rights have been evolving. The relationship is complex and mutable, and I can report that the current status is far from where matters stood back in the early 1980s. In an era of unsettling changes to the status quo, perceptions of the Islam and human rights nexus have proven to be politically sensitive. In these circumstances, the position that Islam and human rights are inherently in conflict, which assumes two settled entities in a stable relationship, is becoming even harder to sustain — as is the view that human rights are ineluctably tied to Western civilization.

At a time when Muslims have been struggling to define where they stand vis-à-vis international human rights law, the United States has been an obtrusive factor and a disruptive influence. As U.S. connections to the international human rights system become more attenuated and as official U.S. human rights rhetoric becomes progressively more discredited, it should become easier for at least some Muslims to differentiate U.S. policies from the actual principles set forth in international human rights documents and to evaluate the latter based on what they actually offer to Muslim societies. Some recent developments are encouraging Muslims to conceive of the relationship of Islam and human rights as harmonious and to promote an appreciation of the merits of human rights universality.

Thus, a potential shift lies before us; we may be facing decades in which the United States will be moving farther away from the international human rights system while Islamic thinkers and people in Muslim countries more generally will be growing more attracted to international human rights law, seeing in it principles that acknowledge the legitimacy of their most pressing concerns and complaints. However, as noted, there are also factors on the current scene that could work in the opposite direction and that could energize Islamist hostility to human rights, confirming suspicions that human rights are part of a nefarious Western plot. Taking stock, we must recognize that the Islam and human rights relationship is regularly readjusting in response to a changing environment, so that the questions that will be addressed over the next decades will not likely be the same ones that Muslim societies and Islamic thinkers have been wrestling with to date.

CHAPTER 20

William Wilberforce: Progenitor
of the Global Human Rights Movement

Scott Horton

> *As soon as ever I had arrived thus far in my investigation of the slave trade, I confess to you sir, so enormous, so dreadful, so irremediable did its wickedness appear that my own mind was completely made up for the abolition. A trade founded in iniquity, and carried on as this was, must be abolished, let the policy be what it might, — let the consequences be what they would, I from this time determined that I would never rest till I had effected its abolition.*
>
> William Wilberforce, speech before the
> House of Commons, May 12, 1789

Early in 2007, the cause of universal human rights celebrated an important anniversary. On February 23, 1807, the Parliament at Westminster voted an act for the abolition of the slave trade. A few decades later, Parliament also voted the manumission of slaves throughout the British Empire. By that time, in the 1830s, the trafficking in slaves was viewed as a *jus cogens* crime by legal scholars around the world and the global movement to abolish slavery altogether was well launched.

Charting the origins of the modern human rights movement is an exercise in an uncertain and problematic geography, but if we follow it back along its swiftest channels to its ultimate source, past the American Civil Rights Movement, the cause of voting rights for women, the great American abolitionist movement of the first half of the nineteenth century, we inevitably come to William Wilberforce and his sisters and brothers who launched the effort to ban the slave trade. Of course there were the French and American Revolutions with their call for the rights of man; there was Jean-Jacques Rousseau's theory of social contract and Immanuel Kant's conceptualization of a philosophy of right. These things have their vital role.

But conceiving human rights as a social movement and propagating it to a rising class of educated citizens — this was Wilberforce's genius. In the process he developed the techniques of "blame and shame," the circulation of mass petitions, the concept of spotlighting the victims and their plight, the use of modern mass media, the use of civil society organizations — all things which continue today to be the stock-in-trade of the human rights advocate. His name may be barely known in the United States today. But William Wilberforce was the great progenitor of the global human rights movement, and on this day he deserves to be recognized as such.

He launched his movement in a dark hour and against great odds. The revolution in France and the slave uprisings in the Caribbean (especially the Haitian rising) made the cause an unpopular distraction in many circles. The economic interests arrayed against Wilberforce were enormous. But Wilberforce and his friends waged their battle with fortitude and unrelenting resolve over decades. They waged it with passion. And they waged it with religious conviction. No less than John Wesley wrote to Wilberforce, in what proved to be his last letter, "Unless God has raised you up . . . I see not how you can go through with your glorious enterprise in opposing that execrable villainy. . . . You will be worn out by the opposition of men and devils; but if God is with you, who can be against you? Oh, be not weary in well-doing. Go on, in the name of God and in the power of his might, till even American slavery, the vilest that ever saw the sun, shall banish away before it" (Feb. 24, 1793).

Wilberforce's leadership of the abolition movement was marked by a keen intellect and a willingness to adapt argument and technique to changing times. Wilberforce mustered many powerful arguments against the slave trade. At first, recognizing the enormous political power wielded by the slave traders — which extended into the royal family — he avoided denunciations of the slave traders, and instead appealed to their humanity and inherent sense of justice. He was prepared to take a gradual approach if he could not find the votes for more robust measures; he was prepared to bring the pressure of the treasury to bear on the issue. "In the case of every question of political expediency," he wrote to a friend on April 13, 1793,

> there appears to me room for consideration of time and seasons — at one period, under one set of circumstances it may be proper to push, at another, under another set of circumstances to withhold our efforts. But in the present instance, where the actual commission of guilt is in question, a man who fears God is not at liberty. To tell you I will say a strong thing which the motive I have suggested will both explain and justify. . . . Be persuaded then, I shall still even less make this grand cause the sport of caprice, or sacrifice it to motives of political convenience or personal feeling.

Wilberforce was also conscious of the gains achieved by the developing notion of humanitarian law — the intersection of human rights law and the law of war. That great Tory of the Augustan Age, Samuel Johnson, had been among the leaders in England promoting the idea that prisoners of war — those who had laid down their arms and been removed from combat — were entitled to be protected by the law. In his great appeal for the relief of French prisoners of war from 1760, Johnson wrote:

> That charity is best of which the consequences are most extensive: the relief of enemies has a tendency to unite mankind in fraternal affection; to soften the acrimony of adverse nations, and dispose them to peace and amity: in the mean time, it alleviates captivity, and takes away something from the miseries of war. The rage of war, however mitigated, will always fill the world with calamity and horror: let it not then be unnecessarily extended; let animosity and hostility cease together; and no man be longer deemed an enemy than while his sword is drawn against us. . . .
> The effects of these contributions may, perhaps, reach still further. Truth is best supported by virtue: we may hope from those who feel or who see our charity that they shall no longer detest as heresy that religion which makes its professors the followers of Him who has commanded us to do good to them that hate us.

Johnson's initiative drew still more public attention during the American Revolution. The British Army treated captured American soldiers as insurrectionists, not as soldiers engaged in lawful combat. They were treated harshly, and an exceptionally high percentage of the captured Americans died in captivity, frequently exhibiting signs of malnourishment and physical mistreatment. For instance, of the 2,607 Americans taken prisoner at the capitulation of Fort Washington in September 1776, all but 800 had died by the end of 1778. The American commander-in-chief, George Washington, resolved not to reciprocate the British practices in dealing with prisoners. Rather, he made the humane treatment of prisoners a matter of principle. Both Wilberforce and Pitt expressed their admiration for Washington and his noble gesture; both came ultimately to advocate a cessation of the war in North America on terms favorable to American independence.

Throughout the Napoleonic Wars, Wilberforce was also a persistent advocate of the doctrine of humane warfare and raised his powerful voice repeatedly for the humane treatment of all prisoners taken in time of war. It occurred to him at length that this law could equally be mobilized to protect Africans impressed into slavery and put in the Middle Passage for labor in the new world. The Africans sold into bondage in the great slaving stations of West Africa were by and large prisoners of war. In one of the most important contemporary records of the slave trade in the English-speaking world, *A New and Accurate Description of Guinea* (1705), William Bosman had written:

> Most of the Slaves that are offered to us are Prisoners of War, which are sold the Victors as their Booty. When these slaves come to Fida [in present-day Benin], they are put in Prison all together, and when we treat concerning buying them, they are all brought together in a large Plain; where by our Chirurgeons [surgeons], whose Providence it is, they are thoroughly examined, even to the smallest Member, and that naked too both Men and Women, without the least Distinction or Modesty. Those which are approved as good are set on one side; and the lame or faulty are set by as Invalides, which are here called Mackrons.

Wilberforce noted this in mobilizing the emerging humanitarian law doctrine of protection for prisoners to oppose the slave trade. A large part of the West Africans impressed into bondage and shipped across the sea to be sold were, he pointed out, actually prisoners taken in warfare on the African continent. As such, he argued, they were entitled to humane treatment which could not be squared with the revolting conditions found on board of the slave trading ships. This shows the close, mutually reinforcing relationship between humanitarian law and human rights law that has continued to this day.

For Wilberforce's campaign, opposition to torture was the critical element. Given biblical texts which explicitly or implicitly condoned the Peculiar Institution, it was difficult to frame a theological attack on slavery per se. But torture was another matter. The cruel abuse of a human being held in captivity was accepted by Wilberforce and most of his colleagues as an offense against Divine Law. Consequently the slave trade was thought a far more vulnerable target than slavery itself. In Wilberforce's great opening speech of 1789, frequently cited as the most important parliamentary address delivered in that memorable era, he dwelled heavily on the physical conditions of the slave ships: how slaves were stripped naked, bound and shackled, packed into the holds of the ship like sardines in a can, subjected to unbearable fluctuations of heat and cold, given inadequate water and food, deprived of sanitation. In such conditions the slaves screamed in agony, many calling out to be killed to put an end to their misery. And very many, by some reckonings most, expired in the process. Wilberforce's speech is a masterpiece of parliamentary rhetoric, and it deserves to be recalled in some detail:

> Having now disposed of the first part of this subject, I must speak of the transit of the slaves in the West Indies. This I confess, in my own opinion, is the most wretched part of the whole subject. So much misery condensed in so little room, is more than the human imagination had ever before conceived. I will not accuse the Liverpool merchants: I will allow them, nay, I will believe them to be men of humanity; and I will therefore believe, if it were not for the enormous magnitude and extent of the evil which distracts their attention from individual cases, and makes them think generally, and therefore less feelingly on the subject, they would never have persisted in the trade. I verily believe therefore, if the wretchedness of any one of the many hundred Negroes stowed in each ship could be brought before their view, and remain within the sight of the African Merchant, that there is no one among them whose heart would bear it. Let any one imagine to himself 6 or 700 of these wretches chained two and two, surrounded with every object that is nauseous and disgusting, diseased, and struggling under every kind of wretchedness! How can we bear to think of such a scene as this? One would think it had been de-

termined to heap upon them all the varieties of bodily pain, for the purpose of blunting the feelings of the mind; and yet, in this very point (to show the power of human prejudice) the situation of the slaves has been described by Mr. Norris, one of the Liverpool delegates, in a manner which, I am sure will convince the House how interest can draw a film across the eyes, so thick, that total blindness could do no more; and how it is our duty therefore to trust not to the reasonings of interested men, or to their way of colouring a transaction. "Their apartments," says Mr. Norris, "are fitted up as much for their advantage as circumstances will admit. The right ancle of one, indeed is connected with the left ancle of another by a small iron fetter, and if they are turbulent, by another on their wrists. They have several meals a day; some of their own country provisions, with the best sauces of African cookery; and by way of variety, another meal of pulse, &c. according to European taste. After breakfast they have water to wash themselves, while their apartments are perfumed with frankincense and lime-juice. Before dinner, they are amused after the manner of their country. The song and dance are promoted," and, as if the whole was really a scene of pleasure and dissipation it is added, that games of chance are furnished. "The men play and sing, while the women and girls make fanciful ornaments with beads, which they are plentifully supplied with." Such is the sort of strain in which the Liverpool delegates, and particularly Mr. Norris, gave evidence before the privy council. What will the House think when, by the concurring testimony of other witnesses, the true history is laid open. The slaves who are sometimes described as rejoicing at their captivity, are so wrung with misery at leaving their country, that it is the constant practice to set sail at night, lest they should be sensible of their departure. The pulse which Mr. Norris talks of are horse beans; and the scantiness, both of water and provision, was suggested by the very legislature of Jamaica in the report of their committee, to be a subject that called for the interference of parliament. Mr. Norris talks of frankincense and lime juice; when surgeons tell you the slaves are stowed so close, that there is not room to tread among them: and when you have it in evidence from sir George Yonge, that even in a ship which wanted 200 of her complement, the stench was intolerable. The song and the dance, says Mr. Norris, are promoted. It had been more fair, perhaps, if he had explained that word promoted. The truth is, that for the sake of exercise, these miserable wretches, loaded with chains, oppressed with disease and wretchedness, are forced to dance by the terror of the lash, and sometimes by the actual use of it. "I," says one of the other evidences, "was employed to dance the men, while another person danced the women." Such, then is the meaning of the word promoted; and it may be observed too, with respect to food, that an instrument is sometimes carried out, in order to force them to eat which is the same sort of proof how much they enjoy themselves in that instance also. As to their singing, what shall we say when we are told that their songs are songs of lamentation upon their departure which, while they sing, are always in tears, insomuch that one captain (more humane as I should conceive him, therefore, than the rest) threatened one of the women with a flogging, because the mournfulness of her song was too painful for his feelings. In order, however, not to trust too much to any sort of description, I will call the attention of the House to one species of evidence which is absolutely infallible. Death, at least, is a sure ground of evidence, and the proportion of deaths will not only confirm, but if possible will even aggravate our suspicion of their misery in the transit. It will be found, upon an average of all the ships of which evidence has been given at the privy council, that exclusive of those who perish before they sail, not less than 12 1/2 per cent. perish in the passage. Besides these, the Jamaica report tells you, that not less than 4 1/2 per cent. die on shore before the day of sale, which is only a week or two from the time of landing. One third more die in the seasoning, and this in a country exactly like their own, where they are healthy and happy as some of the evidences would pretend. The diseases, however, which they contract on shipboard, the astringent washes which are to hide their wounds, and the mischievous tricks used to make them up for sale, are, as the Jamaica report says, (a most precious and valuable report, which I shall often have to advert to) one principle cause of this mortality. Upon the whole, however, here is a mortality of about 50 per cent. and this among negroes who are not bought unless (as the phrase is with cattle) they are sound in wind and limb. How then can the House refuse its belief to the multiplied testimonies before the privy council, of the savage treatment of the negroes in the middle passage? Nay, indeed, what need is there of any evidence? The number of deaths speaks for itself, and makes all such enquiry superfluous.

The greatest blows struck by Wilberforce thus involved the physical mistreatment of the slaves, and the law that he cites is "Divine Doctrine."

He holds the human body created in the image of God and thus sanctified. Acts of cruelty against it are thus acts of depravity. Indeed, Wilberforce was driven by the consequences of this depraved conduct both for the torturer and his victim. Wilberforce's contemporaries readily accepted this thesis: that torture could not be permitted, even torture of slaves whose humanity was doubted. It is curious that today, two centuries later, the notion of slavery is a nonstarter, while under official tutelage, torture is staging a dramatic comeback. There can be no doubt that William Wilberforce would be appalled to make this discovery.

And we should quickly note, this same logic he advanced as the era's greatest defender of animals. Wilberforce was the founder of the Society for the Prevention of Cruelty to Animals. The acts of cruelty, Wilberforce said, deformed those who practiced them. Wilberforce's great undertaking to "reform the manners" of his fellow Englishmen had as its practical outcome the prohibition of bearbaiting, cockfighting, and similar acts of cruelty involving animals, which were still widespread in England in the early nineteenth century.

William Wilberforce may be something of an unwanted model for some of today's human rights advocates. He was an evangelical Christian and, moreover, a Conservative. He sat for decades as a Tory MP for a Yorkshire constituency in Parliament, and his success comes at least to some extent from his close friendship with William Pitt, the youngest prime minister in Britain's history. But these are, I think, among the traits that make Wilberforce such an important figure for us today. He demonstrates the universality of the human rights message and its appeal across partisan and philosophical boundaries. He demonstrates that a political conservative who builds from traditional religious values, who embraces the joys of private property, who advocates a restrained government of limited powers, has every reason to advocate the cause of human rights. He demonstrates that there are and always were compassionate conservatives — men and women who truly earned this label.

But most importantly, Wilberforce reminds us that evangelical Christianity, in its late eighteenth- and nineteenth-century manifestations, was intensely engaged with the cause of human rights. The campaign to end the slave trade, and later to abolish slavery, was above all their cause. Wilberforce saw his ministry as inextricably intertwined with this cause — bringing comfort to those afflicted by torture, brutalized and stripped of their humanity by the slave trade, and in this vision he had the support of

John Wesley and hundreds of other ministers. He was not a social engineer or a man who scorned property. But he had harsh words for religious hypocrites who outwardly manifested their faith while ignoring the mandate to do justice, to support the poor and afflicted. He saved his special contempt for those who used the tropes of religion to justify slavery and the oppression of their fellow man:

> When their conversations get really serious, you will see how little of their Christianity has anything to do with the faith taught by Jesus. Everything becomes subjective. Their conduct is not measured against the standard set by the gospel. They have developed their own philosophies, which they attempt to pawn off as Christianity. (*A Practical View of the Prevailing Religious System of Professed Christians in the Higher and Middle Classes of this Country Contrasted with Real Christianity* [1797])

It is impossible for me to read these words today and not think of leaders of America's Religious Right who observed complete silence when reports surfaced from Abu Ghraib, from Bagram, from Guantánamo — religious leaders who offered apologies and excuses for those in authority even as documents were published that showed that the practice of torture was a matter of formal policy of a government they embraced uncritically. Wilberforce also stood close to politics, and to government. But he never hesitated to raise his voice in condemnation when torture, slave trade, and slavery were an issue. This is the conduct of a man for whom moral principle, not political expedience, was the lodestar:

> Policy, Sir, is not my principle, and I am not ashamed to say it. There is a principle above everything that is political. And when I reflect on the command that says, "Thou shalt do no murder," believing the authority to be divine, how can I dare set up any reasonings of my own against it? And, Sir, when we think of eternity, and of the future consequences of all human conduct, what is here in this life [that] should make any man contradict the principles of his own conscience, the principles of justice, the laws of religion and of God?

Hollywood, it appears, has marked Wilberforce's accomplishment with the 2006 release of *Amazing Grace* — a movie named for the tune once understood around the world as the anthem of the abolitionist cause, forever associated with Wilberforce and his friend John Newton. Wilberforce began his great oration against slavery with this observation:

> When I consider the magnitude of the subject which I am to bring before the House — a subject, in which the interests, not of this country, nor of Europe alone, but of the whole world, and of posterity, are involved: and when I think, at the same time, on the weakness of the advocate who has undertaken this great cause — when these reflections press upon my mind, it is impossible for me not to feel both terrified and concerned at my own inadequacy to such a task.

Wilberforce's profession of modesty of his own talents in the face of a great cause rings hollow in a sense. He was a powerful orator. Joined with his friends inside of Parliament and the crowd of Quakers, Methodists, and evangelical Anglicans who propelled the abolitionist movement in England, he was sufficient to the cause. Wilberforce reminds us that we must never despair out of concern for our own powerlessness in the face of a towering adversary — an adversary moreover which commands the resources of government, which dominates the media and the commercial world. John Wesley was right to remind him of the force inherent in speaking truth to power; and of the certainty that others will hear that truth and be moved by it.

The decision of some in authority to embrace torture has caused a great moral cloud to descend over America. Against this darkness, the memory of William Wilberforce and his cause is a brilliant example in many ways, and most importantly, a reminder that passionate adherence to the truth and determination to overcome an evil enshrined by authority can prevail, though the course be a long and difficult one. Oh, be not weary in well-doing.

CHAPTER 21

What Terrorists Want: An Overview

Louise Richardson

Terrorism is the deliberate targeting of noncombatants for political purposes. It is the means used, and not the ends pursued, that determines whether a group is a terrorist group. Until we are willing to label as terrorists the members of a group that is fighting for a cause we consider legitimate, but deliberately targeting civilians to achieve this cause, we are never going to make progress and certainly never going to forge effective international cooperation against terrorism.

Terrorism is a tactic employed by many different types of groups in many parts of the world in pursuit of many different kinds of objectives. So it makes no more sense to declare war on terrorism, much less terror, than it does to declare war on any other tactic — say, precision-guided bombing. I am convinced that when the history of these years is written, the declaration of a war on terrorism will be seen to have been a colossal mistake.

Taking a longer and a broader perspective, one discovers that many of the widely accepted verities about terrorism today are misplaced:

1. Terrorism is not new, and indeed the recent emergence of terrorist groups which have a mixture of religious and political motives is not new either. Such groups have been documented at least as far back as the *Sicarii* in the first century after Christ.
2. Nor is terrorism the sole or even primary preserve of Islam. There have been Christian, Jewish, Hindu, Muslim, atheist, and secular terrorists.

3. Terrorists are not irrational.
   * Psychologists who have interviewed former terrorists and imprisoned terrorists are unanimous on this point.
   * I would even argue that suicide terrorists are not irrational. From an organization point of view, suicide terrorism is extremely rational in terms of expending minimum effort for maximum effect. Indeed, when the leaders of groups who deploy suicide terrorism talk about the tactic they talk in precisely these calculating cost/benefit terms.
4. Terrorists are not amoral.
   * I have never met a terrorist who did not believe in the morality of his cause or the immorality of his adversary.
   * Fatwas of a certain type are an effort to justify terrorist action. Al-Qaeda pronouncements and those of Osama bin Laden regularly seek to justify their actions.
   * An internal Al-Qaeda document seeking to justify the 9/11 attacks and written by Ramzi Bin al-Scheib spoke of the importance of not killing more than 4 million Westerners or displacing more than 10 million in order to keep the contest reciprocal.
   * Muhammad Sidique Khan's videotape shown on Al Jazeera in September 2006 sought to justify the July 7 bombings in terms of a just war.

I appreciate that it is hardly encouraging that Al-Qaeda feels justified in killing up to 4 million of us, but it does speak to the fact that they do operate under self-imposed constraints.

Causes of Terrorism

There are two reasons why it is very difficult to explain the causes of terrorism. The first is because there are so many terrorists: how can we find a single explanation for the behavior of a Peruvian peasant, a German professor, a radical Saudi imam, a Tamil teenager, a young cricket player from Leeds?

The second is because there are so few terrorists: we cannot convincingly use meta-explanations for microphenomena. If poverty caused terrorism there would be far more terrorists. The social revolutionary movements that bedeviled Europe in the 1970s were explained by the alienation of young people, yet there were far more alienated young people than there were terrorists.

Terrorism is a complicated phenomenon and the search for simplistic explanations is understandable, often ideologically driven, and unlikely to be successful. One characteristic that terrorists share is a highly oversimplified view of the world, a Manichean view that sees the world in black-and-white terms. There is no reason that those of us trying to understand the phenomenon need to adopt this very limited perspective, even if the current U.S. administration has tended to mirror its adversary by responding in oversimplified and Manichean terms.

Rather than poverty and inequality being causes of terrorism, for example, I prefer to see them as risk factors. They increase the likelihood of terrorism, and once a terrorist group forms they increase the likelihood that it will win adherents. Terrorist groups like Hamas and Hezbollah have been extraordinarily successful in exploiting social conditions to win adherents.

My own view is that what causes terrorism is a lethal cocktail of a disaffected individual, an enabling community, and a legitimizing ideology. It is important to see that the enabling community is an absolutely essential ingredient. Terrorists cannot operate unless they have complicit support. People do not have to agree with their atrocities, but simply agree enough with their objectives that they won't turn them in. If a group can operate within this kind of complicit community they can be enormously effective and very difficult to counteract.

The conflict is more likely to be intractable if the legitimizing ideology is a religious one but it certainly does not need to be. The ideology can be anything from religion to nationalism to jihadism, and so on.

One of the sinister aspects of the current jihadi movement is that through their exploitation of the high-tech attributes of the globalization they decry, they are able to create virtual communities to support their adherents whether these adherents are in Leeds, Chechnya, or Detroit. Terrorists have been able to use the Internet to create a virtual enabling community. Take, for example, the three men from Leeds who were behind the London bombings in July 2005. They clearly were not operating within a complicit community, they didn't belong to radical mosques, their families were not aware of what was going on; but they all had access to the Internet. They were able to communicate with people in other parts of the world and feel themselves to be part of that community, instead of the community comprised of the people with whom they worked, played, and went to school every day. One of these young men, 22 years old, was an avid cricket player and sportsman. He had been to college, he liked to drive his father's Mercedes, and yet, instead of identifying with the people around him, through the Internet he started to identify with another community.

The Role of Religion in Terrorist Groups

Certainly over the past thirty years and especially over the past ten we have seen a dramatic increase in the role of religion and the mixture of religious and political motives among terrorist groups. In the nineteenth and early twentieth centuries, terrorists were secular, reflecting the secularization of society in general. The current wave of terrorism began in the late 1960s, yet none of the terrorist groups extant at that time had religious motives; by contrast, of about fifty terrorist groups active today, at least fifteen have very clear religious motives.

Interestingly, this mixture of religious and political motives is also what we find when we look at every single terrorist group that existed prior to the French Revolution. It is the case with ancient groups like the first-century Zealots; it is the case with medieval groups like the assassins of the eleventh through thirteenth centuries; it is also the case with non-Islamic religious groups like those which operated in India for many years.

So this mixture of religious and political motives is not something entirely new, and it has always been particularly dangerous. Religious terrorist groups have generally had two characteristics that set them apart from other terrorist groups. The first is that they have always exercised less constraint. Most experts think that this is because their audience is God rather than the population from which they draw support. Secular terrorists by and large have not taken the opportunities available to them to kill as many people as possible; they haven't needed to do that to achieve their ends. Religious terrorist groups have. The second characteristic is that religious terrorist groups have always tended to transcend the boundaries between nations, which is partly why many of them have lasted longer than others. They have been harder to defeat because they have operated across political borders.

I have observed that religion plays three different roles in terrorist groups, although these three are often mistakenly lumped together. First, religion sometimes simply plays the role of a tag of ethnic identity, which is clearly the case in Northern Ireland. The conflict there is not a religious conflict at all; rather, the use of religious appellations simply makes it easier to identify one's friends and one's enemies.

The second and by far the most common role religion plays in terrorist groups is as a recruitment tool, a mask for political motives, a means of acquiring or claiming legitimacy. An example, I would argue, is Hamas. The literature of Hamas is suffused with religious rhetoric, yet the actions of Hamas can be explained in terms of the very political ambition to replace the PLO as the legitimate voice of the Palestinians. So religion in this case is simply a tool.

And the third role religion plays is as an ideology, as a guide to action, as an alternate claim to legitimacy and sovereignty, as is the case, for example, in certain religious cults like Aum Shinrikyo, the group that released sarin gas in a Tokyo subway.

In sum, there can be religious motives for terrorism. Religion is a possible factor, especially when it promotes a Manichean worldview in which the terrorists are good and their targets evil. Religion, however, is never the sole cause of terrorism; rather, religious motivations are interwoven with economic and political factors, and generally with the "three R's" to which we now turn: revenge, renown, and reaction.

What Terrorists Want

Quite a lot of hot air is expended in debating the point that terrorism works. But one actually cannot sensibly decide whether terrorism works without first establishing what it is that terrorists are trying to achieve.

I find it helpful to think in terms of terrorists having primary and secondary motives. The primary motives differ across different kinds of groups: nationalist groups seek autonomy or secession, religious groups see the replacement of secular with religious law, social revolutionary groups seek to overthrow capitalism, and so on.

Secondary motives, on the other hand, are held across all types of groups, and it has to be said that in seeking these secondary motives terrorists have been altogether more successful than in seeking the fundamental political change they are also trying to effect.

The key secondary motives are what I call the "three R's": revenge, renown, and reaction. I believe that this is what terrorists want:

Revenge: The desire to exact revenge is by far the most common motive for their actions given by current terrorists and former terrorists of every ideological hue from every part of the world. Sometimes this is revenge for something they or their family suffered; often it is revenge for a wrong inflicted on the community with which they identify.

Far from matching our description of them as selfishly pursuing their own ends, they generally identify with others and see themselves as sacrificing themselves for others. (Consider, for example, the young Briton, Omar Sheik, convicted of murdering the American reporter Daniel Pearl: Sheik once leaped down onto the tracks of a London subway train to rescue a man who had fallen in front of an oncoming train, and another time invited a beggar to share his apartment.) While we see terrorists as aggressors and ourselves as defenders, they see us as aggressors and themselves as defenders. Statements by Al-Qaeda and all other terrorist groups, whether intended for internal or external consumption, are suffused with the language of revenge. It would be hard to overestimate the importance of revenge as a motive for terrorism.

Renown: Publicity has always been a central objective of terrorism. It brings attention to the cause and spreads the fear terrorism instills. Renown, however, implies more than simply publicity. It also implies glory. Terrorists seek both individual glory and glory for their cause. For leaders, this glory is manifested on a national or increasingly global stage. For followers, glory within their own community is enough.

Humiliation is a very important factor here. Terrorists seek to attain glory in order to redress their sense of humiliation. They believe their cultures have been humiliated in various ways — for example, by the fact that they have clearly done much less well than the capitalist cultures of the West, and they are resentful of that. The complicating factor is that different people can experience the same situation in different ways. Some may find it deeply humiliating and some not. These differences show that there is nothing simple about understanding terrorism, reminding us again that those who try to cast it in oversimplified terms are doing us all a disservice.

Osama bin Laden is claiming that the U.S. wants to wage war on Islam. It is not hard to look at the War in Iraq as evidence in favor of the argument he is making against us. Certainly nothing could have done more damage than the photographs from Abu Ghraib, which undoubtedly persuaded large numbers of people, many of whom already perceive a sense of humiliation, that we have absolutely no respect for Muslims and that our treatment of prisoners proves that we do not believe in the principles we claim for ourselves.

Reaction: Terrorists, no matter what their ultimate objectives, invariably are action-oriented people operating in action-oriented groups. It is through action that they communicate to the world, through what used to be called "propaganda by deed." Action demonstrates their existence and their strength. In taking action, therefore, they want to elicit a reaction.

Terrorists often have wildly optimistic expectations of the reactions their action will elicit: American and Israeli withdrawal from the Middle East, British withdrawal from Northern Ireland, the collapse of capitalism. Yet it actually appears as though they rarely have a very coherent idea of what kind of reaction they will get. We don't actually know if bin Laden was anticipating American capitulation and withdrawal in response to 9/11 or whether he was anticipating an American war on Islam. He may well have concluded that either reaction would suit him. So long as there is a reaction, the terrorist purpose is served.

Once we understand the powerful appeal of revenge, renown, and reaction, the escalating tactic of suicide terrorism seems much more readily comprehensible. Those who train the volunteers for "martyrdom operations," as they prefer to call them, understand this and use the training period to guarantee glory in the form of songs, posters, and videos to the martyrs, who flock to volunteer to exact vengeance for atrocities committed by the adversary.

Seen in these terms, too, we realize that the desire for glory, belief that one is fighting for a just cause, and intense loyalty to one's small band of brothers that one finds among suicide terrorists is not unlike the motives that have animated soldiers for centuries. When we realize, moreover, that terrorists are motivated by a desire to exact revenge, attain renown, and elicit a reaction, we realize that declaring war on terrorism is playing directly into their hands.

By declaring war on terrorism we are providing both more opportunities to exact vengeance by the forward deployment of our military and more actions to be avenged due to the conduct of war. (It is perhaps worth pointing out that within six months of our invasion of Afghanistan, more Afghan civilians had been killed than people were killed on 9/11.)

When the most powerful countries in the world declare a war on what was, after all, a motley collection of extremists living under the protection of one of the most impoverished countries in the world, they elevate the stature of these terrorists to a height of which they could have only dreamed.

The goal of defensive warfare is to deny the adversary the objectives he seeks, but by declaring war on terrorism we conceded the very objectives the terrorists were trying to achieve — revenge, renown, and reaction — and thereby ensured that it was a war we could not win.

The urge to declare war in response to an atrocity on the scale of 9/11 is very powerful and the decision to do so is very understandable, but I believe it is also very unwise. I believe we should adopt an alternative strategy, one that replaces the overly ambitious goals to "rid the world of the evildoers" and "to root terrorists out of the world" with the more modest and more achievable goal of containing the threat from terrorism.

This strategy would be based on the following six principles derived from the experience of other democracies in successfully countering terrorism:

1) Have a Defensible and Achievable Goal

Instead of eliminating terror, which is an emotion that will never disappear, and instead of abolishing the "tactic" of terrorism, which will be used as long as it seems effective, we should have the goal of reducing the threat from particular terrorists. This is a goal — containment — that I think we can achieve. The particular brand of terrorism that threatens us today comes from Islamic militants. Our goal should therefore be to counteract the spread of Islamic militancy. We need to isolate the terrorists and inoculate potential recruits against them.

2) Live by Our Principles

Our principles must be upheld for both moral and pragmatic reasons. In the struggle against terrorism they are completely aligned with our interests. Far from disabling us, our democratic principles are among the strongest weapons in our arsenal. Unfortunately, we have failed to live by them for the last five years. Had we done so the world would never have seen those wrenching photos of Abu Ghraib, which have done so much to discredit our moral authority in the world. In the eyes of our allies and the

237

uncommitted they have undermined our legitimacy, while in the eyes of many others they have confirmed our perfidy.

3) Know the Enemy

There is no substitute for good intelligence. Every government that has faced a terrorist threat has found it to be indispensable. It is essential that we be able to penetrate terrorist groups. If young Americans like Jose Padilla and John Walker Lindh can join Al-Qaeda and the Taliban, then we should have our operatives in every cell of these groups that we can identify. Moreover, history is replete with examples in which negotiating with terrorist leaders has been relatively successful. It is an understandable but misguided objection to argue that negotiations must never be undertaken. What actually feeds terrorism is a military response that serves to win more recruits to terrorism. When we look at the war in Iraq we see a whole generation of young Muslims from around the world who have been radicalized by our military response, flocking to Iraq to volunteer to fight. So it does not seem that sitting down and talking to our adversary, and particularly when that is another state, as in the case of Iran and Syria, would be a mistake. On the contrary, it is something we should absolutely be doing.

4) Separate Terrorists from Their Communities

We need to understand the ways terrorists garner support among the communities in which they operate. We need to focus on undermining that support. Enabling communities are the ones who can most effectively repudiate the terrorists in their midst. We need to persuade them that we are not in fact their enemies but their friends. We need to show them that the motives and qualities which the Islamic militants attribute to us are untrue. Unfortunately, we have not done a good job of that. If our actions make it seem that what the militants say about us is true, then we are never going to thwart the terrorists by separating them from their communities.

5) Engage Others with Us in the Campaign Against Terrorists

It will not be possible to monitor the activities of known and emerging terrorist cells without extensive cooperation and intelligence-sharing with other countries. This cooperation is more likely to succeed if these countries believe in our legitimacy and if we consult with them in defining the problems and devising a response. Effective multilateral institutions need to be established that can facilitate the tracking of terrorists. Terrorists, furthermore, often make mistakes and go too far, even for their own supporters. At such times it is crucial to be in a position to mobilize opinion against them. Governments need to remember, especially in times of crisis, that the goal is isolating the terrorists and preventing the spread of their ideology. Draconian measures in response to terrorist atrocities will be counterproductive if they alienate popular opinion that might be turned decisively against the terrorists.

6) Have Patience and Keep Perspective

Ghastly as the atrocity of 9/11 was, we need to keep our perspective. The likelihood that any one American citizen will be killed by a terrorist is low indeed. We are at far greater risk every day when we get behind the wheel of a car. We need to keep our perspective and have patience. It will take time to resolve this conflict, but with the right policies it can be done. Terrorism was around well before September 11. There will always be persons with a sense of grievance and humiliation who will want to exact some kind of revenge. Nevertheless, the only threshold we have to reach is that people not be prepared to kill our civilians. Because this is unacceptable behavior in most conventional readings of every single religious tradition, it should be possible.

We will never eliminate all possible attempts to resort to terrorism, but that is the price of living in a complex world. What we have to protect against is that terrorists ever be able to deploy truly lethal weapons against us. To succeed in doing that, they would need to be very organized. One of the problems looking forward is the kind of trends we are seeing in technology. Ever more lethal weapons are becoming smaller and cheaper and hence easier to fall into the hands of smaller and smaller groups. It is, of course, much easier to detect a large group, or attack a large group, than a small group. We can certainly live with a certain level of terrorism, but we cannot live with regular attacks on the scale of 9/11. The British and Israeli publics have lived with terrorist violence for years without allowing it to stop the way they live their lives. We should do that too.

Conclusions

In fighting against terrorism we have, I believe wrongly, assumed that our side has a monopoly on virtue and have assumed that the purity of our motives was self-evident. We have casually assumed that being "tough on terrorism" is equivalent to being effective against terrorism, and so political debate has been hamstrung by the fear of opposition parties that they might be labeled "soft on terrorism."

Instead of worrying about what is tough or soft on terrorism, we should focus exclusively on what is effective against terrorism.

Every time we consider a new counterterrorism law or policy we should ask ourselves one question: Is it effective? And only if the answer is yes should we then ask the second question: At what cost?

Ultimately our democracy cannot be derailed by someone placing a bomb in our midst. It can only be derailed if we conclude that democracy, constitutional government, and the rule of law are inadequate to protect us.

When the U.S. government decided that the Geneva Conventions did not apply to the War on Terror, it violated fundamental principles and behaved in a manner unworthy of our country's traditions. Indefinite detention and the notorious mistreatment of suspects were the direct result. No democracy worthy of the name ought ever to engage in torture. Furthermore, there is the practical matter of whether torture is effective. Here is where we seem too quickly to have assumed that being tough means being effective. A great deal of evidence exists, unfortunately, that torture as a means of interrogation is unreliable. If we had inquired about the costs in terms of undermining our moral legitimacy both at home and abroad, not to mention the shakiness of the legal position, we would never have sanctioned torture.

Only by a return to our fundamental principles and the adoption of attainable goals will we be effective in combating terrorists — as opposed to giving them, unwittingly, what they want.

CHAPTER 22

Speaking Truth to the Not So Powerful

Carol Wickersham

I come to the issue of torture as a pastor, patriot, activist, and sociologist. As a sociologist, I am appalled at the attempts by the Bush administration to normalize the practice of torture. As an activist, I am frustrated at the relative lack of public outrage even after the photographs from Abu Ghraib made the allegations undeniable. As a patriot, I feel the burden of complicity because of what is being done by my country and thus in my name. As a pastor, I believe that my faith will not let me be silent.

In all these roles, my work has primarily been at the grassroots level. By this I mean that I have worked primarily with people in pews, in college classrooms, and in community organizations. The people I work with are far outside the Washington Beltway and are certainly not power brokers; nonetheless, when they speak up their voices can move mountains.

Because of my faith in the collective power of the not so powerful and my horror at the institutionally sanctioned practice of torture, I have worked to catalyze a new faith-based, grassroots effort, the No2Torture movement. Reflecting on this movement through the prism of my various roles, I offer the following guidelines to assist others who are working to mobilize rank-and-file believers on this issue.

First, I offer a few words about the origins of the No2Torture efforts. No2Torture was born at Ghost Ranch Conference Center in New Mexico in late June of 2005, at the twenty-fifth anniversary conference of the Presbyterian Peacemaking Program. At that gathering, General Assembly moderator Rick Ufford-Chase and I issued an impromptu invitation to all who wished to talk about the church's response to the issue of torture. More than fifty people crowded onto the portico, adamant that the church needed to speak out. Very quickly a plan was developed to issue a call to Presbyterians to pray, study, and act on the issue of torture; to develop a curriculum to enable this effort; to create a communication network through the Internet; and to hold a national gathering to plan further action. In the ensuing six months all of these initiatives bore fruit. It is important to note that the group had no budget, and, though its stance was squarely within the church's traditions, it did not emerge from an official church body. Scripture, Reformed theology, and previous General Assembly actions gave those gathered their marching orders. It was and is a truly grassroots movement.

In many ways, this movement represents a new way to do business for religious activists. The guidelines below offer possible ways to approach not just torture but other social justice issues as well. They represent currently evolving insights rather than polished analysis.

Six Guidelines for Discussing Torture with Grassroots Groups

A Conservative Movement

First, the movement to end torture is a profoundly *conservative* movement, and we should claim it as such. It is conservative because we believe we have something in this nation and in our faith worth conserving. Torture undermines what we stand for. When the president or the secretary of state stands before us and claims, "We do not torture," we want to believe him or her, but the evidence to the contrary is overwhelming. Alberto Gonzales and other officials apparently believe that Americans are ready to normalize torture as just the way we do business, but they are wrong. While torture has always been a part of the underside of our history, it has existed in the shadows of plausible deniability, and when it could not be denied it was denounced as shameful and illegal. To speak with legitimacy on this issue, we must say no to torture in order to uphold what is best in our nation and our faith.

Maintaining Control of Language

Second, *we must not cede language* to our opponents. Cognitive linguist George Lakoff's work on the mechanisms and efficacy of moral language makes it clear that we cannot hand over value-laden terms such as "patriotism," "our way of life," "democracy," "security," or "strength" to those who would use them to inculcate fear and justify torture. If language is taken prisoner, so are our arguments. We need to stand up and shout that we oppose torture because we love God and country, and we must be ready to say what this means. We should be able to quote chapter and verse from the core documents of our particular traditions, whether it be the U.S. Constitution, the Talmud, or Calvin's *Institutes.* If we are labeled as unpatriotic, or un-Christian, or un-anything, we should immediately counter with the reasons why we stand squarely within our traditions. Even more importantly, we must choose language that has deep moral resonance for us and for those with whom we speak.

Using Existing Resources

Third, *we must use existing resources.* Lobbyists are fond of saying that to effect change you have to have either the money or the many. Religious communities do not have the money, at least not compared to other groups, but we do have the many and, if we can ignite them about this issue, we have clout.

Every denomination has accrued networks of many kinds — advocacy networks, education networks, clergy networks, women's networks, and so on. Activists should inventory and analyze these networks to understand their unique concerns. With this information we can frame the torture issue in such a way that it will connect with the mission of each particular group. For instance, the No2Torture movement was possible because for the past twenty-five years the Presbyterian Peacemaking Program carefully educated and nurtured a nationwide network of thousands of local advocates concerned about such issues. To build this network from scratch would have taken years and an inconceivable budget. Such networks exist in many denominations but are often underused and undervalued.

Denominational staff on the national level are also an invaluable resource. Yes, in these times of denominational downsizing, staff has shrunk and those who remain are often overextended. Gone are the days (if they ever existed) when staff would organize and run programs for us. However, I have found that staff members are very enthusiastic about supporting grassroots efforts, often going above and beyond the call of duty, as long as those efforts are within sanctioned, documented denominational bounds. The expertise, experience, and perspective of staff are invaluable in identifying potential allies and strategies.

Finally, as the movement works to build legitimacy, it is key to ask those with authority to act as spokespersons, whether they are elected leaders or staff. This means approaching not only the "usual suspects," but others whose voices may resonate with different audiences. Again, an example from the No2Torture effort illustrates this point. The movement was launched by issuing a statement: "A Call for Presbyterians to Say No! to Torture," cosigned by the elected Moderator of the General Assembly, Rick Ufford-Chase, a longtime peace activist, and Ed Brogan, the Director of the Presbyterian Council of Military Chaplains. This unusual partnership made it less likely that the statement would be dismissed as partisan and thus a more diverse constituency was reached.

Creating Coherence

Fourth, *discourse creates coherence.* Discussion of resources leads to a paradoxical reality. On the one hand, the most likely way to create ownership of an issue within a particular constituency is to reach down deep into the particular richness of that community. On the other hand, unless we want to remain in an enclave speaking only to those who are already convinced, we need to reach across traditional divides to find points of commonality. Both of these gestures are possible and necessary — reaching into and reaching across — for thus we can find common cause with those who come to the same conclusion by different routes, as reflected in the joint statement by Ufford-Chase and Brogan. Grassroots activists are most effective speaking to the communities within which they are rooted. This is true for two reasons. First, people listen to and follow those they trust. Second, people need familiar hooks upon which to hang their beliefs, particularly if they are being asked to apply those beliefs in new ways or venues.

Both these aims can only be accomplished through the painstaking work of respectful dialogue. In particular, listening builds trust. To use an economic metaphor, listening is "money in the bank" that can be drawn down when we, in turn, want to be listened to. Listening also allows those who would speak to draw upon and reinforce the particular images, narratives, ethical traditions, and historic voices that carry authority and authenticity for the community. It takes deep, respectful listening to bring nuanced interpretation to bear. Outsiders are often clumsy interpreters and may actually alienate those whom they would sway. Listening allows for genuine authenticity because as the listener is no longer perceived as an outsider but is able to speak from within the community. This can take years, so it is usually best if this work is done by someone already fluent in the community's discourse.

To speak of torture also requires that outside information be brought to bear, in particular the voices of those who have been tortured. Elimination of torture is most often an advocacy issue; in other words, we are not appealing to direct self-interest (though indirectly all of us are affected by the policy and practice of torture), rather we are asking people to speak up for strangers, some of whom they may consider enemies. It is a difficult "ask." This makes it all the more important to allow for dialogue so that people begin to feel empathy. As "they" become "us," the listener can acknowledge that "there, but for the grace of God, go I."

We must respect our allies who arrive at the same conclusions by other routes. We do not all have to get there the same way; in fact we cannot. My community comes to this issue as Reformed Christians, by way of Judeo-Christian Scripture and the Barmen Declaration. Other allies in the cause will come by way of other traditions, which we may deeply respect but do not necessarily share. Since at this juncture the goal is to take action, we do not have to agree about fine points of doctrine, only about the steps to be taken. Recognition that torture threatens us all is a starting point; common faith in God will keep us going. Through dialogue we not only find but also create points of commonality that allow us to move forward together.

A particular caveat is needed as we seek dialogue on this issue among grassroots constituencies. We will very often be speaking with those who have served or have family members serving in the armed forces. Though there is not a complete lack of intersection between "them and us" — those in the military and those speaking against torture — this is a fledgling alliance that needs more nurturing. "Oppose torture, support the troops" is a coherent message; the challenge is for it to be heard as such. If we do not sound this note, we will be seen as disrespecting the deeply cherished beliefs of many.

Leveraging Technology and the Media

Fifth, we must *leverage technology and the media.* While there is no substitute for the painstaking work of face-to-face conversations, we must at the same time be savvy about amplifying our message. Fortunately, in the age of the Internet we have access like never before; and here it is relevant to speak specifically about the beginnings of the No2Torture movement. The No2Torture movement was able to be launched, even though it had zero funding, not only by using the above-mentioned resources of the Presbyterian Church (U.S.A.) but also by using the Internet to eliminate the need for mailing, phone calls, and even meetings.

The group began by initiating a conversation through a free Yahoo group whose initial members were those who had indicated interest at a conference. This small nucleus invited others, thus growing organically. Since the strategy of the founding group was always to reach the grassroots, writing the curriculum was a key step, enabling congregational groups to study the issue in light of Scripture and theology. The next step was to create a web site. With donated time, the cost was only $100. This site enabled us to post the curriculum in HTML and PDF formats, so that it could be read and printed easily and without charge. The curriculum was also written pro bono, by authors from within the tradition who were familiar with how to make it "user-friendly" for congregations. The web allowed us to post action alerts and links to other organizations.

Through conference calls, a small group organized a national gathering in Miami in January 2006. Promotion and registration was handled through the web site. This meeting was organized without funding. People were invited to travel using their own money, or to ask for funds from local sponsors. Fifty people came from across the country, across the generations, and across the theological spectrum to sleep on a church floor or in nearby motels. Even the speakers donated their time and paid for their own travel. This example yields two lessons. First, a small investment in communication can have a large payoff. Second, lack of material resources can turn out to have unexpected benefits. People may be more likely to respond if they are asked to do a lot than if they are asked to do a little. People are looking for significant involvement that is commensurate with the seriousness of the issue.

In addition, we must continually work to establish and maintain media contacts locally and nationally. A meeting of fifty Presbyterians in a church hall is not news — unless it is picked up in a photo essay by Presbyterian News Service, which is then circulated and published in outlets nationwide. Media coverage amplifies the message. The fact is that religious groups have been opposing torture for a long time but their voices have not been heard above the background noise. To get media attention takes research, contacts, and a lot of legwork. We need to learn how to write press releases. We need to frame our message in ways that are likely to be broadcast or published. We also need to build momentum. Sometimes by publishing in small venues the message begins to permeate in ways that one big splash cannot. We should not disregard local papers, local radio, or church newsletters. Denominational newsletters and web sites also have significant and receptive audiences, particularly if the author already has credibility with the readership. Alliances are also forged by links to our allies' web sites. We may not own Fox News or CNN, but there are ways to get our message out.

Affirming Our Reliance on God

Last but not least, we must *affirm our reliance on the mercy of God*. Torture is not a "feel-good" issue. There are many people who are involved in religious communities in order to get the support they need to get through the day. These are the not so powerful people who have all they can handle making the mortgage payments and raising their children. They are not looking to take on a tough issue that makes them squirm. Yet the issue is so central to what we all believe that we cannot turn away. When we bring up the issue of torture, we should anticipate strong emotions — anger, grief, disgust, and fear — feelings people would prefer to avoid. We must let people know that these feelings are to be expected and that they are not alone in experiencing them. People will also need the best factual information available from sources that they trust, or else they will embrace denial to avoid ugly truths.

Among the many strong emotions, there are two in particular we should anticipate. For those who may have experienced abuse in their past, descriptions of torture may trigger painful memories. Those who lead discussions of these issues should be prepared to offer pastoral support and refrain from pushing people beyond where they are capable of going. Much more could be said here, but for now it is important just to flag this statistically likely possibility.

We should also be prepared to help people acknowledge a sense of shame or guilt. It is important to recognize the reality of complicity early in the discussion. As citizens of a democratically elected government, we are corporately responsible for actions done in our name. This truth allows us to demand accountability from our government, while resisting the temptation to scapegoat "a few bad apples." We need to help people see that we are all caught up in a system that has come close to normalizing torture as the way we do things. This is particularly important to those in the military and their families. We are attempting to support the troops by ensuring that they are never put in situations where torture is acceptable or even encouraged. We also support them by acknowledging that we, too, are part of the problem, and all of us together must say no if torture is to be abolished.

People should be encouraged to acknowledge a proportional sense of complicity — no, we are not solely or even primarily responsible; however, we all bear responsibility to hold those in power to account. Confessing complicity is not an invitation to become mired in guilt; just the opposite. It is an invitation to tell the truth, so the truth can set us free to act.

Because we come to this issue as faithful people, we come with hope. As grim as the entrenched realities are, we know that the love and justice of God are stronger. We do what we must do with confidence not in our own efforts but in the mercy and power of God.

CHAPTER 23

How to End Torture

George Hunsinger

In May 2007 I had the privilege of speaking at a conference sponsored by the University of Santa Barbara where one of the other presenters was Darius Rejali, the distinguished torture researcher and analyst. During a break, he turned to me and said, "You know, of course, that there are five steps which would bring torture to an end." No, I said, I didn't know. I will never forget him ticking the five steps off on his fingers one by one.

Although I expected these steps to be included in Rejali's soon-to-appear magnum opus *Torture and Democracy* (Princeton University Press, 2007), I was surprised to discover they weren't there. Perhaps at some point he will develop them in print. Until then, they seem important enough to summarize here.

Here are Rejali's five steps by which U.S. torture could be brought to an end.

First, the rules of interrogation must be clear. Where conflicting directives exist, as was the case at Abu Ghraib, the situation is rife for abuse. Double bookkeeping cannot be tolerated. It is imperative that intelligence operatives of the CIA, for example, or the Navy SEALs, be held to the same high standards — without loopholes — as are required by the Army Field Manual.

Second, the chain of command must be equally clear. Again, Abu Ghraib shows what happens when the lines of authority are blurred. In interrogation, conflicting jurisdictions between military and intelligence services (or independent contractors) must be eliminated.

Third, outside visitation is essential in venues where interrogation occurs. The International Committee of the Red Cross and similar watchdog agencies must receive free access to all detainees as well as authority to publicize the findings. It is alarming that our government has systematically blocked such access at Guantánamo and other facilities around the world, even resorting to the use of "black sites."

Fourth, detainees with grievances must have timely access to a fair hearing. Where the access is not timely or the hearings not fair, the conditions for abuse are obvious.[1]

Finally, and perhaps most importantly, structures of accountability must be strictly observed. Where there is no clear accountability, situations can rapidly deteriorate. Not only does abuse start to proliferate, but professional interrogators who pride themselves on obtaining reliable information by honorable means eventually get disgusted and leave the system. A process that drives out the professionals, while at the same time rewarding the abusers, can only lead to multiple disasters.

In short, there must be (1) a single set of operating procedures, (2) a clear chain of command, (3) outside monitoring by accredited agencies, (4) a fair and timely grievance procedure, and (5) above all a strict observance of procedures for accountability.

"It's totally within our power to stop these things from happening," Rejali remarked in a recent interview. "One of the things we do know from experimental work is that most of the violence doesn't happen because of a disposition toward violence, it happens because of situations where perfectly normal people end up doing violence. It's a question of vigilance, it's not about nature."[2]

Elsewhere he stated to the press:

> One of the main points about what I'm saying is that when we watch, torturers care. Torturers actually care about what your church group, or

---

1. Torture survivors should also have access to justice and reparations. See "Taking Complaints of Torture Seriously: Rights of Victims and Responsibilities of Authorities" (London: The Redress Trust, 2004). Available online at http://www.redress.org/publications/PoliceComplaints.pdf.

2. Brian Stuckmeyer, "Iranian-American Professor: Not All Torture Leaves Visible Scars," *The Journal* (Webster University), February 23, 2006. Available online at http://media.www.webujournal.com/media/storage/paper245/news/2006/02/23/News/IranianAmerican.Professor.Not.All.Torture.Leaves.Visible.Scars-1623926-page2.shtml.

your newspaper, or anybody says. Public monitoring really works. This is one of the important points. . . . The harder thing is to persuade governments to stop creating the conditions that produce torture. Even harder than that for us is going to be that once you have torture in the system it is very hard to get it out. There are all sorts of problems that will take us years and years to fix.[3]

In the effort to end torture Rejali thus envisions, on the basis of his historical research, an important role for religious communities.

3. Lawrence J. Maushard, "Interview with Darius Rejali," *Willamette Week* (Portland, Ore.), November 28, 2007. Available online at http://wweek.com/editorial/3403/10018/.

Torture Always Comes Home:
An Interview with Darius Rejali

Scott Horton

Reed College Professor Darius Rejali is one of the world's leading thinkers and writers on the subject of torture and the consequences of its use for modern society. Princeton University Press has just published his magisterial study of torture and how it has developed as a social and moral issue through the last century. Rejali tracks the question in many different settings and societies — from the French colonial wars to totalitarian states in the mid-twentieth century, down to America in the age of George W. Bush. I put six questions to Rejali about his book and its relevance to the current debate in the United States.

1. Your new book, *Torture and Democracy,* reflects a lengthy engagement with the subject of torture as a phenomenon over a vast stretch of time and among many different societies. But in the preface, you start by relating something about your own background as an Iranian-American, trying to understand how torture was transforming Iran and complicating its evolution in modern times. Did developments in Iran lead you to this subject? In what ways do you think torture has affected the political culture of Iran and its extremely awkward relations with the rest of the world?

Most people think torture is a barbaric survivor and that it will disappear over time with progress. This is a mistake, and my experience growing up in Iran taught me that and led me to write *Torture and Modernity: Self, State, and Society in Iran* (1994). I used Iran to show that while old ritualistic, public torture would disappear over time, other tortures would survive and new techniques would appear; let's call these modern torture.

I remember one distinguished expert who reviewed my work said, basically, how can Rejali say torture is part of modernity? If that was true, America would torture too. It really was amazing, in retrospect, how willfully blind people wanted to be. I grew up in Iran at a time when the Shah's secret police, the SAVAK, did not hesitate torturing Islamic and Marxist insurgents. No one thought torture was something incompatible with cars, fast food, washing machines and other parts of modern life. I remember talking to a high-ranking SAVAK officer years after the Shah was gone, and he certainly felt he played an important role in modernization. It wasn't the last time I've heard torturers say how important they are in making their country safe for economic opportunity.

Another point: Everyone forgets that the Iranian revolution of 1978-1979 was the revolution against torture. When the Shah criticized Khomeini as a black-robed Islamic medieval throwback, Khomeini replied, look who is talking, the man who tortures. This was powerful rhetoric for recruiting people, then as it is now. People joined the revolutionary opposition because of the Shah's brutality, and they remembered who installed him. If anyone wants to know why Iranians hated the U.S. so, all they have to do is ask what America's role was in promoting torture in Iran. Torture not only shaped the revolution, it was the factor that has deeply poisoned the relationship of Iran with the West. So why trust the West again? And the Iranian leadership doesn't.

2. One of the themes that circulates through your book is that we are mistaken in attaching torture only to non-democratic states; your special focus is on how democratic states use torture, and you give examples stretching from Athens in the golden age to America under George W. Bush, but with France in its waning colonial phase as perhaps the best illustration of them all. But isn't it the case that modern democratic concepts rest on the rejection of torture? I think back to figures like Voltaire. When he describes torture in great detail and attacks its crudeness, its stupidity — as in his brilliant description of the cruel execution of the nineteen-year-old Chevalier de la Barre — he seems to be making a political statement by it. This system, he says, does not value the worth of the individual human being, and indeed that is the essence of its tyranny. Conversely, the post-Enlightenment democracies took rejection of torture as an element of

their identity, as we saw in Washington's orders, or as the first article of the German *Grundgesetz,* which states, "The dignity of the human being is inviolable. The respect and protection of that dignity is the obligation of all state power." Leaving aside the differing concept of democracy in classical antiquity, do you not see a fundamental crisis of identity with a democratic state that adopts and uses torture?

Torture involves giving absolute power to one individual over another. Our founders knew that absolute power corrupts absolutely and that we shouldn't even trust ourselves with absolute power. That is why they promoted limited government in politics, toleration of minorities in social life, and dignity in our relations with strangers. The history of slavery teaches us that this kind of power corrupts society, and history of torture shows how badly it damages states. Thomas Hobbes, whose national security credentials are impeccable, says it quite clearly in *The Leviathan:* "Accusations upon torture, are not to be reputed as testimonies" for what each prisoner confesses "tendeth to the ease of him that is tortured, not to the informing of the torturers." People will say anything under torture to ease pain, says Hobbes, and this, as far as he is concerned, corrupted the judicial process and made all of us unsafe.

Torture may be compatible with democracy, but it is not compatible with liberalism, and we live in liberal democracies today. What I document in *Torture and Democracy* is how modern liberal democratic states try to get around violating the dignity of others by becoming hypocrites. To this end, they use a lot of techniques that are physically painful, but don't leave marks. A prisoner who doesn't have marks is simply not credible when he makes the accusation of torture. So now they can say, "There was no torture, see? So go home now." Instead of embracing the ideals of dignity and freedom, states become cleverer in methods of oppression and deception. As John Locke said brilliantly in his *Letter Concerning Toleration,* a state that tortures is always a state of hypocrites. I also document how authoritarian states became cleaner in their torture as liberalism developed into a worldwide human rights movement after World War II. These dictators, especially our allies, realized their legitimacy and foreign aid depended on being clean. Hypocrisy isn't just a monopoly of democratic states.

The good news here is that liberal democratic leaders actually care enough about legitimacy that they fear clear outrages will cause people, the voters, to do something about it. If they didn't, scarring tortures would still be common. So when we watch them, they get sneaky. Could things get worse? Sure. Locke believed that history was committed to liberalism's triumph, but the question today is whether history will even tolerate liberalism surviving into the twenty-second century. Everywhere, blind nationalism seems to threaten liberalism. Documenting clean torture in this respect is like the canary in the coal mine. As long as torture remains clean — and so far it has — it means that government leaders know that people are watching, and I find that hopeful.

3. In America today, the debate seems to focus on the efficacy of torture — whether it is a useful tool for getting at the truth. You note the flow from the Roman Ulpian, who accepts torture as something quite normal to be used in interrogation (though he does at some points express skepticism about its usefulness), to Cesare Beccaria, whose monumental denunciation of torture did so much to influence European ideas about torture and criminal justice in the eighteenth century. But today we seem stuck in a debate in which those who use torture are eager to try to justify themselves but unwilling to let a bright light shine into their conduct, ostensibly for national security reasons, though many will inevitably suspect that secrecy is driven by concerns for their own culpability. You offer up a very lengthy and nuanced discussion on the efficacy of torture, and in your *Washington Post* column on five myths you have pulled some chestnuts out of it. One of them is that "people will say anything under torture." But isn't the claim rather the way Shakespeare put it in Act III of *The Merchant of Venice,* that people will say what they think the torturer wants them to say? And doesn't that explain why societies that put a premium on confessions like torture to extract them, and why al-Libi told the CIA about Saddam Hussein's nonexistent WMD plans? Don't you think that the efficacy discussion has to address the broader consequences that a decision to use torture has to reputation, and conversely to the ability of a terrorist foe to recruit?

Yes, I do. During the Islamic Revolution in Iran, the Shah's torture was the best recruiting tool the opposition had. Prisons were places where prisoners met each other and professionalized their skills, as I and others have documented. It feels like a nightmare watching American politicians make the same mistake as the Shah. I like to believe that with every mistake we must surely be learning, but sometimes it is hard to believe.

When I talked about people under torture saying anything, I was especially interested in the cases where torturers interrogate for true information. That's what I document doesn't work. But it seems pretty clear that torture works to generate false confessions, which serve equally as well as true confessions for many state purposes. When judges and juries value confessions as decisive proof, police are happy to generate confessions for convictions. This can happen in domestic crime, as it happened in Chicago in the 1980s, where African Americans were sentenced to death on the basis of coerced confessions. They're also good for international show trials, trials that exonerate the state's failures. Stalin wanted show trials to demonstrate that terrorists and saboteurs caused his failures, and he wasn't the last leader who liked show trials to vindicate his decisions. And lastly, states use false confessions as blackmail to turn prisoners into unwilling informants. Torture allows one to collect dependent and insular individuals, spreading a net of fear across a population. This can happen locally, as in a ghetto, or in a whole state, like East Germany.

It's also true that torturers often hear what they want to hear. In fact, that's one of the big problems with torture that I document in the book and the "Five Myths" article. Even if torture could actually break a person and they told you the truth, the torturer has to recognize it was the truth, and too often that doesn't happen because torturers come into a situation with their own assumptions and don't believe the victim. Moreover, intelligence gathering is especially vulnerable to deception. In police work, the crime is already known; all one wants is the confession. In intelligence, one must gather information about things that one does not know.

And let's remember, torturers aren't chosen for intelligence; they are chosen for devotion and loyalty, and they are terrible at spotting the truth when they see it. In the "Five Myths" piece I talk about how the Chilean secret service lost valuable information in that way when they broke Sheila Cassidy, an English doctor, and she told them everything but they didn't believe her. And one can just repeat dozens of stories like this. My favorite is when Senator John McCain tried to explain the concept of Easter to his North Vietnamese torturer. "We believe there was a guy who walked the earth, did great things, was killed, and three days later, he rose from the dead and went up to heaven." His interrogator was puzzled and asked him to explain it again and again. He left, and when he came back, he was angry and threatened to beat him. Americans couldn't possibly believe in "Easter" since no one lives again; McCain had to be making this up.

4. You talk about a "national security model" for torture and discuss in particular the way the French adopted torture to use in the Algerian War and how they reconciled this with a legal regime which condemned torture. I was most taken by the discussion of the judicial aspect. Allegations of torture, you report, were referred to a specific examining magistrate, Jacques Batigne, who served as a dead-letter office. You also point how the democratic process failed to engage this, in part because the leftist opposition was so badly discredited with its own Stalinist torture baggage. The analysis you present seems to me to closely parallel what Albert Camus writes in his diary, the *Chroniques algériennes,* in which he dwells very heavily on torture and how it corrupted France's democratic process. In America today, the Bush administration seems to have developed its own repertoire of legal tricks. Judges refuse to consider torture cases by noting that immunity of public officials precludes them, or state secrets, or some combination of the two. And we recently saw Michael Mukasey tell us that because opinions had been given by the Office of Legal Counsel which declared torture techniques lawful, the use of those techniques could not be criminally investigated. It seems very close to the French approach. But assuming the political process produces a change to an anti-torture political leadership, what are the prospects for a democratic society going back and holding torturers to account? Have you given that any systematic study?

Stopping torture is actually the easiest part; the harder part is undoing the long-term damage. To stop torture, all one really needs is clear leadership that spells clear rules and punishes the slightest violations of the rules. It also protects whistleblowers, and requires regular and open medical inspection, not to mention fair and open trials for all prisoners. This was the way we stopped most torture in the U.S. in the 1940s and 1950s after three or four decades of abysmal police torture in America, in cities both large and small.

Torture casts a very long shadow. When a state tortures, many decent professionals retire, leaving the police forces, the military, and the intelligence services in disgust. So those who stay behind create a culture of impunity. Torture also has a powerful deprofessionalizing ethic, damaging other intelligence efforts. Why do the hard work of using proper police and interrogation techniques when you've got a bat? Considering that most recent whistleblowers have had to hide in fear, including the man who revealed the Abu Ghraib tortures, it will be difficult to recruit good people to do this work. How can you prevent waste or fraud, much less torture, if you are not going to protect whistleblowers? You can't.

Americans think in the fantasy terms of Jack Bauer and ticking time bombs, while our hospitals fill with soldiers who clearly are suffering the traumatic side effects of being involved in torture, what is now called "perpetrator induced traumatic stress." Americans seem less willing to acknowledge what our nation asked them to do than fund what is needed for their recovery. Fifty years after the Algerian War, the French have thousands of soldiers in therapy, including their DOPS interrogators who are described as "spiritually wounded men, often ravaged by the weight of their guilt and shame." We have yet to acknowledge that, much less the damage to victims and innocents we tortured.

A lot of people want trials, not just trials for those who did terrible things but also trials for those who had command responsibility and should have, and could have, prevented torture. And nothing predicts future torture quite like past impunity. But trials are an imperfect solution. They can deeply divide a society. The Argentine government tried the generals, but when it tried notorious junior officers responsible for torture, it faced a series of rebellions. And we certainly need to have a final, open accounting of what was done, but truth commissions also have a mixed history, sometimes helping and other times promoting amnesia.

I would like to think that changing leaders will make a difference. But then remember, I lived through a revolution where the most important thing was to throw out the Shah and stop torture. The irony is that it didn't stop. Changing leaders doesn't automatically change torture. In fact, states usually change their interrogation practices after wars, not during them or when leaders change. This is what happened in Iran. People are too scared in wars and uncertain in crises, so they repeatedly reach for the same techniques that the people they opposed used.

But having said that, it is possible to change course in mid-war successfully. As I show in *Torture and Democracy,* the Battle of Algiers turned in favor of the French only after Paul Aussaresses, who ran the torture policy, was replaced by the very smart and canny Col. Yves Godard, and it was his informants, not Aussaresses' torture policy, that gave the French the big breaks they needed. Godard knew how intelligence really worked.

So it can be done. And whoever does it is going to have the backing of the American people. Every scientific national poll I've looked at since 9/11, for example, shows consistently anti-torture majorities in America. This number hasn't varied, always hovering between 55 to 65% opposition, and includes both Republicans and Democrats. When pollsters ask not about "torture" in general but specific techniques like waterboarding, the opposition spikes to 80% opposed even if there is a ticking time bomb. What best predicts whether you're for torture turns out not to be a partisan issue, though there is a slight Republican trend. What predicts whether you're for torture best is if you approve of President Bush's policies; basically it's a loyalty vote. The pro-torture folk have always — and I mean always, in every poll I've seen — been a minority of 35-45% and I'm pretty sure the number is shrinking as the president's approval numbers dip.

So the good news is that opponents of torture are not alone. I suspect people think the majority of Americans are for torture, but this just isn't supported by any of the polling. It's just hype from partisan media, talking heads, and the politicians. The real truth is that there is intelligence out there. What it requires is for government to tap into it and start using it.

5. In the United States, the debate seems to be increasingly focused on waterboarding, which I suspect you'll agree doesn't really present any serious questions on the definitional front. Obviously it is torture. But there are other techniques which are much more problematic. One is the sensory-deprivation/sensory-overload technique associated with Kubark. Waterboarding has not been used frequently, at least according to General Hayden, but the sensory-deprivation technique seems to have developed into something close to standard operating procedure, and was even used on a U.S. citizen, Jose Padilla. A psychologist who evaluated him says he was essentially destroyed as a self-actuated human being, capable of independent thought and direction. Is the Bush administration accomplishing a sort of victory by keeping the debate focused on waterboarding while avoiding discussion of the techniques more commonly employed?

Yes, that's right. The historical record is clear. Waterboarding is torture, and yes, focusing on just waterboarding is a distraction. Waterboarding is serious, but only the tip of the iceberg. There have only been three documented cases of waterboarding, but the CIA has subjected at least 30 others to "enhanced interrogation," as Director Hayden says, so there are other kinds of techniques as well. And there are unaccounted prisoners last seen in U.S. custody as well as secret prisons out there where these things continue to happen.

One day we'll know more, but the historical record now shows that American interrogators and soldiers, whether authorized or not, have used forced standing, forced kneeling, sleep deprivation, exposure to extremes of heat and cold, beatings on the soles of the feet, sexual humiliation, and psychological coercion, as well as, in some cases, electrotorture. So it would be a mistake, then, to confuse the forest with the three tallest trees in it. Waterboarding highlights the huge dangers of torture, but it is only the beginning of political literacy, not the end of it.

And the same applies to domestic policing. I'm less worried about our police learning how to waterboard criminals than I am with the use of stun guns and tasers. Any inspector would wonder what straps and a bucket of water would be doing in an interrogation room, and investigate for torture. But they can't prohibit police from using stun guns and tasers, which have authorized police uses, and it is very hard for them to tell when these devices have been used illegally to torture, as they leave few marks.

Lastly, I think we need to understand that torture doesn't just hide in a vault in the CIA. It hides in all the dark pockets of society — military barracks, schools, frat houses, our supermax prisons, and immigration lockups. When torture happens, the top authorizes, and the people at the bottom come running with the techniques. Vigilance has to extend far beyond our intelligence agencies to all these other areas.

Most dangerously, I think we need to pay attention to our new culture of irresponsibility. We live now in an age where something is or is not torture depending on when and who it is done to. Zapping an angry businessman in an airplane cabin will be called torture, but zapping a foreigner might just be good security and completely excusable. This is bad. All my students at Reed have good intentions, but they don't all deserve A's because what they do matters regardless of their intention. Yet police and intelligence officers, not to mention politicians, want to get A's just because they had good intentions. They want to be exonerated for having done no torture at all; it's only torture if they had bad intentions. And that is very dangerous and irresponsible because judging people solely on their intentions, as William Blake said, is the road to hell.

6. This week Congress will again take up the intelligence bill, and the proposal to clarify that the ban on torture accepted by the uniformed services is applicable to all U.S. actors, including the intelligence community. Of course, the Detainee Treatment Act of 2005 already says that, but the Bush

administration has apparently developed its own secret understanding to the contrary. Part of the argument that has been made in favor of this measure is that the idea of compartmentalization or limitation of torture doesn't work, that once it is known that certain techniques are being used they spread, or "migrate" in the language of the Army's Faye-Jones Report. You seem to chart the same sort of migration many times in your study. Are the proponents of the torture ban correct on this?

Yes, torture does migrate, and there are some good examples of it both in American and French history. The basic idea here is that soldiers who get ahead torturing come back and take jobs as policemen, and private security, and they get ahead doing the same things they did in the Army. And so torture comes home. Everyone knows waterboarding, but no one remembers that it was American soldiers coming back from the Philippines who introduced it to police in the early twentieth century. During the Philippine insurgency in 1902, soldiers learned the old Spanish technique of using water tortures, and soon these same techniques appeared in police stations, especially throughout the South, as well as in military lockups during World War I. Likewise, the electrical techniques used in Vietnam in the 1960s appeared in torturing African Americans on the south side of Chicago in the 1970s and 1980s, and, as I argue in the book, that wasn't just an accident.

So torture always comes home. And the techniques of this war are likely to show up in a neighborhood near you. Likewise, the techniques that appeared in the War on Terror were already documented in INS lockups in Miami in the 1990s. There is no bright line between domestic and foreign torture; the stuff circulates.

Yes, I am opposed to two-track systems, where one group of people can torture and the other people can't. And it is not hard to understand why. Suppose you're an interrogator who is not allowed to use some technique, but the guy from the Other Governmental Agency can. What is more, you believe that these techniques work. So why should you be stuck using techniques that are slow and time-consuming, when the guy from the OGA can get good results and win all the glory? Aren't you just an idiot for sticking to the rules? Of course not, and so torture will spread, and that slippery slope is a lot slicker in counterinsurgency conflicts than in domestic policing, as I show in the book.

There are good reasons to believe that whatever these "enhanced techniques" are, they will seep into other agencies and organizations. And since many of these techniques leave no marks, it will be impossible to prove that they were even used. We saw this pattern in Iraq and Afghanistan, where soldiers reported having learned their interrogation techniques by imitating CIA field officers.

So I think it is only a matter of time now before new rot sets into the U.S. military thanks to the two-track system our government has endorsed. This is inevitable when you codify two-track interrogation systems into law. In the 1970s, the Brazilian military had a similar system, and the state had to turn on and kill its torturers in order to preserve itself. As the Brazilian journalist Elio Gaspari observed at the time, "Unless everyone in the army participates in torture, you very quickly develop two kinds of soldiers." He called them the "combatants," who fight the terrorists with torture, and the "bureaucrats," who are committed to preserving the military's everyday functioning and discipline. In Brazil, the day came when the combatant-torturers refused to accept the orders of the bureaucrats and regarded with contempt their peers who were committed to army disciplines. The generals reluctantly concluded that the "torturers were going to have to be isolated, marginalized, and eliminated, so as to save the Army."

Torture Is a Moral Issue:
A Statement of Conscience by the
National Religious Campaign Against Torture

Torture violates the basic dignity of the human person that all religions, in their highest ideals, hold dear. It degrades everyone involved — policy-makers, perpetrators, and victims.

It contradicts our nation's most cherished values. Any policies that permit torture and inhumane treatment are shocking and morally intolerable. Nothing less is at stake in the torture abuse crisis than the soul of our nation. What does it signify if torture is condemned in word but allowed in deed?

Let America abolish torture now — without exceptions.

Signatories: A Partial List

Organizations listed for identification purposes only.

Rev. William J. Byron, S.J.
Former President, Catholic University of America

President Jimmy Carter
Nobel laureate

Rev. Richard Cizik
Vice President for Governmental Affairs, National Association of Evangelicals

Appendix 1

ARCHBISHOP DEMETRIOS
Primate, Greek Orthodox Archdiocese of America

REV. DR. BOB EDGAR
Former General Secretary, National Council of Churches

RABBI JEROME M. EPSTEIN
Executive Vice President, United Synagogue of Conservative Judaism

DR. DAVID P. GUSHEE
President, Evangelicals for Human Rights; Distinguished University
Professor of Ethics, McAfee School of Theology, Mercer University

DR. MAHER HATHOUT
Muslim Public Affairs Council

DR. STANLEY HAUERWAS
Gilbert T. Rowe Professor of Theological Ethics, Duke University

GARY HAUGEN
President, International Justice Mission

DR. ROBERTA HESTENES
Minister-at-Large, World Vision

DR. GEORGE HUNSINGER
McCord Professor of Theology, Princeton Theological Seminary

THE MOST REVEREND KATHARINE JEFFERTS SCHORI
Presiding Bishop and Primate, The Episcopal Church

REV. KERMIT D. JOHNSON
Chaplain (Major General), U.S. Army (Ret.)

HONORABLE THOMAS H. KEAN
Former Governor, New Jersey, and co-chair of the 9/11 Commission

Rev. Dr. Clifton Kirkpatrick
Stated Clerk, Presbyterian Church (U.S.A.)

Rev. Joseph Lowery
Co-Founder, Southern Christian Leadership Conference

Ron Mahurin
Vice President of Professional Development and Research, Council for
Christian Colleges & Universities

Frederica Mathewes-Green
Author and commentator

Dr. Ingrid Mattson
President, Islamic Society of North America

Theodore Cardinal McCarrick
Archbishop Emeritus of Washington

Dr. Brian McLaren
Founder, Cedar Ridge Community Church, Spencerville, Maryland

Dr. Richard Mouw
President, Fuller Theological Seminary

Prof. Mary Ellen O'Connell
Robert and Marion Short Professor of Law, University of Notre Dame

Rev. Samuel Rodriguez
President, National Hispanic Christian Leadership Coalition

Rabbi David Saperstein
Director, Religious Action Center of Reform Judaism

Rabbi Gerry Serotta
Chair, Rabbis for Human Rights — North America

Dr. Ron Sider
Professor of Theology and Culture and Director of the Sider Center on Ministry and Public Policy, Palmer Theological Seminary; Founder, Evangelicals for Social Action

Dr. Glen Stassen
Lewis B. Smedes Professor of Christian Ethics, Fuller Theological Seminary

Dr. Leonard Sweet
E. Stanley Jones Professor of Evangelism, Drew University

Dr. Sayyid M. Syeed
National Director, Islamic Society of North America

Major General (Ret.) Antonio M. Taguba
U.S. Army

Dr. Frank A. Thomas
Editor, *The African-American Pulpit;* Pastor, Mississippi Boulevard Christian Church, Memphis

Rev. Dr. John H. Thomas
General Minister and President, United Church of Christ

Rev. Jim Wallis
Editor-in-Chief / Executive Director, Sojourners

Dr. Rick Warren
Founder and Pastor, Saddleback Church

Rabbi Arthur Waskow
Director, The Shalom Center

Rev. Dr. Sharon E. Watkins
General Minister and President, Christian Church (Disciples of Christ)

ELIE WIESEL
Nobel laureate

COLONEL (RET.) LAWRENCE B. WILKERSON
Chief of Staff, U.S. State Department (2002-2005)

DR. NICHOLAS WOLTERSTORFF
Noah Porter Professor of Philosophical Theology, Yale University

BRIGADIER GENERAL (RET.) STEPHEN N. XENAKIS, M.D.
Greek Orthodox

National Religious Campaign Against Torture
316 F St. NE, Suite 200, Washington, DC 20002
202-547-1920
http://www.nrcat.org

Founder: Dr. George Hunsinger
President: Linda Gustitus
Executive Director: Richard Killmer

Statement on Interrogation Practices

Honorable Member of the Committee on the Armed Services,

Attached please find the *Statement on Interrogation Practices,* signed by 20 former US Army Interrogators and Interrogation Technicians. In the *Statement* you will find that trained and experienced interrogators refute the assertion that so-called "coercive interrogation techniques" and torture are necessary to win the "War on Terror." Trained and experienced interrogators can, in fact, accomplish the intelligence gathering mission using only those techniques, developed and proven effective over decades, found in the Army Field Manual 34-52 (1992). You will also see that experienced interrogators find prisoner/detainee abuse and torture to be counter-productive to the intelligence gathering mission.

The signatories to the *Statement* represent over 200 years of combined interrogation service and experience, including Chief Warrant Officer 5 Donald Marquis who, at the time of his retirement earlier this year, was the Army's most senior interrogator. [As you may know, the Army utilizes only enlisted personnel and warrant officers as interrogators. No commissioned officers serve as interrogators in the Army.] The experience of the signatories to the *Statement* ranges from the Vietnam era to Afghanistan, Guantanamo Bay, and Iraq. Of the interrogators with whom we were able to establish contact, 100% have expressed total agreement with the Statement. The names of active-duty interrogators have not been added to the list of signatories because of conflicts between the *Statement* and public comments by the Secretary of Defense and his staff, and the Vice President and his staff.

We, the signatories and subject-matter experts, ask that you ensure unhampered operation of the intelligence gathering mission by refusing to authorize or accept any interrogation practices that differ from the techniques and standards established in FM 34-52 (1992). We urge you to listen to the subject-matter experts — the actual Interrogators to whom you entrust intelligence gathering — and refute any efforts to condone or authorize techniques we find to be counter-productive to the intelligence collection mission.

The Statement on Interrogation Practices and the list of signatories will be distributed to the Press and select Non-Governmental Organizations (NGOs) later today.

Submitted on behalf of the signatories 31 July 2006 with all due respect,

Peter Bauer
Former US Army Interrogator , 1986-1997

Statement on Interrogation Practices
July 31, 2006

We the undersigned, former active-duty Army Interrogators (97E) and Interrogation Technicians (351E), believe the following two statements to be true:

- Trained and skilled interrogators can accomplish the intelligence gathering mission using only those interrogation techniques found in Army Field Manual 34-52 (1992).
- Prisoner/detainee abuse and torture are to be avoided at all costs, in part because they can degrade the intelligence collection effort by interfering with a skilled interrogator's efforts to establish rapport with the subject.

(signed)
Chief Warrant Officer 5 (retired) Donald Marquis
Chief Warrant Officer 3 (retired) Marney Mason
Chief Warrant Officer 3 (retired) Kirk Wilmore
Chief Warrant Officer 3 (resigned) Ronald E. Anderson
Sergeant Major (retired) Lucinda K. Rost
Sergeant First Class (retired) Tom Roberts
Staff Sergeant (retired) Timothy Fredrickson
Peter Bauer
Justin Camp
Mirko Hall
Christopher Goyette
Brian Sands
Charles Zinner
Darin Klein
Richard Kedzior
Travis Hall
Chris McLean
Richard Dickerson
Shaun Beijan
Darrin Babin

Permissions and Sources

Ch. 1 — Kenneth Roth, "Getting Away with Torture." Originally published in *Global Governance: A Review of Multilateralism and International Organizations*, vol. 11, no. 3 (2005). Copyright Lynne Rienner Publishers, Inc. All rights reserved. Used with permission of the publisher.

Ch. 2 — Dianna Ortiz, OSU, "A Survivor's View of Torture." Originally published as "Theology, International Law, and Torture: A Survivor's View" in *Theology Today*, vol. 63, no. 3 (October 2006). All rights reserved. Used with permission of the publisher.

Ch. 3 — Tony Lagouranis as told to John Conroy, "Confessions of a Torturer." An abridged version of the original, published as "Confessions of a Torturer: An Army Interrogator's Story," by John Conroy, *Chicago Reader*, March 2, 2007. All rights reserved. Used with permission of the publisher. Available online at http://www.chicagoreader.com/features/stories/torture/.

Ch. 7 — David Gushee, "Six Reasons Why Torture Is Always Wrong." Originally published as "Against Torture: An Evangelical Perspective" in *Theology Today*, vol. 63, no. 3 (October 2006). All rights reserved. Used with permission of the publisher.

Ch. 8 — William T. Cavanaugh, "Torture and Eucharist: An Update." Originally published as "Making Enemies: The Imagination of Torture in Chile and the United States" in *Theology Today*, vol. 63, no. 3 (October 2006). All rights reserved. Used with permission of the publisher.

Ch. 9 — Fleming Rutledge, "My Enemy, Myself." Originally published in *Theology Today*, vol. 63, no. 3 (October 2006). All rights reserved. Used with permission of the publisher.

Ch. 11 — Edward Feld, "Developing a Jewish Theology Regarding Torture." Originally published in *Theology Today,* vol. 63, no. 3 (October 2006). All rights reserved. Used with permission of the publisher.

Ch. 12 — Ellen Lippmann, "These Things I Remember as I Pour Out My Heart: A Sermon for Kol Nidre 5766." An abridged version of the original, available online at http://www.kolotchayeinu.org/rabbi/KolNidre5766.pdf.

Ch. 13 — Rabbis for Human Rights, "What We Pray For." Available online as "Principles of Faith: What We Pray For" at http://rhr.israel.net/profile/principles offaith.shtml.

Ch. 14 — Ingrid Mattson, "Stopping Oppression: An Islamic Obligation." Available online at http://macdonald.hartsem.edu/mattsonart6.htm.

Ch. 15 — Taha Jabir Alalwani, "Of Torture and Abuse." Excerpted from a call-in interview, June 6, 2004. Available online at http://www.islamonline.net/english/introducingislam/politics/System/article07.shtml.

Ch. 16 — Yahya Hendi, "A Call for Dialogue." Available online at http://www.imamyahyahendi.com/library_articles_9.htm.

Ch. 17 — Fiqh Council of North America, "Fatwa Against Terrorism." Available online at http://www.fiqhcouncil.org/FatwaBank/tabid/79/Default.aspx.

Ch. 18 — "Universal Islamic Declaration of Human Rights." Available online at http://www.alhewar.com/ISLAMDECL.html.

Ch. 19 — Ann Elizabeth Mayer, "Islam and Human Rights Today." An abridged version of the original, published as "The Islam and Human Rights Nexus: Shifting Dimensions" in *The Muslim World Journal of Human Rights,* vol. 4, no. 1 (2007). All rights reserved. Used with permission from the publisher, The Berkeley Electronic Press. Available online at http://www.bepress.com/mwjhr/vol4/iss1/art4/.

Ch. 21 — Louise Richardson, "What Terrorists Want: An Overview." A compilation of several talks, used with permission of the author.

Afterword — "Torture Always Comes Home: An Interview with Darius Rejali." *Harper's,* February 13, 2008. Available online at http://harpers.org/archive/2008/02/hbc-90002387.

Appendix 2 — "Statement on Interrogation Practices" used with permission of Peter Bauer.

Except where noted, all essays in this volume are contributed with permission from the authors, who retain copyrights.